KU-379-571

CONVEYANCING SOLUTIONS
2: THE CONTRACT

AUSTRALIA AND NEW ZEALAND
The Law Book Company Ltd.
Sydney : Melbourne : Perth

CANADA AND U.S.A.
The Carswell Company Ltd.
Agincourt, Ontario

INDIA
N.M. Tripathi Private Ltd.
Bombay
and
Eastern Law House Private Ltd.
Calcutta and Delhi
M.P.P. House
Bangalore

ISRAEL
Steimatzky's Agency Ltd.
Jerusalem : Tel Aviv : Haifa

MALAYSIA : SINGAPORE : BRUNEI
Malayan Law Journal (Pte.) Ltd.
Singapore and Kuala Lumpur

PAKISTAN
Pakistan Law House
Karachi

CONVEYANCING SOLUTIONS 2: THE CONTRACT

RUTH ANNAND, B.A.

Solicitor,
Lecturer in Law, University of Bristol

RICHARD WHISH, B.A., B.C.L. (Oxon)

Solicitor,
Lecturer in Law, University of Bristol

LONDON   SWEET & MAXWELL   1987

Published in 1987 by
Sweet & Maxwell Limited
11 New Fetter Lane, London
Computerset by Promenade Graphics Limited, Cheltenham
Printed in Great Britain by
Robert Hartnoll (1985) Limited
Bodmin, Cornwall

British Library Cataloguing in Publication Data
Annand, Ruth
    The contract.—(Conveyancing solutions; v. 2).
    1. Conveyancing—England
    2. Contracts for deeds—England
    I. Title II. Whish, Richard III.
    Series 344.2064'38   KD979

    ISBN 0–421–36240–5

All rights reserved. No part of this publication
may be reproduced or transmitted, in any form or by any
means, electronic, mechanical, photocopying, recording
or otherwise, or stored in any retrieval system of
any nature, without the written permission of the
copyright holder and the publisher, application for
which shall be made to the publisher.

© RUTH ANNAND & RICHARD WHISH   1987

CONTENTS

TABLE OF CASES

TABLE OF STATUTES

TABLE OF STANDARD CONDITIONS OF SALE

The standard conditions are set out in full at Appendices G and H.

1 INTRODUCTION

This is the second in a series of conveyancing manuals for practitioners. The idea for the series was formulated at a time of growing public dissatisfaction with the system of residential conveyancing. Now the Administration of Justice Act 1985 contains provisions which extend the procedures for dealing with complaints against solicitors[1] and allow licensed non-solicitors to undertake conveyancing for reward.[2] The manuals will concentrate in the main on residential conveyancing, although much of what will be said applies equally to commercial and agricultural conveyancing. References to "solicitor" should be read as including licensed conveyancers where appropriate.

There follows, in chart form, a basic description of the conveyancing process. The topics covered by this manual—matters relating to the contract—are identified in bold type.

Conveyancing procedure

Preliminary agreement to buy
|
Vendor and Purchaser instruct conveyancers

Vendor's conveyancer	*Purchaser's conveyancer*
Sends **draft contract with copy Register entries and filed plan and, or other copy documents** to ⎯⎯⎯⎯⎯→	
	Peruses draft contract and other documents
	Private surveyor instructed
	Application for mortgage made
	Searches Public Index Map (unregistered land)
	Makes local land charges search and enquiries of the local authority
←⎯⎯⎯⎯⎯⎯	Raises enquiries before contract
Answers enquiries before contract ⎯⎯⎯⎯⎯→	
(refers to client where necessary)	
	Search of Commons Register and, or Register of rents?
	Other enquiries?
	Considers replies to searches and enquiries with client together with mortgage offer and surveyor's report
Agrees contract	**Agrees contract**
Obtains vendor's signature to contract	**Obtains purchaser's signature to contract and deposit**

PRELIMINARY

---

[1] s.5.
[2] s.7.

EXCHANGE OF CONTRACTS

CONTRACT
TO
COMPLETION

Insurance is necessary as from date of contract as risk passes to purchaser
Protection of contract by registration?

Supplies abstract of title or authority to inspect Register ⟶

Investigates title
Prepares draft conveyance or transfer and requisitions on title. Reserves right to raise further requisitions on behalf of mortgagee

⟵ Notifies mortgagee of redemption and obtains redemption figure and "daily rate"

Replies to requisitions and approves conveyance or transfer ⟶

If not acting for mortgagee—sends all documents to mortgagee's conveyancer; receives mortgagee's requisitions and draft mortgage from mortgagee's conveyancer, replies to mortgagee's requisitions by raising further requisitions with vendor's conveyancer if necessary; mortgagee agrees loan
If acting for purchaser and mortgagee—reports on vendor's title to mortgagee; drafts mortgage

Replies to any additional requisitions ⟶

Makes land charges search or official search of register (and "Bankruptcy only" land charges search if necessary)
Search of Companies register?

Prepares completion statement ⟶

Mortgage executed
Dispatches engrossed
⟵ conveyance or transfer (sometimes bearing purchaser's signature)

Makes final arrangements for completion

Confirms arrangements for completion
Obtains completion moneys from mortgagee and purchaser

COMPLETION

AFTER
COMPLETION

Redeems mortgage
Accounts to client

If not acting for mortgagee sends all documents to mortgagee's conveyancer
Otherwise attends to stamping and registration where appropriate

Forwards receipted mortgage or Form 53 ⟶

Reform   The proposals for reform in this area towards the overall
simplification and speeding up of conveyancing, include, as a
matter of law, all contracts for the sale of land to be in writing[3] (at
present they are only required to be evidenced in writing), and as
a matter of practice, pre-contract deposits[4] and deposit
guarantees.[5]

---

[3] This solution has emerged as the most popular from comments received in
response to Law Com. Working Paper No. 92 "Transfer of Land. Formalities
for Contracts for Sale etc. of land."
[4] See "Pre-Contract Deposits. A Practice Recommendation by the Conveyancing
Standing Committee", reproduced as App. A.
[5] The Second Report of the Conveyancing Committee 1985, para. 9.32. See
Chap. 5.

2 FORMALITIES

Introduction

A contract for the sale or other disposition of land can be made in the same way as a contract for the sale of any other property. Provided there is complete and final agreement between the parties on at least its essential terms, namely the parties, the property, the price, and in the case of a lease the commencement and the period of the lease,[1] the contract will be valid, even if oral. However, statute decrees that it cannot be enforced unless the party one wishes to sue or someone on his behalf has signed a written version of the contract or there is sufficient act of part performance.

L.P.A. 1925, s.40

Section 40 of the Law of Property Act 1925 reads:

> "(1) No action may be brought upon any contract for the sale or other disposition of land or any interest in land, unless the agreement upon which such action is brought, or some memorandum or note thereof, is in writing and signed by the party to be charged or by some other person thereunto by him lawfully authorised.
>
> (2) This section applies to contracts whether made before or after the commencement of this Act and does not affect the law relating to part performance or sales by the court."

Statute of Frauds 1677, s.4

Section 40(1) substantially re-enacts section 4 of the Statute of Frauds 1677, introduced to avoid parties being held to an alleged bargain the terms of which they had not agreed. By 1686 equity had invented the doctrine of part performance (given statutory recognition in section 40(2))—seen as an extension of the rule that equity will not permit a statute to be used as an instrument of fraud—which robs the provision of many of its terrors. In addition the judiciary have devised exceptions and extensions to the statute other than the doctrine of part performance, anxious not to allow the absence of sufficient writing to defeat an otherwise established contract. The result is said to be that section 40 has 'acquired a thick crustation of legal authority and judicial gloss, much of it inconsistent and unsupported by the enactment itself."[2]

The cases on section 4 of the Statute of Frauds apply equally to section 40.

Contracts within section 40

Sale or other disposition

Section 40 applies to any contract for the sale or other disposition of land or any interest in land. It covers a contract for the creation of a new interest in land as well as a contract for the transfer of an existing interest, "disposition" being defined as including a

---

[1] *Harvey* v. *Pratt* [1965] 1 W.L.R. 1025. The issue of whether there is an agreement or not is dealt with in the following chapter.

[2] Barnsley's *Conveyancing Law and Practice* (2nd ed), p. 102.

mortgage, charge, lease, disclaimer or release, and a devise or appointment of property by will.[3] This definition of disposition is not however exhaustive.[4] In *Daulia Ltd.* v. *Four Millbank Nominees*[5] the term was held to include an agreement to exchange contracts for the sale of land, and in *Re Gonin*[6] an agreement that a daughter should be given a house in return for looking after her parents for life. Sales by the court are expressly excluded by section 40(2).

Land or any interest in land

Difficulties have arisen with the proper interpretation of the words "land or any interest in land"; "land" being widely defined by section 205(1)(ix) of the Law of Property Act 1925. Contracts which have been held to fall within section 40 as contracts relating to "land or any interest in land" include, an agreement to sell land with chattels[7]; an agreement to grant or assign a lease[8] or to procure the transfer of a lease[9]; an agreement to charge land[10] or to sell a debenture charged on company land[11] and to shoot and take away game from land.[12] Also included have been an agreement to submit to arbitration a dispute relating to land or an interest in land[13] and an agreement concluded in the course of arbitration.[14]

An undivided share

Despite the express exclusion of an "undivided share in land" from the definition of land in section 205(1)(ix), it is generally accepted[15] that section 40 applies to a contract for the sale of an undivided share in land.

Fixtures

Fixtures form part of the land to which they are attached, so that a contract for their sale or other disposition (even if separate from the land) must be evidenced in writing.[16] However, an agreement by a tenant to sell fixtures to his landlord needs no formality.[17] It is regarded as a renunciation by the tenant of his right to remove those fixtures.

Right of pre-emption. Board and lodgings

Licences

A right of pre-emption creates no interest in land[18] nor does a right to board and lodgings.[19] Oral agreements relating to either are enforceable.

The orthodox view is that a contractual licence does not create a proprietary interest in land, in which case there would be

---

[3] Law of Property Act 1925, s.205(1)(ii).
[4] *Grey* v. *I.R.C.* [1960] A.C. 1.
[5] [1978] Ch. 231.
[6] [1979] Ch. 16.
[7] *Hawkesworth* v. *Turner* (1930) 46 T.L.R. 389, *Ram Narayan* v. *Rishad Hussain Shah* [1979] 1 W.L.R. 1349; unless the contract is divisible into two separate agreements, one relating to land and the other to chattels: *Bigg* v. *Whisking* (1853) 14 C.B. 195, *Morgan* v. *Griffith* (1871) L.R. 6 Exch. 70, *De Lasalle* v. *Guildford* [1901] 2 K.B. 215.
[8] *Thursby* v. *Eccles* (1900) 70 L.J.Q.B. 91, *Biss* v. *Hygate* [1918] 2 K.B. 314.
[9] *Horsey* v. *Graham* (1869) L.R. 5 C.P. 9.
[10] *Mounsey* v. *Rankin* (1885) 1 Cab. & E. 496, *Pattle* v. *Anstruther* (1893) 69 L.T. 175.
[11] *Driver* v. *Broad* [1893] 1 Q.B. 744.
[12] *Webber* v. *Lee* (1882) 9 Q.B.D. 315.
[13] *Rainforth* v. *Harmer* (1855) 25 L.T. (O.S.) 247.
[14] *Walters* v. *Morgan* (1792) 2 Cox Eq. Cas. 369.
[15] *Cooper* v. *Critchley* [1955] Ch. 431 accepted in *Steadman* v. *Steadman* [1976] A.C. 536, *Liddell* v. *Hopkinson* (1974) 233 E.G. 512, and *Sutton* v. *Sutton* [1984] Ch. 184.
[16] *Morgan* v. *Russell* [1909] 1 K.B. 357 and s.61(1) of the Sale of Goods Act 1979.
[17] *Lee* v. *Gaskell* (1876) 1 Q.B.D. 700.
[18] *Pritchard* v. *Briggs* [1980] Ch. 338.
[19] *Wright* v. *Stavert* (1860) 2 El. & El. 721.

no need to satisfy the requirements of section 40.[20] It may be that the courts are in the process of developing a doctrine whereby contractual licences to occupy a property as a dwelling-house will bind third parties in some circumstances, in which case they may be interests in land.[21] However, in these circumstances there would presumably be no problem of formality as the taking of possession is part performance.

Crops   A contract for the sale of natural crops (*fructus naturales*) is within section 40,[22] unless the title in the crop is not to pass until it is severed from the land.[23] Cultivated crops (*fructus industriales*) are goods,[24] and oral contracts to sell them are enforceable.

Sufficient writing

Several points must be considered here:

Some memorandum or note   **A. Form**   The contract itself need not be in writing, so long as "some memorandum or note thereof is in writing." The memorandum need not be in any special form, nor need the writer intend his document to satisfy section 40(1). In *Re Hoyle*[25] the testator's will supplied the necessary memorandum: "the question is not one of intention of the party who signs the document but simply one of evidence against him. The court is not in quest of the intention of parties, but only of evidence under the hand of one of the parties to the contract that he has entered into it. Any document signed by him and containing the terms of the contract is sufficient."[26] Indeed memoranda have commonly been found in letters[27] and receipts.[28]

Time of memorandum   The memorandum can be made either at the time of or at any time after the contract is made,[29] but it must be in existence at the date of action.[30] It can even be made before the contract it evidences is made, in the situation where one party makes an offer in writing intending to contract, which is subsequently accepted by the other party by words or conduct.[31] It has however been observed that this rule has: "pushed the literal construction of the Statute of Frauds to a limit beyond which it would perhaps be not easy to go."[32]

[20] *National Provincial Bank Ltd.* v. *Ainsworth* [1965] A.C. 1175.

[21] *Midland Bank Ltd.* v. *Farmpride Hatcheries Ltd.* (1981) 260 E.G. 493.

[22] *Crosby* v. *Wadsworth* (1805) 6 East. 602, *Rodwell* v. *Phillips* (1842) 9 M. & W. 501.

[23] (1953) 22 Conv. 137, *Smith* v. *Surman* (1829) 9 & Cr. 561.

[24] *Morgan* v. *Russell* [1909] 1 K.B. 357.

[25] [1893] 1 Ch. 84.

[26] *Ibid. Per* Bowen L.J. at p. 99, and see *Hill* v. *Hill* [1947] Ch. 231.

[27] *Smith-Bird* v. *Blower* [1939] 2 All E.R. 406, *Smith* v. *Mansi* [1963] 1 W.L.R. 26.

[28] *Auerbach* v. *Nelson* [1919] 2 Ch. 383; *Davies* v. *Sweet* [1962] 2 Q.B. 300.

[29] *Barkworth* v. *Young* (1856) 4 Drew. 1.

[30] *Re Holland* [1902] 2 Ch. 360.

[31] *Warner* v. *Willington* (1856) 3 Drew 523, *Smith* v. *Neale* (1857) 2 C.B. (N.S.) 67, *Renos* v. *Picksley* (1866) L.R. 1 Exch. 342. In *Tiverton Estates Ltd.* v. *Wearwell Ltd.* [1975] 1 Ch. 146 at p. 156 Lord Denning M.R. explained that as these cases were decided at a time when the common law knew nothing of part performance: "these decisions were very necessary to meet the justice of the case."

[32] *Per* Bowen L.J. in *Re New Erbhardt Co., ex p. Menzies* (1889) 43 Ch.D. 118 at p. 129.

Where a plaintiff can establish that a memorandum has been lost or destroyed, oral evidence is admissible to prove that it did satisfy section 40(1).[33]

"in writing" "Writing" is defined[34] as including "typing, printing, lithography, photography, and other modes of representing or reproducing words in a visible form." Thus it was tacitly accepted in *Aquis Estates Ltd.* v. *Minton*[35] that a contract for the sale of property by telex was "in writing."

B. All terms The memorandum must contain all the terms of the contract,[36] that is the names of the parties (parties), a description of the subject matter of the sale or other disposition (property), the consideration (price), and any other agreed terms (provisions).

(i) *Parties*[37] The memorandum must either name the parties or describe them in a way that precludes any fair dispute as to their identity. Oral evidence is then admissible to complete their identification.

Sufficient For instance in *Sale* v. *Lambert*[38] land was described in
identification auction particulars as being sold "by direction of the proprietor" but he was not named in the contract. This was held to be sufficient identification for there was only one person who answered the description of proprietor.[39] In *Carr* v. *Lynch*,[40] "you" was enough to identify the purchaser, referred to as being the person who paid the deposit.

Similarly calling the vendor "mortgagee,"[41] or "trustee for sale,"[42] or "personal representative"[43] will suffice; his identity can be fairly ascertained. It was argued in *F. Goldsmith (Sicklesmere) Ltd.* v. *Baxter*[44] that the process of looking for identifying factors outside the name was appropriate to identify a personal vendor but inappropriate to identify a limited company, which has no physical characteristics. In that case the company-vendor was incorrectly named in the contract. This was no bar to its claim for specific performance of the contract. The vendor was sufficiently described in the contract by matters other than name. The registered office given in the agreement was the same as that of the true owner, the property was correctly described and the name of the director who signed the contract was correctly stated and was the same as that of the director of the owner company.

Insufficient A description that is too general will fail to satisfy section
identification 40(1). Calling the seller, "vendor,"[45] or either party, "my

---

[33] *Barber* v. *Rowe* [1948] 1 K.B. 535.
[34] Interpretation Act 1978, s.5, Sched 1.
[35] [1975] 1 W.L.R. 1452.
[36] *Beckett* v. *Nurse* [1948] 1 K.B. 535.
[37] H.W. Wilkinson (1969) 129 New L.J. 990.
[38] (1874) L.R. 18 Eq. 1.
[39] Explained in *Potter* v. *Duffield* (1874) L.R. 18 Eq. 4.
[40] [1900] 1 Ch. 613.
[41] *Jarrett* v. *Hunter* (1886) 34 Ch.D. 182, *Allen & Co. Ltd.* v. *Whiteman* (1920) 123 L.T.R. 773.
[42] *Catling* v. *King* (1877) 5 Ch.D. 660.
[43] *Fay* v. *Miller, Wilkins & Co.* [1941] 1 Ch. 360.
[44] [1970] Ch. 85 following *Commins* v. *Scott* (1875) 20 L.R. Eq. 11.
[45] *Potter* v. *Duffield* (1874) L.R. 18 Eq. 4. "Landlord" is also insufficient, *Coombs* v. *Wilkes* [1891] 3 Ch. 77.

client"[46] is useless. Any number of persons could satisfy either description. In *Lovesey* v. *Palmer*[47] a solicitor acting for an intending lessee mentioned only "my clients" when agreeing heads of agreement. Lovesey was his client, but Lovesey intended to form a company to take the lease which is why the solicitor referred to "my clients." Lovesey failed to get specific performance of the agreement because "my clients" was not a good description of him. It was irrelevant that the defendants knew that "my clients" were in fact Lovesey.[48]

Undisclosed principal   Provided the memorandum states the names of two parties who are contractually bound to one another, then section 40(1) is satisfied even though it is known at the time, or later discovered, that one of the parties is an agent for either the vendor or the purchaser.[49]

(ii) *Property*   Although the description of the property may be vague, if it is clear enough to enable the property to be **Sufficient description** ascertained, then oral evidence is admissible to complete the description. "Twenty-four acres of land, freehold, . . . at Totmonslow, in the parish of Draycott, in the county of Stafford" was held to be a sufficiently certain description of the property in *Plant* v. *Bourne*.[50] The court will assume that a man is selling his own property. Similarly in *Auerbach* v. *Nelson*,[51] a description of the property as: "House being sold by Nelson to Auerbach for 500." was sufficient to let in parol evidence identifying the only house answering that description—Mr Nelson's. Parol evidence was also allowed to identify properties described as: "my house,"[52] "Mr Ogilvie's house,"[53] and "property purchased at 420l. at Sun Inn, Pinxton, on the above date. Mr George Cotterell, Pinxton, Owner."[54]

Insufficient description   However, extrinsic evidence cannot be called in to provide a description where there is none in the contract. Suppose X contracts to sell "my property in AB street." If X has more than one property in AB street the description is uncertain.[55]

It is only necessary for the property to be described in the physical sense. In the absence of specific mention, the estate or interest being disposed of is governed by implied terms.[56]

In the case of a contract for a lease, the duration and commencement date of the lease must appear in writing.[57]

(iii) *Price*   The memorandum must state the price or allow for its objective determination by the court. Where no price is agreed,

---

[46] *Lovesey* v. *Palmer* [1916] 2 Ch. 233.
[47] *Ibid.*
[48] See also *Jarrett* v. *Hunter* (1886) 34 Ch.D. 182.
[49] *Davies* v. *Sweet* [1962] 2 Q.B. 300.
[50] [1897] 2 Ch. 281.
[51] [1919] 2 Ch. 383.
[52] *Cowley* v. *Watts* (1853) 17 Jur. 172.
[53] *Ogilvie* v. *Foljambe* (1817) 3 Mer. 53.
[54] *Shardlow* v. *Cotterell* (1881) 20 Ch.D. 90. See also *Davies* v. *Sweet* [1962] 2 Q.B. 300.
[55] This example of an uncertain description was given in *Plant* v. *Bourne* [1897] 2 Ch. 281.
[56] *Timmins* v. *Moreland Street Property Co. Ltd.* [1958] Ch. 110.
[57] *Harvey* v. *Pratt* [1965] 1 W.L.R. 1025.

the court will not imply a term that a reasonable price must be paid.[58]

Objective formula   Thus an agreement to sell at a "fair price" or "fair valuation,"[59] or an option to renew a lease "at a rent to be fixed having regard to the market value,"[60] will be valid and enforceable. The use of such objective formulae renders the price sufficiently ascertainable by making appropriate enquiries. "The court is reluctant to hold void for uncertainty any provision intended to have legal effect."[61]

No formula   By way of contrast, an agreement to sell at "a price to be agreed between the parties," or an option to renew a lease "at such rental as may be agreed upon between the parties"[62] will be void for uncertainty. The court is provided with no formula for determining the price and an agreement to agree is unenforceable.[63]

Inessential machinery   Where the parties provide machinery for arriving at a price and that machinery breaks down, the court will substitute its own, unless the machinery is an essential term of the contract. *Sudbrook Trading Estate Ltd.* v. *Eggleton*[64] concerned an option to purchase at a valuation price. Each side, lessor and lessee, had to appoint valuers and in the event of their being unable to agree a valuation, the valuers were to appoint an umpire. The House of Lords held that the valuation machinery was an inessential term of the option. Its breakdown could not prevent the option from being valid and enforceable. The price was sufficiently certain because the term "valuer" implied that it should be fair and reasonable as between the parties. Lord Fraser thought that the valuation machinery might be vital to the enforceability of an agreement which stated that the price was to be fixed by a named valuer.[65] However in *Re Malpass*,[66] the participation of the district valuer was not considered to be an essential part of an option to purchase a farm: "at the agricultural value thereof determined for probate purposes . . . as agreed with the District Valuer." Since he refused to agree a proper price for the farm the court directed an enquiry as to its agricultural value.

Note   It should be remembered that if any of the above terms are uncertain (parties, property or price) the contract will not only be unenforceable but also non-existent.

(iv) *Provisions*   The contract must be in writing or there must be a written record of *all* its terms; "some note or memorandum

[58] *Gourlay* v. *Somerset* (1815) 19 Ves. 429.
[59] *Milnes* v. *Gery* (1807) 14 Ves. 400, *Talbot* v. *Talbot* [1968] A.C. 1.
[60] *Brown* v. *Gould* [1972] Ch. 53.
[61] *Per Megarry J., ibid.* at p. 56.
[62] *Kings Motors (Oxford) Ltd.* v. *Lax* [1970] 1 W.L.R. 421.
[63] *Courtney and Fairburn Ltd.* v. *Tolani Brothers (Hotels) Ltd.* [1975] 1 W.L.R. 297; *Milnes* v. *Gery* (1807) 14 Ves. 400. Contrast the position where the contract has been partly performed, see *Beer* v. *Bowden* (1976) [1981] 1 W.L.R. 522 and *Thomas Bates & Sons Ltd.* v. *Windham Lingerie Ltd.* [1981] 1 W.L.R. 505.
[64] [1983] A.C. 444.
[65] *Ibid.* at pp. 483–484. *Cf.* the position where the contract has been partly performed, *Trustees of National Deposit Friendly Society* v. *Beatties of London Ltd.* (1985) 275 E.G. 54, (1985) 82 L.S.Gaz. 3601–3605; or where it is a subsidiary part of a wider enforceable contract, *Smith* v. *Peters* (1875) L.R. 20 Eq. 11.
[66] [1985] Ch. 42.

thereof." A memorandum that does not accurately reflect the parties' bargain will not satisfy section 40(1), even though on its face it shows a concluded contract. In *Ram Narayan* v. *Rishad Hussain Shah*[67] there was an oral agreement for the sale of two farms, two bullocks, two ploughshares, and one tractor but the written memorandum only mentioned the land. The whole agreement was unenforceable.

No specific performance

A written contract cannot be varied or contradicted by oral evidence. But oral evidence is admissible to show that an alleged memorandum of an oral agreement does not contain all the terms agreed on, and this will be a good defence to an action for specific performance. In *Johnson* v. *Humphrey*[68] the defendant orally agreed to sell her bungalow to the plaintiff, vacant possession to be given when she had found somewhere else to live. The written memorandum of sale was silent as to the question of vacant possession and therefore did not contain all the terms agreed on. The plaintiff failed to get an order for specific performance.

There are the following qualifications to the "all terms" rule:

Waived term

(a) "[I]f a term is exclusively for the benefit of one party, that party may sometimes waive the benefit of it and sue on the contract for enforcement, even though the memorandum contain no evidence of that term."[69] So for example in *North* v. *Loomes*[70] the court permitted the plaintiff to waive an undertaking by the defendant to pay the plaintiff's legal costs and enforce the contract for sale. It has been said that to be capable of waiver the term must not be "really an essential part of the bargain."[71]

No question can arise of a plaintiff waiving a term for his benefit unless he can first show a concluded contract.

Term submitted to

(b) If the missing term is beneficial to the defendant, it is probable that the plaintiff can agree to perform the term and enforce the contract. In *Martin* v. *Pycroft*[72] a tenant sued for specific performance of an agreement for sub-lease contained in a written document. The document omitted a term that the tenant would pay a premium of £200. The Court of Appeal allowed the tenant to pay the premium and enforce the contract. On this authority the rule was accepted in *Williams on Vendor and Purchaser*,[73] but in *Burgess* v. *Cox*[74] a contrary result was reached by Harman J. Subsequently *Martin* v. *Pycroft* and *Williams* were followed in *Scott* v. *Bradley*[75] where the plaintiff was awarded a decree of specific performance on submitting to perform the missing term that he pay half the defendant's costs.

Implied term

(c) The memorandum need not mention terms that are implied into the parties' agreement.[76] In *Farrell* v. *Green*[77] the plaintiff successfully sued for specific performance of his oral

---

[67] [1979] 1 W.L.R. 1349.
[68] [1946] 1 All E.R. 460, and see *Beckett* v. *Nurse* [1948] 1 K.B. 535, *Tweddell* v. *Henderson* [1975] 1 W.L.R. 1496.
[69] *Hawkins* v. *Price* [1947] 1 Ch. 645 at p. 649 *per* Evershed J.
[70] [1919] 1 Ch. 378.
[71] *Hawkins* v. *Price* [1947] 1 Ch. 645.
[72] (1852) 22 L.J. Ch. 94.
[73] (4th ed., 1936), Vol. 1, p. 5.
[74] [1951] Ch. 383.
[75] [1971] 1 Ch. 850.
[76] *Timmins* v. *Moreland Street Property Co. Ltd.* [1958] Ch. 110.
[77] (1974) 232 E.G. 587.

agreement to buy a Georgian mansion. The defendant tried to resist his claim by arguing that the written memorandum of sale failed to mention vacant possession on completion. Pennycuick V.C. held that the omission was irrelevant, because the law implies, in the absence of contrary expression, completion within a reasonable time and vacant possession on completion. He also confirmed the rule that a memorandum is not defective if it omits an expressly agreed term which exactly coincides with an implied term.

Rectification

(d) Where the missing terms are a result of a mistake common to both parties, the court may in one action rectify the agreement and decree specific performance. It was once thought that the court only had jurisdiction to rectify where a concluded contract was shown to exist prior to the written agreement in hand. However in *Joscelyne* v. *Nissen*[78] the Court of Appeal held that it was not necessary to find a concluded contract antecedent to the agreement, they had jurisdiction to rectify on the basis of a common continuing intention of the parties, "with the qualification that some outward expression of accord is required."[79] This led *Emmet on Title*[80] to comment: "Consequently, considerable inroads into the 'all terms' rule of section 40(1) could be achieved with sales of land where the negotiations customarily proceed throughout on a basis of various common continuing intentions expressed in correspondence up to a formal exchange of contracts."

"agreement"?

C. Acknowledgment Although it is clear that a memorandum cannot deny the existence of a contract,[81] it is uncertain whether a memorandum need acknowledge the existence of a contract. The controversy[82] turns on the interpretation of "the agreement" in section 40(1), for it is "the agreement" that the memorandum must evidence. Does it mean the fact of consensus, the terms of agreement or a document which records that agreement? In *Law* v. *Jones*[83] the Court of Appeal held that a memorandum need only record the terms agreed, and that there was nothing to prevent a letter headed "subject to contract" from being a valid memorandum. However, *Law* v. *Jones* was not followed in *Tiverton Estates Ltd.* v. *Wearwell Ltd.*[84] by a differently constituted Court of Appeal, which held that a section 40 memorandum must not only record all the terms of the contract but also acknowledge its existence. Use of the words "subject to contract" in correspondence was tantamount to denial of liability under the contract. Although these two cases are "undoubtedly

Law v. Jones

Tiverton Estates Ltd. v. Wearwell Ltd.

---

[78] [1970] 2 Q.B. 86.
[79] *Ibid. per* Lord Russell at p. 98. In *Agip SpA* v. *Navigazione Alta Italia SpA* [1984] 1 Lloyd's Rep. 353 Slade L.J. said (at p. 359): "The standard of proof required in an action of rectification to establish the common intention of the parties is the civil standard of balance of probability. Nevertheless, parties who append their signature to a written instrument prima facie indicate, by the very fact of their signatures, their assent to all the terms contained in it."
[80] 19th ed. 2/63.
[81] *Goodman* v. *Griffiths* (1857) 1 H. & N. 574, *Archer* v. *Baines* (1850) 5 Exch. 625, *Thirkell* v. *Cambi* [1919] 2 K.B. 590.
[82] The Law Commission Working Paper No. 92, p. 15.
[83] [1974] Ch. 112.
[84] [1975] Ch. 146.

in conflict"[85] the *Tiverton* case is more often preferred as deciding the law.[86]

D. Signature The writing must be "signed by the party to be charged" or his agent, or in other words the defendant to the action. The plaintiff can enforce the contract even though he has signed nothing.[87] A rule which allows a party to enforce a contract which is unenforceable against him, has been said to be: "distasteful to one's idea of fairness."[88] Nevertheless the rule is beyond dispute.

The signature can appear anywhere in the writing relied on, provided it governs the whole agreement. The defendant's printed name[89] or initials[90] will do, if appended in order to authenticate the writing.[91] In *McBlain* v. *Cross*[92] a signature on a telegram form was held to be a sufficient signature to the contract contained in the telegram. It is open to question whether a contract by telex is "signed" for the purpose of section 40(1),[93] especially where the defendant does not send the telex message himself.[94]

Printed names or initials inserted into a document will not suffice if it is clear that the parties intended further signing to make the contract binding. In *Hubert* v. *Treherne*[95] the words: "As witness to our hand . . . " at the end of the agreement were found to indicate such an intention. However, the presence of an attestation clause is not conclusive. *Leeman* v. *Stocks*[96] concerned a sale of property by auction. The vendor's initials and surname were put into the memorandum of sale by the auctioneer before the auction took place. It was held that the memorandum was sufficient to bind the vendor to the sale, despite the fact that it contained an attestation clause signed by the purchaser alone. The evidence showed that both the auctioneer and the purchaser considered that the purchaser's signature was all that was required to conclude the contract.

A further signature may be necessary where a document is altered after it has been properly signed. Oral approval of an alteration to a signed document will suffice to revive the original signature if the alteration is made to correct the documents

"signed by the party to be charged"

Signature

Attestation clauses

Alterations

---

[85] *Daulia Ltd.* v. *Four Millbank Nominees Ltd.* [1978] Ch. 231 at p. 250.
[86] See *Cohen* v. *Nessdale*[1981] 3 All E.R. 118; Cheshire and Burn, *Modern Law of Real Property* (13th ed., 1982), p. 112; letter dated December 12, 1974, from the Law Society to the Law Commission: "The Council consider that, following the decision in the case of *Tiverton Estates Ltd.*v. *Wearwell Ltd.* current conveyancing practice is now reasonably satisfactory"; but in *Alpenstow Ltd.* v. *Regalian Properties plc* [1985] 1 W.L.R. 721 an enforceable contract was spelt out of "subject to contract" correspondence. Lack of s.40(1) formality on the basis of *Tiverton* was not argued in the case, see (1985) 135 New L.J. 1101.
[87] *Auerbach* v. *Nelson* [1919] 2 Ch. 383.
[88] *Farrell* v. *Green* (1974) 232 E.G. 587, *per* Pennycuick V.C. at p. 588.
[89] *Leeman* v. *Stocks* [1951] Ch. 941, *Cohen* v. *Roche* [1927] 1 K.B. 169.
[90] *Knight* v. *Luckford* (1794) 1 Esp. 190, *Saunderson* v. *Jackson* (1800) All E.R. 126.
[91] *Hill* v, *Hill* [1947] Ch. 231.
[92] (1871) 25 L.T. 804.
[93] Despite the assumption that it would be in *Aquis Estates Ltd.* v. *Minton* [1975] 1 W.L.R. 1452 at p. 1454.
[94] *Brinkibon Ltd.* v. *Stahag Stahl mbH* [1983] 2 A.C. 34.
[95] (1842) 3 M. & 9G. 743.
[96] [1951] Ch. 941.

inaccurate formulation of the parties agreement,[97] or before the
parties are contractually bound.[98] But once a concluded contract
has been reduced to signed writing, any variation or addition to
its terms must be re-signed.[99] Consequently: "problems may
arise in practice where due initialling of alterations is overlooked,
or is not insisted upon, for example in the common situation
where the completion date is only agreed after exchange of
contracts: strictly speaking, without initialling, there will be no
"signed" contract or memorandum."[1]

(*i*) *Agents*   The writing need not be signed by the defendant
personally; it can be signed by "some other person thereunto by
him lawfully authorised." "Lawfully authorised" is not defined
in the statute therefore ordinary agency principles apply. An
agent will be "lawfully authorised" to sign on behalf of his
principal if he has express authority to do so, in writing or
orally,[2] or if he signs whilst acting within the scope of his
authority.[3]

Auctioneer   An auctioneer has implied authority to sign the contract for
both parties. In the case of the vendor, his authority lasts for as
long as he has authority to sell and it is not dependent on his
receiving a deposit from the purchaser.[4] His authority to sign on
behalf of the purchaser is limited to the time of sale.[5]

Solicitor   A solicitor has no implied authority to sign the actual
contract of sale,[6] but his authority to sign a memorandum of an
already existing contract may be implied from his instructions to
act.[7] Thus the inadvertent signing of a letter by him may produce

Litigation   an earlier enforceable contract than expected.[8] Another trap for
the unwary was exposed by *Grindell* v. *Bass*.[9] Counsel signed a
defence in an action which recognised as existing, and contained,
the terms of an oral contract. The defence was held to be an
adequate section 40 memorandum; the defendant had clearly
authorised her counsel to sign it. "[I]t matters not that the fact
that a memorandum within the Statute of Frauds would thereby
be brought into existence was not present to the minds of either
counsellor or client."[10] Where a solicitor is authorised to sign on

---

[97] *Buck* v. *Gompertz* (1852) 7 Exch. 862.
[98] *Koenigsblatt* v. *Sweet* [1923] 2 Ch. 314.
[99] *New Hart Builders Ltd.* v. *Brindley* [1975] Ch. 342. Goulding J. criticised the
  rule as "illogical," see C.T. Emery (1975) 39 Conv. 336.
[1] Law Commission Working Paper No. 92, pp. 20–21, para. 3.19.
[2] Since the statute does not prescribe how the authority must be given, written
  authorisation is unnecessary: *Daniel* v. *Trefusis* [1914] 788.
[3] *John Griffiths Cycle Corporation Ltd.* v. *Humber & Co. Ltd.* [1899] 2 Q.B. 414.
  It seems that signature on behalf of a company of its duly authorised agent
  acting within the scope of his authority will be the signature of the company for
  the purposes of s.40(1): *UBAF Ltd.* v. *European American Banking Corporation*
  [1984] Q.B. 713.
[4] *Phillips* v. *Butler* [1945] Ch. 358.
[5] *Ibid.* What counts as "the time of sale" is a question of fact in each case:
  Chaney v. *Maclow* [1929] 1 Ch. 461; *Bell* v. *Balls* [1897] 1 Ch. 663. *Bell* v. *Balls*
  also establishes the rule that this authority does not extend to an auctioneer's
  clerk.
[6] *Smith* v. *Webster* (1876) 3 Ch.D. 49; *H. Clark (Doncaster) Ltd.* v. *Wilkinson*
  [1965] Ch. 694.
[7] *North* v. *Loomes* [1919] 1 Ch. 378.
[8] *Thirkell* v. *Cambi* [1919] 2 K.B. 590; *Horner* v. *Walker* [1923] 2 Ch. 218.
[9] [1920] 2 Ch. 487.
[10] *Ibid.* at p. 492, *per* Russell J.

behalf of the vendor, it is immaterial whether he accepts the purchaser's deposit as stakeholder or as agent for the vendor.[11]

Estate agent   An estate agent has no such implied authority to sign a memorandum of sale: "the mere appointment by an owner of an estate agent to dispose of a house confers no authority to make a contract; the agent is solely employed to find persons to negotiate with the owner; but, if the agent is definitely instructed to sell at a defined price, those instructions involve authority to make a binding contract and to sign an agreement."[12]

Ratification and estoppel   The unauthorised signing by an agent may subsequently be ratified by a principal (but not an undisclosed principal[13]). The principal is then bound to perform the contract.[14] Alternatively a principal may be estopped from denying that the contract was entered into by an agent without his authority, if by his conduct he leads the plaintiff to believe that such agent did have the authority to enter a binding contract on his behalf, and the plaintiff has acted to his detriment in reliance on this representation.[15]

E. Joinder   In certain cases, where no *one* document satisfies section 40(1), two or more incomplete documents may be joined together to form a complete memorandum.

Two or more documents   The first case is where the defendant has signed all the documents sought to be joined. If when laid "side by side" they clearly refer to the same transaction, they may be read together to form a complete memorandum.[16]

Timmins v. Moreland Street Property Co. Ltd.   The second arises where there is: "a document signed by the party to be charged, which, while not containing in itself all the necessary ingredients of the required memorandum, does contain some reference, express or implied, to some other document or transaction. Where any such reference can be spelt out of a document so signed, then parol evidence may be given to identify the other document referred to, or, as the case may be, to explain the other transaction, and to identify any document relating to it. If by this process a document is brought to light which contains in writing all the terms of the bargain so far as not contained in the document signed by the party to be charged, then the two documents can be read together so as to constitute a sufficient memorandum for the purposes of section 40." This statement of the present law was made by Jenkins L.J. in *Timmins* v. *Moreland Street Property Co. Ltd.*[17] In that case the plaintiff was refused permission to join his cheque for the deposit with a receipt containing the agreed terms of sale. The cheque was only evidence of "the mere fact that the payment must have been made for some purpose or for some consideration," and it was "impossible to spell out of this cheque any reference, express or implied, to any other document or to any transaction other than

---

[11] *Elias* v. *George Sakely & Co. (Barbados) Ltd.* [1983] A.C. 646.
[12] *Keen* v. *Mear* [1920] 2 Ch. 574 at p. 579, *per* Romer J. see also *Wragg* v. *Lovett* [1948] 2 All E.R. 968.
[13] *Spiro* v. *Lintern* [1973] 1 W.L.R. 1002.
[14] *Keen* v. *Mear, supra.*
[15] *Spiro* v. *Lintern, supra.*
[16] *Sheers* v. *Thimbleby & Son* (1879) 76 L.T. 709, *Burgess* v. *Cox* [1951] Ch. 583.
[17] [1958] 1 Ch. 110 at p. 130.

the order to pay a sum of money constituted by the cheque itself."[18]

Privy Council approval

The dicta of Jenkins L.J. in *Timmins* v. *Moreland Street Property Co. Ltd.* were approved by the Privy Council in *Elias* v. *George Sahely & Co. (Barbados) Ltd.*[19] The parties had orally agreed on the sale of business premises and the purchaser's lawyer wrote to the vendor's lawyer setting out the essential terms and enclosing a 10 per cent. deposit. The vendor's lawyer responded by sending a receipt in the following terms:

> "RECEIVED from Fauzi Elias the sum of Thirty nine thousand Dollars and . . . Cents being deposit on Property at Swan Street B'town agreed to be sold by George Sahely & Co. B'dos Ltd. to Fauzi Elias and/or his nominees.
> R. G. MANDEVILLE & CO.
> Per E. Clarke."

The purchaser was able to join the receipt, which implied the existence of another document or transaction, with the letter, to produce a memorandum sufficient to satisfy section 40(1).

A document signed by the defendant cannot be treated as referring to a document not in existence when the first document was signed.[20] The court will not however involve itself in minute investigations to discover the order in which documents were signed if they were, more or less, contemporaneously executed.[21]

Non-compliance

"no action may be brought"

Non-compliance with section 40(1) prevents an action for damages or claim for specific performance being brought on the contract. In *Delaney* v. *T. P. Smith Ltd.*[22] the plaintiff needed to rely on an oral agreement for lease as an essential part of his cause of action against the defendant freeholders for trespass. His action failed because he could not show that the agreement satisfied section 40(1) or that circumstances existed to take it outside the section.

Section 40 must be pleaded as a defence

The plaintiff's action on the contract will not however fail for lack of formality unless this is specifically pleaded as a defence. In *North* v. *Loomes*[23] the defendant pleaded the Statute of Frauds generally but did not plead that the alleged memorandum omitted an essential term of the parties' agreement. He was ordered to specifically perform the agreement as set out in the memorandum. The court does however have discretion to allow pleadings to be amended, so that the defendant can take advantage of the section, where for example, an innocent mistake was made or a new matter has come to light since the pleadings were drawn up.[24]

---

[18] *Ibid. per* Jenkins L.J. at pp. 130–131.
[19] [1983] 3 A.C. 646.
[20] *Turnley* v. *Hartley* (1848) 3 New Pr. Cas. 96.
[21] *Timmins* v. *Moreland Street Property Co. Ltd.* [1958] Ch. 110.
[22] [1946] 1 K.B. 393.
[23] [1919] 1 Ch. 378.
[24] *Re Gonin* [1979] Ch. 16.

Enforceable otherwise than by action

Non-compliance does not render a contract invalid, merely unenforceable. Provided of course a concluded contract exists, it can be enforced by other means. *Low* v. *Fry*[25] concerned an oral agreement for the sale of a house. The purchaser gave a cheque in part payment of the purchase price, but before it was presented changed his mind about proceeding with the purchase. The vendor successfully brought an action to recover the deposit on the cheque. Similarly in *Monnickendam* v. *Leanse*,[26] the vendor was allowed to forfeit the deposit when his purchaser defaulted under the oral contract of sale.

An oral contract of sale between joint tenants, although unenforceable between them, may effect a severance of their beneficial joint tenancy.[27]

Part performance—section 40(2)

Section 40(2)

Despite the absence of sufficient writing the contract may still be enforceable in Equity, by a decree of specific performance, if there has been a sufficient act of part performance by the plaintiff.[28]

Act of part performance

To amount to an act of part performance the act must, on a balance of probability,[29] point to the existence of some contract between the parties and either show the nature of or be consistent with the contract alleged. Thus in *Kingswood Estate Co. Ltd.* v. *Anderson*[30] a widow's moving out of her rent-controlled house into a flat provided by her landlord was an act of part performance sufficient to make their oral agreement for a life tenancy enforceable.

Not all acts done in performance of a contract will aid the plaintiff, but several acts when joined together "may throw light on each other; and there is no reason to exclude light."[31] Even "spoken words may themselves be part performance of a contract."[31]

Acts of part performance most commonly relate to a change of possession, but this is not a requirement. In *Rawlinson* v. *Ames*[32] a landlord made alterations to a flat at the request of the defendant who had orally agreed to take a lease of it. The court granted the landlord a decree of specific performance.

Steadman v. Steadman

Although the payment of money is not usually sufficient act of part performance, it was accepted in *Steadman* v. *Steadman*[33] that in some circumstances it can be. In *Steadman*, a husband and wife in proceedings following divorce agreed (*inter alia*) that the husband would buy out the wife's interest in the matrimonial home for £1,500 plus £100 in full satisfaction of arrears of maintenance. The husband paid the £100 and his solicitors

---

[25] (1935) 15 L.T. 585.
[26] (1923) 39 T.L.R. 445.
[27] *Burgess* v. *Rawnsley* [1975] Ch. 429.
[28] Law of Property Act 1925, s.40(2).
[29] *Steadman* v. *Steadman* [1976] A.C. 536 at pp. 564–565, *per* Lord Simon and at pp. 541–542, *per* Lord Reid.
[30] [1963] 2 Q.B. 169.
[31] *Steadman* v. *Steadman* [1976] A.C. 536 at p. 564, *per* Lord Simon.
[32] [1925] Ch. 26.
[33] [1976] A.C. 536.

prepared and sent a deed of transfer to the wife for her to sign. The wife refused to proceed and sought to rely on section 40(1). The House of Lords held (by a majority of four to one) that both the payment of the £100 and the preparation and sending of the deed of transfer were sufficient acts of part performance to render the agreement enforceable against her.

Repercussions The case has important repercussions for the conveyancer. Two of their Lordships[34] suggested that payment of a deposit or part payment of the purchase price would only be an act of part performance if the vendor could not repay the purchaser.[35] And the majority were of the opinion that in the ordinary circumstances of a contract for the sale of land, a sufficient act of part performance could be found in the fact of a purchaser instructing his solicitors to prepare and submit a draft conveyance or transfer. It therefore seems that an oral contract for sale can unilaterally be rendered enforceable by the purchaser.[36] And it has been suggested that a vendor might rely on the unilateral act of (part) performance constituted by actually executing the conveyance or transfer.[37]

The principles of *Steadman* were applied by Goff J. in *Re Windle*[38] to an oral contract between husband and wife for the transfer of property. He held that instructions to solicitors to prepare the transfer and the payment of their costs and disbursements were sufficient acts of part performance, but that payment of mortgage arrears and instalments were not.

One question that was unresolved by their Lordships in *Steadman* was whether the act of part performance had to be referable to some contract between the parties, or some contract concerning land. In the later case of *Re Gonin*,[39] Walton J. preferred to follow the traditional view that the act of part performance must refer to the land.

Limitations Limitations on the operation of the doctrine of part performance? The act must be done in part performance of an existing contract, not in contemplation of the making of a contract.[40] It must be of such a nature that it would be a fraud on the defendant's part to take advantage of section 40(1). And even then, the equitable remedy of specific performance is discretionary and can be refused if, for example, the plaintiff has behaved inequitably, or has an equally effective common law remedy.[41]

---

[34] *Ibid., per* Lord Salmon at p. 571 and Lord Reid at p. 541.

[35] *Emmet on Title* (19th ed), p. 2/102 says this suggestion is illogical and impractical.

[36] Followed in *Re Windle* [1975] 1 W.L.R. 1628.

[37] See [1974] Conv. (N.S.) 388–391; and M.P. Thompson [1979] Conv. 402.

[38] [1975] 1 W.L.R. 1628 and see also *Sutton* v. *Sutton* [1984] Ch. 184: wife's consent to divorce sufficiently linked to oral contract as to transfer of beneficial interest in matrimonial home to be an act of part performance within *Steadman*.

[39] [1979] Ch. 16.

[40] *Daulia Ltd.* v. *Four Millbank Nominees Ltd.* [1978] Ch. 231; *New Hart Builders Ltd.* v. *Brindley* [1975] Ch. 342.

[41] *Turner* v. *Melladew* (1903) 19 T.L.R. 273.

Reform?

Working Paper No. 92

The property law team of the Law Commission has recently produced a working paper on section 40 as part of its programme for the simplification of conveyancing. Working Paper No. 92[42] makes no provisional proposals of the commission itself but puts **Five proposals** forward five proposals: that no substantial change should be made in the present law; that in future no formalities should be required for the making of a contract for the sale, etc., of land; that all such contracts should themselves be in writing, not merely evidenced in writing; that contracts for sale should be in a prescribed form; or that there should be a "cooling-off" period after an oral or written contract during which either party can withdraw.

Need for reform

Panic swept conveyancers in 1974 when the Court of Appeal in *Law* v. *Jones*,[43] held that a solicitor's "subject to contract" letter was sufficient to satisfy section 40. Their fears were allayed by a differently constituted Court of Appeal in the later case of *Tiverton Estates Ltd.* v. *Wearwell Ltd.*[44]; "subject to contract" correspondence could not make an oral agreement enforceable. The Law Society declared itself reasonably satisfied with current conveyancing practice but still pressed for reform of the statute.

Apart from the "subject to contract" controversy, section 40 presents difficulties with its interpretation and its interaction with part performance, especially since *Steadman* v. *Steadman*.[45] **1937 Law Revision Committee** Although section 40 was not within the terms of reference of the 1937 Law Revision Committee when they considered the Statute of Frauds 1677,[46] these five of their criticisms have been said[47] to be equally applicable to the section 40 requirement:

(1) The requirement for signed written evidence of a contract was introduced at a time when the parties could not give evidence.

(2) It may stop perjury but it may also stop the truth.

(3) It is out of line with how business is conducted.

(4) It can operate unfairly. For example, if A and B make a contract which is evidenced in writing and only A signs in writing, B can sue but not A.

(5) The contract is not void for non–compliance, merely unenforceable by action, and this can lead to anomalous results.[48]

Three general principles

Three general principles govern the present proposals for reform: no reform should increase the likelihood of contracts for sale etc. becoming binding before the parties have been able to obtain legal advice (reform should not increase formalities which can only be undertaken by lawyers); reform if not unable to reduce the risk of injustice should at least not increase it (in particular new formal requirements should not be so inflexible that hardship or unfairness results in cases of minor non-

---

[42] July 1985.

[43] [1974] Ch. 112.

[44] [1975] 1 Ch. 146.

[45] [1976] A.C. 536.

[46] Cmd. 5449 (1937), reprinted 1951.

[47] H.W. Wilkinson [1967] Conv. 182.

[48] *Morris* v. *Baron* [1918] A.C. 1 was cited as an example.

compliance); and reform should simplify, not complicate, conveyancing (but not at the expense of certainty). In addition it must be remembered that since the Administration of Justice Act 1985[49] only qualified persons[50] may prepare an instrument which is a contract for the sale or other disposition of land (other than short leases) for gain or reward. Any reform which insists that all contracts be in writing strengthens this provision, whilst any relaxation of formal requirements weakens it.

Ratings?
No change?
How does the Commission therefore rate its five proposals? It admits that proposal I, to make little or no change, is attractive, and that difficulties with interpretation could be ironed out by statutory definition (the meaning of "agreement," and "signed," and the limits of the joinder of documents rule could be spelt out). However, it concludes that such a piecemeal approach is inconsistent with its prima facie case for overall reform. Proposal II, the repeal of section 40 without replacement, fares no better. This proposal has the advantage that in future cases of dispute attention would be focused on the substantive issue of whether there was a contract, not on whether there was a sufficient memorandum or signature, but it goes against the general principles by which the Commission would like the proposals to be judged. Proposal III, all contracts in writing, is definitely more attractive. We would know with certainty when and if a contract was made and as an added bonus the doctrine of part performance would bite the dust. But should writing be necessary for all contracts? What about short leases? and what has to be in writing? all the terms? or only main terms? and how are they to be defined? Further proposal III offers no more than proposal IV, a prescribed form of contract. It is proposal IV which the Commission tentatively favours because it has three extra advantages over the earlier proposal: a prescribed form could be used to carry warnings regarding the danger of entering a contract without first obtaining legal advice; it offers clarity as to whether a contract has been made; and it could incorporate standard conditions of sale. The Commission is unsure as to whether a prescribed form of contract is appropriate for all contracts for the sale, etc., of land (it favours limiting the requirement to contracts for the sale etc. of legal estates). It also realises that insistence on a prescribed form could lead to injustice in the minority of cases where parties inadvertently use the wrong form. Here however sources of intervention other than part performance would remain possible, on the grounds of, for instance, proprietary estoppel, undue influence or misrepresentation.

No formalities?

All contracts in writing?

A prescribed form?

"cooling-off" period
Finally, a "cooling-off" period? No, this would only aggravate the problems presented by chain transactions in domestic conveyancing.

Note
Proposal III, all contracts in writing, has emerged as the most popular from comments received in response to the working paper.

---

[49] s.6.
[50] Defined by the Solicitors Act 1974, as amended.

3 "SUBJECT TO CONTRACT" AND CONDITIONAL AGREEMENTS

Introduction

As we have seen in the previous chapter, a contract for the sale of land is only enforceable if it is evidenced by a written memorandum or if there is a sufficient act of part performance. However the issue of formalities is not the only important one when considering whether a vendor and purchaser have entered into an enforceable contract. In particular it is necessary to examine the significance and effect of various expressions commonly used in conveyancing transactions such as "subject to contract," "subject to title" and "subject to finance." Before doing so, it may be helpful briefly to say a few words about the law of contract generally in order to place the discussion in context.

Offer and acceptance   There will not be a contract unless the parties have reached agreement, and there will not be agreement

Offer until one party has accepted an offer made by the other.[1] An offer is "an expression of willingness to contract made on certain terms made with the intention (actual or apparent) that it shall become binding as soon as it is accepted by the person to whom it is addressed."[2] An offer must be distinguished from a mere

Invitation to treat "invitation to treat," which precedes the process of offer and acceptance. Whether a statement amounts to an invitation to treat or to an offer may not be easy to divine, since this depends upon the intention of the person making it. However a letter from a prospective vendor saying that a sale at a future date may be considered would be a mere invitation to treat.[3]

Acceptance An acceptance is a final expression of assent to the terms of an offer, and must be unqualified; in particular where a person purports to accept an offer, but subject to the variation or deletion of some aspect of it, this simply acts as a counter-offer which the original offeror is at liberty to accept or refuse.[4] Until the acceptance matches the offer, there will be no contract. Therefore a vendor who accepts an offer from a would-be purchaser subject to an increase in the suggested purchase price of £1,000 would not be accepting the offer in contractual terms at all: the matter would still be in negotiation.

---

[1] On offer and acceptance generally, see *Chitty on Contracts* (25th ed., 1983), Chap. 2; Treitel, *The Law of Contract* (6th ed., 1983), Chap. 2; Cheshire, Fifoot and Furmston, *Law of Contract* (11th ed., 1986), Chap. 3.
[2] *Treitel op. cit.* p. 8.
[3] *Gibson* v. *Manchester City Council* [1979] 1 W.L.R. 294.
[4] *Jones* v. *Daniel* [1894] 2 Ch. 332.

Qualified acceptance

Conditional contracts It is important to distinguish a qualified acceptance of an offer, in which case no contract is created, from the situation in which the parties do enter into a contract but one whose performance is conditional upon the occurrence of a certain event, for example the acquisition of planning permission or the offer of a satisfactory mortgage. There is no reason in principle why the parties should not be free to enter into an agreement, a term of which is that performance under the contract is not to become due until the satisfaction of some condition precedent. However, conditional contracts of this type

Uncertainty

are not without their difficulties. First, it is possible that they will be struck down on grounds of uncertainty[5]: if it is impossible to give meaning to the condition in question, the court cannot

Nature of obligations

enforce the contract.[6] Secondly, where the parties enter into a conditional contract, disputes may arise as to the precise obligations of the parties in relation to the conditions. For example, if a purchaser agrees to buy "subject to finance," is he obliged to use his best endeavours to obtain such finance? Must he do so within a particular time? May he withdraw without even applying for a loan at all? Of course these problems can be avoided by careful drafting of the contract in question, but this has not prevented several cases of this type coming before the courts. They will be examined below in relation to various conveyancing expressions often encountered. A third issue, also dealt with below, is whether it is possible to waive a condition precedent found in a contract.

Intention to enter legal relations Apart from the rules on offer and acceptance, for there to be a binding contract the parties must intend to enter legal relations. This issue is not normally raised in the case of commercial contracts, since the intention to enter a legal relationship is usually obvious from the circumstances; most of the cases therefore have tended to be about agreements in a domestic context, where the matter is not so straightforward.[7] However, the requirement of intention is important in the case of conveyancing contracts, because of the particular way in which such agreements are negotiated and

Subject to contract

entered into. During the early stages of a conveyancing transaction, it is commonplace for the parties and their agents to negotiate with one another "subject to contract." This is the "magic formula" used by conveyancers which, generally speaking, has the effect of negativing contractual intention and thus preventing one party from enforcing the agreement against the other.

Against this background of the rules relevant to the formation of a binding contract, we shall now consider how various expressions commonly used by conveyancers are treated by the courts. As a general point, it is worth emphasizing here that there is no substitute for clear, precise drafting if the cost of litigation (in time and money) is to be avoided.

---

[5] See *Treitel op. cit.* pp. 40–46; *Cheshire, Fifoot and Furmston, op. cit.* pp. 42–45.
[6] See pp. 35–36.
[7] See *Treitel, op. cit.* Chap. 4; *Cheshire, Fifoot and Furmston, op. cit.* Chap. 5.

Subject to contract

It is standard practice in most conveyancing transactions for the parties to agree to a sale and purchase "subject to contract."[8]

Lack of contractual intention
Where this expression is used, the position is almost invariably that the court will hold that the vendor and purchaser lack contractual intention so that there is no enforceable contract. Possible exceptions to this rule are dealt with below, but they are very limited: generally the courts have accepted the "magic" of the "subject to contract" formula and have been keen to protect it. As early as 1857 the House of Lords held that use of the expression, in a letter offering to purchase a property "subject to the terms of a contract being arranged" prevented a binding contract from coming into effect.[9] Similarly, in *Winn* v. *Bull*[10]

Winn v. Bull
the parties agreed to the creation of a lease "subject to the preparation and approval of a formal contract." The prospective lessor drew up a formal contract, but it was never approved by the would-be lessee. The lessor's action for specific performance failed.

Meaning of the term
The precise significance of the "subject to contract" formula was explained by Maugham L.J. in *George Trollope & Sons* v. *Martyn Brothers*[11]: use of the term "means that the matter remains in negotiation until a formal contract is executed, that is, if the contract is recorded in two parts until the formal parts are exchanged." Of course it is normal practice for the contract to be recorded in two parts, so that either party can withdraw at any point before exchange takes place.[12] Lovers of Latin often call this right of withdrawal a *locus poenitentiae*. The right to

Eccles v. Bryant and Pollock
withdraw is well illustrated by *Eccles* v. *Bryant and Pollock*.[13] The parties had agreed to a sale and purchase subject to contract; the vendor's solicitor wrote to the purchaser's to say that his client was ready to exchange; the purchaser's part of the contract was sent to the vendor's solicitor. The vendor then decided to pull out of the sale, and the Court of Appeal upheld his right to do so. However, a vendor who withdraws from a sale without good reason may be contractually liable to pay commission to his estate agent.[14]

Other expressions
It is not only the magic words "subject to contract" which have been held to negative contractual intention. Various other expressions have been held to have the same effect (some *a fortiori*). In each case it is for the court to construe the precise meaning of the terminology used. Examples of expressions negativing intention are "subject to a formal contract to be approved by your solicitors and ourselves"[15]; "subject to a

---

[8] Note the different position in relation to sales by auction: pp. 114–116.
[9] *Honeyman* v. *Marryatt* 6 H.L.C. 113.
[10] (1877) 7 Ch. 29.
[11] [1934] 2 K.B. 436.
[12] If the same solicitor acts for both parties, physical exchange is not necessary: *Smith* v. *Mansi* [1963] 1 W.L.R. 26. As a general rule, solicitors are not permitted to act for both parties anyway: Practice Rule (1972) 69 L.S. Gaz. 1117.
[13] [1948] Ch. 93.
[14] This was the actual point in *George Trollope & Sons* v. *Martyn Bros.* [1934] 2 K.B. 436.
[15] *Santa Fe Land Co.* v. *Forestal Land Timber and Railway Co.* (1910) 26 T.L.R. 534.

proper contract to be prepared by the vendors' solicitors"[16]; and "subject to suitable agreements being arranged between your solicitor and mine."[17]

Policy reasons for retention of the term   In policy terms, there is much to be said for withholding contractual effect from agreements entered into "subject to contract." There are many pre-contract tasks which both a vendor and purchaser must carry out before they cross the Rubicon by exchanging contracts: the purchaser usually has to obtain a mortgage and to make pre-contract searches and enquiries; the vendor will normally be looking for another property and will need to synchronise his sale

Gazumping   and purchase. However the fact that either side may withdraw before exchange takes place also has its disadvantages: a certain sympathy may be felt for a prospective purchaser who incurs legal fees and the cost of a survey only to find that the vendor has decided to pull out. This practice of "gazumping" (dealt with below) is also distasteful to many people. These are the prices that have to be paid for the judicial attachment to the magic formula.

Specific issues

Having considered the general status of the "subject to contract" expression, there are some more specific issues that should be dealt with. In particular, it will be seen that in some rare circumstances, these words may fail to have the effect of negativing contractual intention.

Return of deposit   If the purchaser has handed over any money to the vendor by way of deposit, it is clearly established that he can bring an action to recover this amount if agreement was only reached "subject to contract."[18]

Return of office copies, etc.   Similarly, the vendor is entitled to insist upon the return of any papers he may have sent to the purchaser such as office copies of entries on the register of title or the draft contract.

Pre-contract expenditure   A purchaser who spends money before exchange of contracts cannot recover this sum from the vendor, even if the vendor's conduct is flagrantly unfair. The logic of the situation is quite clear: if the matter is "subject to contract," neither party normally owes any contractual duty to the other and so the risk of wasted expenditure inevitably falls on the person incurring it. This problem is particularly severe when the condition of the property market encourages "gazumping" by vendors, and is considered further below. It may be that in some highly exceptional circumstances, pre-contract expenditure may be recoverable from the other party by bringing an action in quasi-

Brewer Street Investments v. Barclays Woollen Co. Ltd.   contract. In *Brewer Street Investments* v. *Barclays Woollen Co. Ltd.*[19] the parties had reached agreement, subject to contract, on the terms of a lease save that one issue (whether the tenants should be granted an option to purchase the freehold) remained

---

[16] *Chillingworth* v. *Esche* [1924] 1 Ch. 97.
[17] *Lockett* v. *Norman-Wright* [1925] Ch. 56.
[18] *Chillingworth* v. *Esche* [1924] 1 Ch. 97.
[19] [1954] 1 Q.B. 428.

unresolved. While negotiations continued, the landlords carried
out alterations to the property in accordance with the tenants'
specifications. The parties failed to agree on the issue of the
option, the deal fell through and the prospective landlords
stopped the alteration works. They claimed reimbursement from

**Action in quasi-
contract**

the would-be tenants, and the Court of Appeal upheld their
claim. All three judges were of the view that the tenants had
"taken the risk" of the lease falling through and that the loss
should fall on them. Denning L.J. said that "the proper way to
formulate the claim is on a request implied in law, or, as I would
prefer to put it these days, as a claim in restitution," while
Somervell and Romer L.JJ. appeared to consider that there was
some collateral contract between the parties.[20] Presumably, if the
work had been carried out by the prospective tenants, they could
have brought an action in restitution against the freehold
owners.[21]

**Law of Property
Act 1925, s.40(1)**

It is still not entirely clear whether correspondence bearing
the expression "subject to contract" can constitute, or constitute
part of, a written memorandum for the purposes of section 40(1)
of the Law of Property Act 1925. Two Court of Appeal decisions,
Law v. *Jones*[22] and *Tiverton Estates Ltd.* v. *Wearwell Ltd.*[23] are in
conflict on this point, although as stated earlier there is a
tendency to prefer the latter (and later) decision, according to
which such correspondence cannot be used.[24]

Removing the "subject to contract" qualification   A question
which has come before the courts on a number of occasions is
whether, and if so how, it is possible for the parties to waive or
abandon a "subject to contract" qualification. For example,
suppose that a purchaser makes an offer for a house and that
correspondence takes place "subject to contract." It may be that
the negotiations are protracted and that a considerable time
elapses at the end of which a "final" agreement is reached or an
unconditional offer is made which does not contain or refer to the
original "subject to contract" qualification. The important issue
is to decide whether the qualification still has some vitality or
whether it has ceased to be effective. The tendency of the courts

**The "umbrella
principle"**

has been to uphold the efficacy of the "subject to contract"
formula. In *Tevanan* v. *Norman Brett (Builders) Ltd.*[25] Brightman
J. said that "parties could get rid of the qualification of 'subject to
contract' only if they both expressly agreed that it should be
expunged or if such an agreement was necessarily to be implied."
Earlier in his judgment, he invoked what may be termed the

**Tevanan v.
Norman Brett
(Builders) Ltd.**

"umbrella principle": "when the parties started their
negotiations under the umbrella of the 'subject to contract'
formula, or some similar expression of intention, it was really
hopeless for one side or the other to say that a contract came into
existence because the parties became of one mind
notwithstanding that no formal contracts had been

---

[20] See Goff and Jones, *The Law of Restitution* (2nd ed. 1978), pp. 395–396.
[21] *Ibid.* p. 396.
[22] [1974] Ch. 112.
[23] [1975] Ch. 146.
[24] See pp. 11–12, above.
[25] (1972) 223 E.G. 1945.

Sherbrooke v. Dipple

exchanged. . . . " The Court of Appeal in *Sherbrooke* v. *Dipple*[26] approved these passages from Brightman J.'s judgment. In that case, an offer was made by a letter of January 22, 1975 to sell a small piece of land to Mr. Dipple for £200. Nothing came of the matter, however, and by November 1975 negotiations had ceased. The issue was revived in 1976: a further written offer, not expressed to be subject to contract, was made to Mr. Dipple which he orally accepted. When the vendors refused to complete, Mr. Dipple sought specific performance in the county court and was successful. On appeal, however, he lost: all the negotiations were within the ambit of the original "subject to contract" formula.

Cohen v. Nessdale Ltd.

The tenacity of the magic words was also illustrated in *Cohen* v. *Nessdale Ltd.*, another Court of Appeal decision.[27] The appellant was the statutory tenant of a flat. He entered into negotiations with the respondent landlords to purchase a long lease; in March 1977 the latter offered to sell the reversion to him, subject to contract, for £20,000. Negotiations continued, but were broken off in the summer of 1977 when the tenant discovered that the landlord had applied to the rent officer to have the rent increased. In November 1977 the landlords revived the issue, and on November 18 the parties met and entered into an oral agreement, whereby the tenant would be granted a 99-year lease for £17,000. No mention was made at that meeting that the oral agreement was subject to contract. Later that day, the landlords confirmed the agreement in writing, but added the words "subject to contract." Later they refused to proceed with the sale and the tenant sought specific performance. He failed both at first instance and in the Court of Appeal: the November negotiations were a continuation of the original ones and continued to come within the umbrella of the "subject to contract" stipulation. All three lords justices in the Court of Appeal expressed their regret at their decision, as they felt that the landlords' behaviour had been pretty outrageous; their refusal to "bend the rules" even when equity appeared to be on the side of the tenant illustrates just how potent the "subject to contract" formula is.[28]

This is not to say that the courts will never consider that the expression has lost its effect, but that they will only do so in clear cases. In particular it is important to bear in mind that Brightman J. in *Tevanan* v. *Norman Brett (Builders) Ltd.*[29] said that the words can only be waived by *both* parties agreeing to do so expressly or by necessary implication. It would of course be an absurdity if one person, by unilateral action, could be taken to have expunged the words. An example of implied waiver is *Griffiths* v. *Young*.[30] Correspondence relating to a sale and purchase had been going on between solicitors "subject to contract." During a later telephone conversation, an unconditional offer was made and accepted, and the Court of Appeal considered that a contract had been concluded at that

---

[26] (1981) 41 P. & C.R. 173.

[27] [1982] 2 All E.R. 97.

[28] In *Sherbrooke* v. *Dipple* (1981) 41 P. & C.R. 173 the Court of Appeal was clearly not particularly sympathetic to Mr. Dipple's claim.

[29] (1972) 223 E.G. 1945.

[30] [1970] Ch. 675.

time. Perhaps if a similar case were to occur now, the court would be more likely to consider that the conversation was within the protective umbrella of the subject to contract formula, given the tenor of the judgments in *Sherbrooke* v. *Dipple*[31] and *Cohen* v. *Nessdale Ltd.*[32] Nevertheless, *Griffiths* v. *Young*[33] illustrates that great caution is necessary when communicating with the other side in a conveyancing transaction.[34]

Prior agreement   In the normal case, negotiation "subject to contract" prevents a contract from coming into existence at all until exchange takes place. In some cases, however, the parties enter into an agreement, either orally or in writing, without invoking the expression at all. At a later stage, one or other of them may use the words "subject to contract" in correspondence, and the question arises of what effect this has upon the contract. In *Law* v. *Jones* Buckley L.J. said[35] "It is clear that where a principal has entered into a binding contract, neither he nor his solicitor can thereafter deprive it of its binding effect by unilaterally treating the contract as 'subject to contract.' " Of course, it would be possible for *both* parties to agree to terminate the prior agreement and to continue negotiations on a "subject to contract" basis. A different issue that arises in such cases is whether correspondence bearing the words "subject to contract" can ever qualify as a written memorandum of a prior agreement for the purposes of section 40(1) Law of Property Act 1925. The Court of Appeal in *Law* v. *Jones* held that this was possible, though doubt has been cast upon this decision by *Tiverton Estates Ltd.* v. *Wearwell Ltd.*[36] This problem would not arise at all if the person seeking to enforce the contract could prove an act of part performance.[37]

> **Law of Property Act 1925, s.40(1)**

Provisional agreement   As we have seen, where the parties use the expression "subject to contract," it is normally assumed that this means that there will be no contract until exchange takes place. However, the fact that the parties intend to have a formal document drawn up does not inevitably mean that there is to be no contract until that time. It is theoretically possible for them to enter into a binding, albeit provisional, contract which will subsequently be replaced by a more formal one. It is a matter of construction for the court to decide "whether the execution of the further contract is a condition or term of the bargain or whether it is a mere expression of the desire of the parties as to the manner in which the transaction already agreed to will in fact go through."[38] It is highly unlikely that the court would find a binding provisional contract where the "magic" words "subject

---

[31] (1981) 41 P. & C.R. 173.
[32] [1982] 2 All E.R. 97.
[33] [1970] Ch. 675.
[34] It is not clear that there was a satisfactory memorandum for the purposes of s.40(1) of the Law of Property Act 1925 in *Griffiths* v. *Young*: the Court of Appeal held that there was, but this was doubted in *Tiverton Estates Ltd.* v. *Wearwell Ltd.* [1975] Ch. 146.
[35] [1974] Ch. 112 at p. 124.
[36] [1975] Ch. 146: see pp. 11–12, above.
[37] See pp. 16–17, above.
[38] *Von Hatzfeld-Wildenburg* v. *Alexander* [1912] 1 Ch. 284 at p. 288, *per* Parker J.

to contract" are used, but where some similar expression is used the court will have to examine all the surrounding circumstances.

Branca v. Cobarro In *Branca* v. *Cobarro*[39] a written agreement was prepared, a term of which stated that "This is a provisional agreement until a fully legalised agreement drawn up by a solicitor and embodying all the conditions herewith stated is signed." There was held to be a binding provisional agreement.[40]

Meaninglessness An agreement is not a binding contract if it lacks certainty; however the court is permitted to disregard terms which are meaningless.[41] Provided that the terms in question do not govern a vital aspect of the contract, they can simply be ignored, leaving the remainder of the contract enforceable. It is of course highly unlikely that the court would regard the "subject to contract" formula as being meaningless, given that there is a consistent policy of upholding the use of this expression. The possibility cannot be entirely ruled out, however. In *Michael*

Michael Richards v. St. Saviour's *Richards Properties Ltd.* v. *Corporation of Wardens of St. Saviour's, Southwark*[42] a letter of acceptance in response to an offer to tender was sent which, by clerical error, bore the words "subject to contract." Goff J. disregarded them and held that there was a binding contract. The tender document set out all the contractual terms, nothing was left to be negotiated, and there were no further formalities which needed to be satisfied. However, in

Munton v. GLC *Munton* v. *GLC*[43] the same judge, by then elevated to the Court of Appeal, made it quite clear that the *Michael Richards* case had been an unusual one which turned on its own particular facts. It should not be considered to have thrown any doubt upon the "well established and well settled sanctity of the words 'subject to contract.' " In *Munton*, negotiations took place between the local authority and a home owner over the compulsory purchase of his home. In 1969 a price was agreed between the parties of £3,400: the correspondence bore the words "subject to contract." For various reasons, the matter was not completed until December 1972, by when the property was worth £5,100. The authority claimed that there was a concluded agreement to acquire it for £3,400. The Court of Appeal disagreed: as long as the words "subject to contract" were used, then, in the context of compulsory purchase, they were effective to prevent a binding agreement being created. The result therefore was that the authority had to pay the higher figure of £5,100. A similar

Dutton's Brewery v. Leeds City Council conclusion was reached in *Dutton's Brewery Ltd.* v. *Leeds City Council*.[44] There is little doubt that in both of these cases the sympathy of the Court of Appeal lay with the owners rather than the local authorities, which would have made a windfall gain had the decisions gone in their favour.

---

[39] [1947] K.B. 854.
[40] See similarly *Rossiter* v. *Miller* (1878) 3 App. Cas. 1124, H.L.; *Bonnewell* v. *Jenkins* (1878) 8 Ch. D. 70, C.A.; *Filby* v. *Hounsell* (1896) 2 Ch. 737; *Storer* v. *Manchester City Council* (1974) 118 Sol J 599.
[41] *Nicolene Ltd.* v. *Simmonds* [1953] 1 Q.B. 543.
[42] [1975] 3 All E.R. 416.
[43] [1976] 1 W.L.R. 649.
[44] (1982) 43 P. & C.R. 160.

An exceptional case   Just as the court may in exceptional circumstances regard the use of the words "subject to contract" as meaningless, so too there may be occasions on which they will refuse to give them the meaning established in cases such as *George Trollope & Sons* v. *Martyn Brothers*[45] and *Eccles* v. *Bryant and Pollock*.[46] This point is illustrated by *Alpenstow Ltd.* v. *Regalian Properties plc*.[47] The case turns very much on its somewhat unusual facts. The plaintiffs owned the Free Trade Wharf, Tower Hamlets. The defendants were brought in as development design consultants. From February 1983 negotiations took place, in particular with a view to the defendants taking a right of preemption in the event of suitable planning permission for the site being obtained. At one point a binding agreement was entered into, but the parties then abandoned it. On July 12, 1983 a letter was sent from the owner's side setting out a very detailed offer. In particular, paragraph 4 of the letter suggested that:

> (a) if planning permission was obtained, the plaintiffs would serve a notice on the defendants offering them a 51 per cent. stake in the freehold for £1,530,000;
> (b) within 28 days of serving the notice, the defendants "will accept this notice, *subject to contract*," and within seven days thereafter a draft contract would be submitted for approval;
> (c) within 28 days of receipt of the draft contract, the defendants would approve it subject to any reasonable amendments and would then exchange within a further seven days;
> (d) completion would take place 28 days after exchange.

On July 13 the defendants wrote, accepting this offer. Further land was brought into the agreement in December 1983. The defendants registered cautions to protect their position. In 1984, problems emerged in connection with the application for planning permission, when the London Borough of Tower Hamlets brought proceedings challenging the permission granted by the London Docklands Development Corporation. Meanwhile, Denton, Hall & Burgin were instructed by the plaintiffs, and they wrote to the defendants' solicitors claiming that the correspondence of July 1983 was subject to contract and that there was no enforceable contract. The plaintiffs applied to have the defendants' cautions vacated; in a separate action the defendants sought specific performance. Nourse J. heard the motion to have the cautions vacated: all turned on the inclusion of the phrase "subject to contract" in paragraph 4(b) of the letter of July 12. Nourse J. began by saying that "the words 'subject to contract' have a clear prima facie meaning, being in themselves merely conditional. But there might be a very strong and exceptional context which would induce the court not to give them that meaning in a particular case." He then went on to hold that this one of the exceptional cases. Important factors were that:

Alpenstow Ltd. v. Regalian Properties plc

---

[45] [1934] 2 K.B. 436.
[46] [1948] Ch. 93.
[47] [1985] 1 W.L.R. 721; see Wilkinson (1985) 135 New L.J. 1101.

(a) the letter of July 12 was not a "primitive" or "preliminary" document, but written after months of negotiation;

(b) it was possible to give meaning to an obligation on the plaintiffs' part to send a draft contract for approval, in the same way that an agreement to grant an option to purchase land "at a price to be agreed upon" was given meaning in *Smith* v. *Morgan*[48];

(c) there was nothing objectionable about the fact that the defendants' only right was to approve the formal contract subject to reasonable amendments;

(d) the idea that the whole matter was subject to contract was inconsistent with the clear and detailed timetable for exchange and completion set down in the plaintiffs' letter;

(e) indeed it was hard to see how the provisions of paragraph 4 could be given meaning at all, if the matter was subject to contract;

(f) the agreement was professionally drawn by people who must have known what they were doing. "You cannot credit the draftsman with an adherence to the conventional meaning of 'subject to contract' without accusing him of lax and superfluous drafting. I think that he has shown himself to be worth more than that. Why write so much so well to so small effect?"

The case is obviously very significant, since the magic formula failed to prevent contractual liability. The facts were unusual and to suppose that the case somehow undermines the use of the expression "subject to contract" generally would be an overreaction. The clear message, as usual, is that draftsmen must make their intentions abundantly clear, thus eliminating the need for subsequent costly litigation.[49]

Proprietary estoppel In some rare situations it is possible that the magic of the "subject to contract" formula may be outflanked by reliance on the doctrine of proprietary estoppel.[50] Such an attempt failed in *Clark* v. *Follett*[51] and in *Derby & Co. Ltd.* v.

Salvation Army v. West Yorkshire *ITC Pension Trust Ltd.*,[52] but succeeded in *Salvation Army Trustee Co. Ltd.* v. *West Yorkshire Metropolitan County Council.*[53] The Salvation Army agreed, subject to contract, to sell land to the council; the council agreed to sell another site to it on which to build a new hall. In due course, the Salvation Army did acquire its new site and build on it, but the sale of the old site never took place. Eventually the council refused to go ahead with the purchase, claiming there was no contract. Woolf J. held that there was an estoppel in favour of the Salvation Army and that

48 [1971] 1 W.L.R. 803.
49 It should be noted that Nourse J. in *Alpenstow* does *not* say that the words "subject to contract" were meaningless, as in the *Michael Richards* case above, but rather that on the facts of the case they should not be given their usual meaning.
50 On proprietary estoppel generally, see Megarry and Wade, *The Law of Real Property* (5th ed., 1984), pp. 804–805; Cheshire and Burn, *Modern Law of Real Property* (13th ed., 1982), pp. 563–566.
51 [1973] T.R. 43.
52 (1977) 245 E.G. 569.
53 (1981) 41 P & C.R. 179; *cf. Att.-Gen. of Hong Kong* v. *Humphreys Estate (Queen's Gardens) Ltd.* [1987] 2 W.L.R. 343, P.C. (no estoppel).

the sale should be completed. However, the judge also said "I would not want my decision in this case to interfere with the normal conduct of negotiations 'subject to contract'." The intrusion of estoppels into this area has not been met with universal approval.[54] However the facts of this case were unusual: in particular it should be noted that the *same two parties* had agreed to sell *to each other*, and that one of those sales had already taken place. In those circumstances, it is not particularly surprising that the court should have decided to enforce the other sale.

Gazumping   Of course, one of the great problems about negotiations subject to contract is precisely that, since there is no contract, either party can back out at any time up until exchange. This may produce unfairness both for the vendor and the **Pre-contract costs** purchaser, though it is usually the latter who suffers. Having made an offer for a property, the purchaser inevitably has to incur costs on pre-contract tasks (eg paying for a survey, instructing a solicitor). To lose this money through the caprice of a vendor is extremely irksome. The problem is particularly acute when the property market has one of its bouts of escalating prices: in such circumstances, the vendor has everything to gain from the "subject to contract" formula as he plays eager purchasers off against one another. Judicial distaste for "gazumping" has often been expressed,[55] but finding a solution **Law Commission** is not a simple matter. In the mid 1970s the Law Commission **Report** looked into the matter[56] but their conclusion was that there was no change they could recommend. In their Report they said that this was because "the 'subject to contract' procedure is one which has been evolved in order to ensure that those buying and selling houses do not find themselves irrevocably committed to a sale or purchase before being given the chance of taking advice, of making proper inquiries, searches and inspections and of making their financial arrangements. In the context of house purchase it is in our view of paramount importance that the law should place no fetter on the freedom of each of the parties, and in particular the buyer, to refrain from binding commitment if he so wishes."[57]

In early 1987, the Conveyancing Standing Committee set up by the Law Commission recommended a new procedure whereby both vendor and purchaser would pay "pre-contract deposits" which would be forfeited by a party withdrawing from a conveyancing transaction without good reason. It is doubtful however whether this would prevent gazumping to any great extent since, in a buoyant seller's market, a vendor could refuse to participate in the scheme, and because the deposit payable ($\frac{1}{2}$ per cent. of the sale price) would often be insignificant when compared with the "profit" to be made by gazumping.

The risk   The position then is that a purchaser always runs the risk of being gazumped and that the risk increases in times of accelerating

---

[54] See, *e.g.* Farrand, *Contract and Conveyancing* (4th ed., 1983), p. 21.
[55] See, *e.g. Cohen* v. *Nessdale Ltd.* [1982] 2 All E.R. 97.
[56] Working Paper No. 51 *Transfer of Land: "Subject to Contract" Agreements*; Report No. 65 *"Subject to Contract" Agreements*.
[57] Law Comm. Report No. 65, at p. 4.

price rises. It may be that in exceptional cases the courts may be able to come to the assistance of a purchaser by outflanking the "subject to contract" formula in one of the ways suggested above, but most of the cases in which that has happened were highly unusual ones. One of the most effective ways of preventing gazumping would be to speed up the conveyancing procedure: in particular if the period between the first viewing of a property and exchange was shorter, so the opportunity to gazump would

Conveyancing Committee's proposals be decreased. The Conveyancing Committee's proposals in this respect would be of considerable assistance if brought into effect.[58] On the other hand, one could imagine there being more opportunity to gazump if the suggestion that all contracts relating to land should be made in a prescribed form,[59] since then the court would not be able to enforce a concluded agreement entered into orally or in correspondence.

Other terms giving rise to a conditional agreement

Having considered how the courts treat the words "subject to contract," we must now look at the meaning and effect of other expressions, such as "subject to title," "subject to finance" and "subject to survey," sometimes used in the negotiation of conveyancing contracts. Legal analysis of these terms is not always a simple matter and the cases are not always consistent. A few general comments may be helpful.

Generally   When confronted with an agreement expressed to be subject to the satisfaction of some matter such as title or finance, the court may characterise the situation in one of three main

Contractual intention negatived ways. It may say that the use of the expression negatives contractual intention or prevents final agreement, in which case there is no binding contract at all. In this situation, the expression will have achieved the same effect as use of the words

Performance conditional "subject to contract." A second possibility is that the formula used by the parties means that there is undoubtedly a contract in existence between them, but that *performance* of that contract only becomes due after the satisfaction of the condition in question. In practice, this is how many of the cases to come

Term of the contract before the courts have been dealt with. A third possibility is that, by making the agreement subject to some matter, the court will consider the parties to have made that matter a straightforward term of the contract, as opposed to a condition precedent to its performance. It is in the second situation that the greatest problems arise. In the words of one author "An agreement which is subject to a condition precedent is not fully binding until the specified event occurs; nor does either party undertake that it will occur. But an agreement subject to such a condition may impose some degree of obligation on the parties or on one of them. Whether it has this effect, and if so what degree of obligation is

[58] *Conveyancing Simplifications* The Second Report of the Conveyancing Committee (1985).
[59] A proposal tentatively favoured by the Law Commission in its Working Paper No. 92 *Transfer of Land: Formalities for Contracts for Sale, etc., of Land.*

imposed, depends on the true construction of the condition."[60]
The difficulty lies in ascertaining the true construction of the
condition in question.[61] As usual, there is no substitute for clear
and precise drafting, but all too often the parties fail to achieve
this. Five particular problems of construction may arise.

(1) Attempting to satisfy the condition   In most cases, the condition
is imposed for the benefit of the purchaser: for example he will
not want to proceed until he has obtained a suitable mortgage
offer or until he has received detailed planning permission. The
question may arise whether he is under any contractual obligation
to seek a mortgage or to apply for planning permission in such
cases. Of course, if the answer is no, then by pure inactivity the
purchaser can get out of the agreement and the vendor's position
will be very unfavourable. This problem can be overcome by
proper drafting, and the court may anyway be prepared to imply
a term on the purchaser's part to use his best endeavours to
satisfy the condition.[62]

(2) Time   Another problem is to decide how long the purchaser
has got within which to satisfy the condition. It is clearly
undesirable to leave a matter such as this at large, particularly if
the transaction in question is intended to be part of a chain of
other deals. The Privy Council considered the matter of time-
limits in *Aberfoyle Plantations Ltd.* v. *Cheng*[63] and said that the
time within which a condition must be satisfied "must plainly
depend on the true construction of the agreement, or in other
words on the intention of the parties as expressed in, or to be
implied from, the language they have used. But, subject to this
overriding consideration their lordships would adopt, as
warranted by authority and manifestly reasonable in themselves,
the following general principles: (i) where a conditional contract
of sale fixes a date for the completion of the sale, then the
condition must be fulfilled by that date; (ii) where a conditional
contract of sale fixes no date for completion of the sale, then that
condition must be fulfilled within a reasonable time; (iii) where a
conditional contract of sale fixes (whether specifically or by
reference to the date fixed for completion) the date by which the
condition is to be fulfilled, then the date so fixed must be strictly
adhered to, and the time allowed is not to be extended by
reference to equitable principles."[64] *Aberfoyle* itself was an
example of principle (i). It was a condition of the contract
between the parties that the vendor should obtain the renewal of
certain leases. A date for completion was fixed and the purchaser
paid a deposit to the vendor. It was held that the contract was
unenforceable, and the deposit therefore recoverable, since the
vendor had failed to obtain renewal of all the leases by the
completion date. Application of the second principle is illustrated
by *Re Longlands Farm; Alford* v. *Superior Developments Ltd.*[65]

Aberfoyle Plantations Ltd. v. Cheng

Completion date fixed

No completion date fixed

----

[60] Treitel, *The Law of Contract*, (6th ed. 1983), p. 47.
[61] A useful discussion of conditional contracts will be found in the judgment of
  Goff J. in *Wood Preservation* v. *Prior* [1969] 1 W.L.R. 1077 at p. 1090.
[62] See *Treitel op. cit.* p. 49.
[63] [1960] A.C. 115.
[64] *Ibid.* at pp. 124–125.
[65] [1968] 3 All E.R. 552.

The contract was subject to the purchaser obtaining planning permission. More than three and a half years had elapsed and the court held that, as more than a reasonable time had now passed, the vendor was discharged from his obligation to sell. In the course of his judgment, Cross J. remarked that what is reasonable for these purposes must be determined at the time of the contract, and that reasonableness must be judged by an objective **Date fixed for** test applicable to both parties. As for general principle (iii) in **fulfilment of** *Aberfoyle*, it should be noted that this means that time will be of **condition** the essence in such circumstances, contrary to the general rule in conveyancing contracts.[66]

(3) Satisfying the condition   A further difficulty with conditional agreements is to decide whether the condition in question has been satisfied. For example, if an agreement is "subject to planning permission," would the grant of *outline* permission be sufficient? Alternatively, what if detailed permission is granted, but subject to conditions? Similarly, the problem exists of deciding whether the matter is an objective or a subjective one: is it for the court to say whether a condition has been satisfied by applying the criteria of the ordinary bystander, or can a purchaser simply say that as a subjective matter he is not satisfied with a surveyor's report, a mortgage offer or a grant of planning permission? The more detailed and precise the drafting, the less likely it is that these difficulties will arise. Particular problems of this type will be considered below when looking at individual expressions.

(4) Uncertainty   A similar point concerns uncertainty. The court will not enforce a contract whose terms are insufficiently certain: for this reason agreements "subject to finance" have sometimes failed.[67] The parties should therefore state with the greatest particularity possible precisely what is meant by any condition they impose.

(5) Waiver   Where the parties enter into a contract subject to some condition precedent, the question may arise of whether it is possible for one party to waive the condition and to insist on performance. The general answer is that, provided the condition was imposed for the benefit of one person only, that person is **Batten v. White** entitled to waive it. For example, in *Batten* v. *White*[68] a contract for the sale of land was entered into, subject to planning permission. While the purchaser was still seeking permission, the vendor repudiated the contract. The court held that the purchaser was entitled to waive the condition and to sue for specific performance. However, if the condition is imposed for the benefit of *both* parties, or if it is inextricably linked to other terms of the contract from which it cannot be severed, it will **Boobyer v.** require the consent of both parties to waive it. In *Boobyer* v. **Thornville** *Thornville Properties Ltd.*[69] the contract was subject to planning **Properties** permission, and completion was to take place within six weeks of

---

[66] See Ch. 4, below.
[67] See pp. 35–36, below.
[68] (1960) 12 P. & C.R. 66; see similarly *Morrell* v. *Studd and Millington* [1913] 2 Ch. 648.
[69] (1968) 19 P. & C.R. 768.

such permission being obtained. The purchaser sought to waive the condition and to insist upon performance; the court declined to allow him to do so, for without a grant of planning permission it was impossible to give meaning to the provision about

Heron Garage Properties Ltd. v. Moss

completion. The same was true in *Heron Garage Properties Ltd.* v. *Moss*.[70] Not only was the completion date there geared to the grant of planning permission, but it also seemed that the vendor stood to benefit from the condition being satisfied as well as the purchaser.

Equitable ownership

Two final general points about conditional contracts should be made. The first is that where the parties enter into a contract subject to a condition precedent, the purchaser becomes equitable owner of the property in question.[71]

Registration

The second point is that a purchaser under a conditional contract ought to protect his interest by registration under the Land Charges Act 1972 or the Land Registration Act 1925 as the case may be.[72]

Turning now from these general comments about conditional contracts, we shall consider the way in which particular expressions have been dealt with by the courts.

"Subject to title"   The parties may enter into an agreement "subject to title" or "subject to approval of the title by the purchaser's solicitor." Where a vendor agrees to sell land, there is

Implied terms as to good title

an implied term anyway that he will show a good title[73]; in this case it is arguable that this type of condition really adds nothing so that there is an enforceable contract, free from any condition precedent, from the outset. This was the view taken by Lord Cairns (*obiter*) in *Hussey* v. *Horne-Payne*[74]: he was concerned that otherwise a purchaser could change his solicitor from time to time and say whenever he wished to do so that he disliked some aspect of the title. This would leave the vendor in an impossible position. Other cases however have preferred to attribute some meaning to the "subject to title" formula over and above the term implied by law. In *Hudson* v. *Buck*[75] the court held that a purchaser was not bound to proceed with a purchase if his

Solicitor's disapproval

solicitor disapproved of the title offered reasonably and in good faith: the condition meant that if there was any dispute as to title, it was for the purchaser's solicitor to decide whether his client should proceed or not. In *Smallman* v. *Smallman*[76] Lord Denning said that, where the parties agree "subject to title being approved by the purchaser's solicitor" that there is "an implied promise by the buyer that he will appoint a solicitor and shall consult him in good faith, and that the solicitor shall give his honest opinion. If

---

[70] [1974] 1 W.L.R. 148: see Robinson [1975] Conv. 251 at pp. 255 *et seq.*

[71] *Gordon Hill Trust Ltd.* v. *Segall* [1941] 2 All E.R. 379; *Property Discount Corporation Ltd.* v. *Lyon Group Ltd.* [1981] 1 W.L.R. 300.

[72] It may be that conditional contracts cannot be protected by registration (see *e.g.* Smith [1974] C.L.J. 211–214); it is hard to see that this can be correct, however, if as just stated the purchaser in such circumstances has an equitable interest.

[73] *Souter* v. *Drake* (1834) 5 B. & Ad. 992.

[74] (1879) 4 App. Cas. 311.

[75] (1877) 7 Ch. D. 683. See also *Caney* v. *Leith* [1937] 2 All E.R. 532.

[76] [1972] Fam. 25.

the solicitor honestly disapproves, the contract does not bind. But until he does disapprove, the contract binds."[77]

"Subject to preliminary searches and enquiries"   In *Smith and Olley* v. *Townsend*[78] the parties exchanged contracts by post. The purchaser's solicitor wrote in a covering letter that exchange was "subject to preliminary enquiries and to searches." The local search revealed that the property could only be used for residential purposes, whereas the purchasers wished to use it as a saw mill and factory. The purchasers sued for the return of their deposit and succeeded. However, Roxburgh J. refused to decide whether the contract was void for uncertainty and unenforceable for that reason, or whether the condition was an effective one which in the circumstances had not been satisfied. On either analysis, the plaintiff would succeed. The tendency in modern cases is for the court to be reluctant to hold that expressions apparently intended to have meaning by the parties should be struck down on grounds of uncertainty, so that the second ground suggested by Roxburgh J. may well be followed today.` In

Satisfaction   that case, a second issue is whether satisfaction of the condition precedent should be judged objectively or subjectively.[79] In *Aquis Estates Ltd.* v. *Minton*[80] the parties entered into a contract subject to "the property being found free from adverse entry on the purchaser's local land charge and land registry searches." The purchaser wished to demolish the building, whereas in fact the search revealed that it was of special historic interest: this meant that it could not be knocked down. The Court of Appeal held that the matter had to be viewed objectively: the fact that this particular purchaser wished to demolish the building was irrelevant. The important question was whether it could reasonably be said that the entry revealed by the search substantially restricted the use to which the property could be put or substantially diminished its value. Judged objectively, the court considered that the condition was not satisfied; however it went on to hold that the purchaser had waived the right to back out of the agreement since he had continued to negotiate with the vendor after becoming aware of the planning position.

"Subject to finance"   On four occasions, the courts have had to consider agreements expressed to be subject to finance or mortgage.[81] Such cases are relatively rare, since a purchaser almost invariably arranges a mortgage before exchanging contracts. In principle, however, there is no reason why the parties should not enter into an enforceable contract but one whose performance is conditional upon appropriate finance becoming available. The enforceability of such agreements tends

Certainty   to turn on the issue of certainty. In *Re Rich's Will Trusts*[82] a

[77] On "subject to title" and similar expressions, see Wilkinson [1985] Conv. 90, pp. 94–95 and in particular the precedents suggested on p. 95. The same article also deals with other expressions in particular "subject to approval of a lease" and "subject to solicitor's approval" (more commonly used in Commonwealth jurisdictions).

[78] (1949) 1 P. & C.R. 28.

[79] If there is no enforceable contract for want of certainty, the issue does not arise.

[80] [1975] 1 W.L.R. 1452.

[81] See generally Coote "Agreements 'subject to finance' " [1976] Conv. 37.

[82] (1962) 106 S.J. 75.

contract provided that the vendor's solicitors should "be instructed to obtain and fix a suitable mortgage advance on this property." The condition was struck down because of uncertainty. Again in *Lee-Parker* v. *Izzett (No. 2)*[83] there was a contract of sale "subject to the purchaser obtaining a satisfactory mortgage." Goulding J. held that this term was too uncertain, so that there was no enforceable agreement.[84–85]

The courts have tended to relax their attitude towards uncertainty in recent years, and on two occasions have upheld clauses of the type being considered here. In *Lee-Parker* v. *Izzett*[86] (where both the parties and the property were different from the case above), the contract was conditional upon the vendor arranging "a satisfactory mortgage for the purchaser within twenty-eight days." The condition was held to be sufficiently certain, since it meant that a mortgage had to be arranged suitable to the purchaser *acting as a reasonable man*. Similarly in *Jan Mohamed* v. *Hassan*[87] the contract was "subject to a mortgage satisfactory to the purchaser." This was also held to be valid, since a term could be implied that the purchaser would act as a reasonable man in considering whether any mortgage offered was suitable. These cases show that if the courts can construe the condition in a way which avoids the pitfall of uncertainty, they will do so. In particular, if it is possible to set some objective standard, the contract may be saved.

Commonwealth cases   In Commonwealth cases, the courts have been even more willing to uphold "subject to finance" clauses. In particular, in *Meehan* v. *Jones*[88] the Australian Supreme Court upheld a contract "subject to the purchaser or his nominee receiving approval for finance on satisfactory terms and conditions in an amount sufficient to complete the purchase hereunder." Since the issue in the case of "subject to finance" clauses is likely to be one of certainty, it is vital that the parties should be as clear and specific in their drafting as possible, assuming that they both wish and intend to enter a binding contract. In particular they should direct their minds to the amount of the loan required, the interest rate, the other terms of the deal, and the time at which the money is to become available.

"Subject to survey"   It is normal for a prospective purchaser who wishes to commission a survey to do so, and to study the surveyor's report, before exchanging contracts. On some occasions, the courts have been required to consider the effect of **No binding contract**   the parties entering into an agreement "subject to survey." In *Marks* v. *Board*,[89] Rowlatt J. considered that use of this expression had the same effect as the words "subject to contract": in other words there was no binding contract between

---

[83] [1972] 1 W.L.R. 775.
[84–85] The would-be purchaser was in possession of the property. Had the contract have been enforceable, she would have had an overriding interest for the purposes of s.70(1)(g) of the Land Registration Act 1925 which would have bound a later equitable mortgagee.
[86] [1971] 1 W.L.R. 1688; see also [1971] 3 All E.R. 1099.
[87] (1977) 241 E.G. 609.
[88] (1982) 56 A.L.J.R. 813; Wilkinson [1984] Conv. 243.
[89] (1930) 46 T.L.R. 424; see similarly *Graham and Scott* v. *Oxlade* [1950] 2 K.B. 257.

the parties and, in the particular circumstances of the case, the purchaser could not recover damages from the vendor when he refused to complete. In *Astra Trust Ltd.* v. *Adams and Williams*[90] the parties entered into an agreement for the sale of a yacht "subject to satisfactory survey." The prospective purchaser commissioned a survey and then refused to go through with the deal. The vendor retained the deposit which the purchaser had already handed over: the question before the court was whether it should be returned. Megaw J. held that the case was the same as *Marks* v. *Board*; the expression "subject to satisfactory survey" prevented a binding contract from coming into existence at all.

Dissatisfaction with the survey— conditional contract
The purchaser could therefore recover. However he went on to say that, even if his decision in that respect was wrong, he would still have found for the purchaser since he was dissatisfied with the survey on reasonable grounds. While it did not matter on the facts of this particular case which of these two approaches was adopted, it is obviously important to know whether the courts will consider "subject to survey" clauses as preventing a contract at all on the one hand or as constituting conditional contracts on the other. If they give rise to conditional contracts, it is also important to know what rights and obligations will be implied in such agreements in the absence of express terms. These questions are discussed to some extent by *Ee* v. *Kakar*.[91] There the parties agreed to a sale "subject to survey of the property." The vendor wished to withdraw from the sale, and the purchaser sought specific performance. Walton J. concluded that there *was* a conditional contract and went on to spell out the obligations of the purchaser in the circumstances. First, he was under an obligation to obtain a survey within a reasonable time: if he failed to do so, he waived his right to have a survey made and could not withdraw from the purchase. Secondly, he was under an obligation to act bona fide when considering the results of the survey and whether or not to proceed with the purchase. Reasonableness for these purposes would be assessed on an objective basis.

Conclusion
It is submitted that the approach adopted by Walton J. to "subject to survey" clauses is preferable to that shown in the (much earlier) case of *Marks* v. *Board*.[92] It is hard to see why the words "subject to survey" should be treated in the same way as "subject to contract." The latter expression has a unique significance in conveyancing transactions and gives rise to special considerations. Agreements "subject to survey" are more closely related to contracts "subject to finance" (above) and "subject to planning permission" (below) which the courts tend to treat as conditional contracts. The main vice in these cases is the problem of uncertainty, but proper drafting can avoid this difficulty and the courts may well be prepared to imply appropriate terms anyway.

---

[90] [1969] 1 Ll.R. 81.
[91] (1980) 40 P. & C.R. 223; see Adams [1980] Conv. 446; Wilkinson (1981) 131 New L.J. 771; Marksen (1980) 124 S.J. 871; Oakley (1981) 40 C.L.J. 23.
[92] See also two shipping cases, *The Merak* [1976] 2 Ll.R. 250 and *The John S. Darbyshire* [1977] 2 Ll.R. 460 which are consistent with the line adopted in *Ee* v. *Kakar*.

"Subject to planning permission"   The last expression which we need to consider is "subject to planning permission." Planning permission is often a matter of great significance to a prospective purchaser, and someone wanting to alter the use of an existing property or to demolish dwelling-houses to replace them with offices may well be unwilling to exchange contracts at all until the planning position is sorted out to his satisfaction. On the other hand, entering into a contract "subject to planning permission" is not unusual in practice, and the courts have had to consider the effect of this expression several times. It is clear that, as always, it is necessary to construe the actual terms of the

Conditional contract   agreement in question, but in the usual case an agreement "subject to planning permission" will be regarded as a conditional contract. Various issues may then arise.

Certainty   The first point is that, as in other situations, the contract must be sufficiently certain. If it is impossible to give meaning to the condition in question, the contract will be unenforceable. This means that it should be drafted clearly and precisely and that the purpose for which permission is sought should be spelt out. Even when the parties fail in this respect, the court will do its best to give meaning to the words in the contract. In *Batten* v. *White*[93] the parties agreed to a sale "subject to planning permission and satisfactory drainage." The vendor sought to withdraw from the contract before the local authority had dealt with the application, claiming that it was void for uncertainty. The court upheld the agreement: during negotiations between the parties it had been made clear that the purchaser wished to build houses on the land, and this was a relevant consideration when deciding whether the condition was sufficiently certain.

Satisfaction of the condition   The second point about agreements "subject to planning permission" is that disputes may arise as to whether a given condition has been satisfied as a matter of fact. For example, if the local authority grants *outline* planning permission or permission subject to conditions, is the purchaser obliged to proceed? Again, the parties may provide expressly for this situation, in which case there should be no problem. Otherwise the position is less satisfactory, and it may require litigation to determine the matter. Two cases shed some light on this issue. In *Hargreaves Transport* v. *Lynch*[94] the parties agreed to a sale subject to the purchaser obtaining planning permission to use the property as a transport depot. Outline planning permission was granted, but then revoked because of public hostility. The purchaser withdrew from the agreement, but the vendor argued that the condition had been satisfied and that anyway the purchaser was under an obligation to exhaust the appeals procedure before he could withdraw. The court found for the purchaser on both points. Outline planning permission did not entitle the purchaser to go ahead and develop the land: that could only be done once detailed permission had been granted; the condition was therefore not satisfied. Furthermore it would be unreasonable to expect the purchaser to exhaust the appeals procedure before withdrawing, because of the time and expense involved in doing so: this would be disproportionate to the

---

[93] (1960) 12 P. & C.R. 66.
[94] [1969] 1 W.L.R. 215; *cf. Guinness* v. *Pearce* (1971) 22 P. & C.R. 998.

benefit that he might obtain from having the outline permission reinstated.

Permission subject to conditions

The other case concerns planning permission which is granted subject to conditions. In *Richard West & Partners (Inverness) Ltd.* v. *Dick*[95] a contract for the sale of land was conditional "upon planning consent being granted by the local authority following upon the application already lodged for use of the subject of sale as a hotel." When planning permission was granted, two conditions were imposed. First, the purchaser was required to improve the access to the main road, to cope with the inevitable increase in traffic. Secondly, any alterations to the property had to conform to the requirements of the local building inspector. In fact he required extensive work to be done in order to satisfy the fire regulations. The purchaser claimed that the contract was not enforceable against him because of these conditions attached to the planning permission. The court held that the contract was enforceable against the purchaser. The question was whether a true planning permission had been granted for the development: on the facts of the case the answer was yes, for the conditions attached could not be said to be so onerous as to render the permission useless. A further point was that the requirement on the purchaser's part to comply with *fire regulations* was not within the scope of the expression "planning consent" anyway. More specific drafting would have been needed to afford the purchaser a right to withdraw on this ground.

Details of application

The next point about contracts "subject to planning permission" is that they should specify the time within which permission is to be applied for,[96] and the person whose duty it is to make the application. Unless the contract provides to the contrary, it is the purchaser's responsibility to seek the permission which he requires, although he is not obliged to proceed if there is no point in doing so and if he acts in good faith. For example in *Tesco Stores Ltd.* v. *William Gibson & Son Ltd.*[97] the parties agreed to a sale "on the footing that the purchasers obtain planning permission for the total development of the site in accordance with their requirements and this contract is subject to such consent being obtained." It transpired that the property was insufficiently large for the prospective purchasers' purposes, and they withdrew without applying for planning permission. The vendors sued, but unsuccessfully. There was no point in requiring the purchasers to go through the procedure of applying for planning permission when the property could never be developed to their satisfaction anyway.

Consultation before withdrawal of application

The last point to make on planning permission is that, if the vendor himself has already made an application, he is obliged not to withdraw it without first consulting the purchaser.[98]

---

[95] [1969] 2 Ch. 433.
[96] See pp. 32–33, above and in particular *Re Longlands Farm* [1968] 3 All E.R. 552.
[97] (1970) 214 E.G. 835.
[98] *Sinclair-Hill* v. *Sothcott* (1973) 26 P. & C.R. 490.

4 THE CONTRACT

Introduction

In order to comply with the requirements of section 40 of the Law of Property Act 1925 as to the enforceability of the contract, the vendor's conveyancer prepares a written contract and sends it to the purchaser's conveyancer for approval, eventual signing and exchange. Most vendors' conveyancers employ a standard form of contract, usually either the Law Society's Contract for Sale (1984 Revision) or the National Contract of Sale (20th Edition).

The particulars and the conditions   These standard form contracts follow the traditional layout for contracts for the sale of land of bipartite division into particulars and conditions. Malins V.-C., in *Torrance* v. *Bolton*[1] said: "The proper office of the particulars is to describe the subject-matter of the contract, that of the conditions to state the terms on which it is sold." Warrington J. in *Blaiberg* v. *Keeves*[2] added: "It is not the function of the particulars to deal with title at all; that has to be dealt with on evidence, and it is the function of the conditions to state what evidence of title the purchaser is to have." To banish any misapprehension as to what the particulars should or should not contain, the Council of the Law Society have explained[3] that: "the proper description of the subject-matter involves not only a physical description, but also a description of the exact estate or interest sold and of every charge upon it or right restricting the purchaser's absolute enjoyment of it; these matters should appear in the particulars and not merely in the conditions. Reference should accordingly be made in the particulars to onerous covenants, easements and the like, whether or not they are also mentioned in the conditions."

Conditions of sale   Both the Law Society's and National contracts include a comprehensive set of conditions which can be altered or amended to suit the particular transaction. The making of conditions of sale has become so much a part of conveyancing practice, that it is sometimes forgotten that every contract for the sale of land is made on the terms implied by law into an open contract (that is, a contract with no conditions). Conditions may seek to improve the open contract position of the parties by modifying or supplementing these implied terms,[4] but they never displace them entirely. Furthermore: "[in] approaching the question of the construction of the conditions of sale, it is well established that the court should have regard to the normal rules of equity as

---

[1] (1872) L.R. 14 Eq. 124.
[2] [1906] 2 Ch. 175 at p. 184.
[3] (1952) 49 L.S.Gaz. 29.
[4] The current Law Society and National conditions of sale owe their existence first to vendors' and later to purchasers' reluctance to enter an entirely open contract for sale.

regards the respective rights of vendor and purchaser."[5] The result is a "catch-22" situation for:

> "[any] discussion of the terms of contracts for the sale of land must have much in common with the house that Jack built: that is the agreement that incorporates the special conditions that refer to the general conditions that modify the statutory provisions that vary the equitable principles that mitigate the rules of common law."[6]

Open contracts

Implied terms   An open contract is made where agreement is reached as to the parties, property and price. In the absence of contrary stipulation in the contract the terms which will be implied include[7]:

(1) That the vendor is selling an estate in fee simple free from incumbrances.

(2) That the vendor will show good title. Section 110 of the Land Registration Act 1925 prescribes the mode of deducing title to registered land and for the most part cannot be contracted out of.

(3) That vacant possession will be given on completion. This presumption may be rebutted if the property was occupied by someone other than the vendor when the purchaser inspected it, or if the contract states that the sale is subject to tenancies.

(4) That the purchase shall be completed as soon as good title has been shown to the property and good title shall be shown within a reasonable time.

(5) That time is not "of the essence" of the contract unless the contract itself so provides, or the surrounding circumstances show that the parties intended it to be so.[8]

(6) That certain expressions have the following meanings unless the context requires otherwise[9]:
     (i) "month" means calendar month;
     (ii) "person" includes a corporation;
     (iii) the singular includes the plural and vice versa;
     (iv) the masculine includes the feminine and vice versa.

Void conditions

Illegal stipulations   Certain stipulations contrary to the policy of the law are void. These include[10]:

[5] *Re Hewitt's Contract* [1963] 1 W.L.R. 1298 at p. 1301. Take for example a condition in the contract to the effect that no misdescription shall annul a sale. The condition may be ineffective to protect a vendor because of the rule in *Flight* v. *Booth*, that if the misdescription is substantial the purchaser will be able to avoid the contract at law and in equity and recover his deposit with interest and costs.

[6] J.T. Farrand, *Contract and Conveyance* (4th ed.), p. 76.

[7] A full list is given in *Emmet on Title* (19th ed., p. 2/151).

[8] Law of Property Act 1925, s.41.

[9] *Ibid.* s.61 which applies to "all deeds, contracts, wills, orders, and other instruments . . . made . . . after the commencement of this Act."

[10] A full list appears in *Emmet on Title* (19th ed., p. 2/153).

(1) A condition that a purchaser of a legal estate in land shall accept a title made with the concurrence of a person entitled to an equitable interest, if a title can be made discharged from the equitable interest under a trust for sale, or under the Law of Property Act 1925, or the Settled Land Act 1925, or any other statute.[11]

(2) A condition that an outstanding legal estate is to be traced or got in by or at the expense of a purchaser or that no objection is to be taken on account of an outstanding legal estate.[12]

(3) Where a purchaser of a legal estate is entitled to have it discharged from a registered equitable interest which will not be overreached by the conveyance to him, a condition that he shall not require such registration to be cancelled or the person entitled to the equitable interest to concur in the conveyance, and in either case free of expense to the purchaser.[13]

Charges for draft conveyance, etc.

(4) A condition preventing a purchaser from employing a solicitor of his own free choice, or providing that the conveyance to, or the registration of the title of, the purchaser, shall be prepared or carried out at the expense of the purchaser by the vendor's solicitor.[14] However the vendor can reserve the right to furnish the purchaser with a form of conveyance from which the draft can be prepared, and to charge a reasonable fee for it.[15] The Council of the Law Society have drawn attention[16] to the fact that: "what is a reasonable fee will depend on the circumstances, but should not, it is considered, exceed the out-of-pocket expenses of the vendor's solicitors for providing the form. Where the same form is used for more than a few sales, the fee for reproduction should be nominal only. . . .

The practice of providing a form of conveyance in estate development or otherwise is normally to assist the vendor by ensuring conformity and therefore high charges cannot be justified. In the Council's view, subject as above-mentioned, the practice is unobjectionable, but would not generally be appropriate on the sale of a single property." A vendor is free to stipulate in the contract that the purchaser shall pay his conveyancing costs.

(5) A condition barring the purchaser from objecting to lack of stamping on a document forming part of the title or

---

[11] Law of Property Act 1925, s.42(1).

[12] *Ibid.* s.42(3).

[13] *Ibid.* s.43.

[14] *Ibid.* s.48(1). The same protection is afforded to a lessee or underlessee by s.48(2). If such a contractual provision is rendered void it is implied that: "the lessee or underlessee shall register with the lessor or his solicitor within six months of the date thereof, or as soon after the expiration of that period as may be practicable, all conveyances and devolutions (including probates or letters of administration) affecting the lease or underlease and pay a fee of one guinea in respect of such registration, and the power of entry (if any) on breach of any covenant contained in the lease or underlease shall apply and extend to the breach of any covenant so to be implied."

[15] *Ibid.* s.48(1)(2) proviso.

[16] (1965) 62 L.S.Gaz. 184.

requiring the purchaser to pay for the proper stamping of that document.[17]

(6) A condition that the purchaser shall not be entitled to inspect a power of attorney affecting the title, or be supplied with a copy of it, free of charge.[18]

(7) A condition which excludes or restricts any liability or remedy for a misrepresentation made before contract, except insofar as it satisfied the requirement of reasonableness as stated in section 11(1) of the Unfair Contract Terms Act 1977.

Standard conditions[19]

The first set of standard conditions seems to have been those issued by the Liverpool Law Society in 1865. The National conditions were published in 1902 and the Law Society's general conditions were used as from January 1, 1926. The Law Society's general conditions were last revised in 1984 and are materially different from the National conditions now in their twentieth edition.

An effective incorporation is necessary for these standard conditions to apply to the contract. In *McKay* v. *Turner*,[20] the first special condition in some auction particulars stated that the property was sold, "subject to the general conditions printed within. . . . " But in fact nothing was printed within, although the intention had been to incorporate the Law Society's General Conditions of Sale (1973 revision). Fox J. held that the special condition could only be construed on its actual wording in the light of any admissible circumstances of which the vendor's intention was not one. No general conditions were incorporated.

Incorporation of the conditions

However in the later case of *Smith* v. *South Wales Switchgear Co. Ltd.*,[21] a contract for sale was made "subject to . . . our general conditions . . . obtainable on request." Evidence showed that the vendors had at the time of the contract, three different versions of their general conditions of sale, revised at different dates, and if asked would have sent whichever version came to hand. The House of Lords rejected the argument that none of the versions were incorporated by the reference, because "its logical result would seem to be that there was no contract at all." They held that the reference to the general conditions must be taken to incorporate the version current at the date of the contract. It should be mentioned that the *Smith* case involved a contract for the supply of electrical maintenance work. It had nothing to do with land. Nevertheless it is arguable that in a case like *McKay* the general conditions presently used by the vendor's solicitor would be incorporated. This would accord with the final outcome

---

[17] Stamp Act 1891, s.125(2).

[18] Law of Property Act 1925, s.125 as amended by the Law of Property (Amendment) Act 1926 and the Powers of Attorney Act 1971, s.11(3).

[19] The reader is referred generally to H. W. Wilkinson, *Standard Conditions of Sale of Land* (3rd ed.). This does not however deal with the 1984 revision of the 1980 edition of the Law Society's General Conditions of Sale.

[20] (1975) 120 S.J. 367; [1978] Conv. 81.

[21] [1978] 1 W.L.R. 165.

of *McKay*, where a 28–day notice to complete was held effective under the general law even though served under an ineffective condition.

Construction of the conditions

Any ambiguity in the standard conditions will be construed against the vendor, applying the *contra proferentem* principle. Knight-Bruce V.-C., in *Symons* v. *James*,[22] said: "If a vendor means to exclude a purchaser from that which is a matter of common right he is bound to express himself in terms the most clear and unambiguous. And if there be any chance of reasonable doubt, or reasonable misapprehension of his meaning, I think that the construction must be that which is rather favourable to the purchaser than to the vendor." This was recently reaffirmed by Slade J. in *Leominster Properties Ltd.* v. *Broadway Finance Ltd.*,[23] where referring to condition 10 of the National Conditions of Sale (19th edition), he said that if the words of a condition were ambiguous they should be construed against the vendor, "because it was the grantor, and the rights of the plaintiff as purchaser were thereby restricted."

Status of the conditions
Lyme Valley Squash Club Ltd. v. Newcastle under Lyme Borough Council

The judicial calling of a former Law Society general condition "very much part of the small print" of a contract, raises the question of the status of the conditions. *Lyme Valley Squash Club Ltd.* v. *Newcastle under Lyme Borough Council*[24] concerned a sale of land under the 1973 edition of the Law Society's General Conditions of Sale, by the local authority to the squash club for development as a squash club. At the time of sale the land was surrounded on three sides by land owned by the local authority and used as a public car park. After the club was built the local authority contracted with developers for them to construct a retail store and amenities on this land. The club objected the ground, *inter alia*, that the building would affect the light to the club's windows and sought an injunction to restrain its construction.

General condition 4(2)(*c*) of the contract read:

" . . . where all or part of the property adjoins or is near to any other land of the vendor the purchaser shall not acquire any rights or easements thereover which would restrict the free use of the vendor's other land for building or any other purpose and the conveyance shall so provide."

By mistake the conveyance had not so provided but Blackett-Ord, V.-C., decided[25] that the case was not one for the discretionary remedy of rectification, especially since third party mortgagees had acquired rights in the club as bona fide purchasers for value without notice of any claim for rectification: no order could bind them. The main point he had to consider was whether the club had acquired a right of light to its windows having apparently contracted out of it in general condition 4(2)(*c*). He was of the opinion that the parties had given no thought to the condition and that it was therefore right to go behind it. There was a mutual intention at the time of the contract, that the club should have the right to light. Under both

---

[22] 62 E.R. 983.
[23] (1981) 42 P. & C.R. 372 at p. 387.
[24] [1985] 2 All E.R. 405; [1985] Conv. 237.
[25] *Ibid.* at p. 413.

the doctrine of non-derogation from grant and under section 62 of the Law of Property Act 1925, the conveyance carried an easement of light to the windows similar to that which was enjoyed at the time of conveyance. An injunction was refused but the club was awarded £10,000 damages.

General condition 4(2)(c) was replaced by 5(3)(b) in the 1980 edition of the Law Society's general conditions (it was introduced by the 1984 revision). Nevertheless 4(2)(c) *was* in the present contract and *was* ignored. This is nothing new: "the courts have demonstrated a disturbing tendency to dislike and discount general conditions of sale."[26] Other cases showing this trend, notably *Walker* v. *Boyle*[27] and *Faruqi* v. *English Real Estates*[28] are discussed later in the book together with the condition they concern.

The Law Society's Contract for Sale (1984 Revision) (reproduced at pp. 46–47)

The 1984 Revision superseded the 1980 edition of The Law Society's Contract and General Conditions of Sale as from September 3, 1984. The document is distinguishable by its bright pink colour. Opportunity was taken in this latest revision to make minor changes in the layout of the form of contract and of some of the wording of the special conditions.

Agreement

Agreement, parties The agreement for sale and purchase and the names and addresses of the vendor and purchaser appear at the top of the contract, and are separated from the signature-box. The separation is of no consequence, as the signatures are clearly intended to govern the whole contract. The agreement is expressed to be made subject to the special conditions on the back page of the contract form.

Parties

Where the contract is one of sub-sale and purchase, and the land is unregistered, the sub-purchaser's interest must (if necessary) be registered against the name of the head-vendor: registration against the sub-vendor is ineffective[29] because he is not the legal estate owner. The purchaser's solicitor should have discovered by way of preliminary enquiry whether the vendor is the legal estate owner, or if he is not, who the head-vendor is. If not, this information should be elicited by special condition.

The particulars Perfect particulars will state:

Perfect particulars

(1) the physical extent of the land, accurately;
(2) the estate or interest in the land sold (freehold or leasehold);
(3) the rights the benefit of which are to pass with the land sold;
(4) the obligations the burden of which the land is subject to.

---

[26] J.T. Farrand, *Contract and Conveyance* (4th ed.), pp. 79–80.
[27] [1982] 1 W.L.R. 495.
[28] [1979] 1 W.L.R. 963.
[29] Land Charges Act 1972, s.3, *Barrett* v. *Hilton Developments Ltd.* [1975] Ch. 237.

> **IMPORTANT**
> This is a technical document, designed to create specific legal rights and obligations.
> It is recommended for use only in accordance with the advice of your solicitors.

THE LAW SOCIETY'S CONTRACT FOR SALE (1984 REVISION)

AGREEMENT made the   day of   198

BETWEEN

Vendor

Purchaser

IT is agreed that the Vendor shall sell and the Purchaser shall purchase in accordance with the following special conditions the property described in the particulars below at the price of

PARTICULARS—ALL THAT freehold/leasehold property

SPECIAL CONDITIONS OF SALE—SEE BACK PAGE

		SIGNED
Purchase money *less* deposit paid		
Chattels, fittings etc.		
Balance		Vendor/Purchaser

Vendor's Solicitors   Ref.

Purchaser's Solicitors   Ref.

Local Authorities

SPECIAL CONDITIONS

A. The property is sold subject to The Law Society's General Conditions of Sale (1984 Revision) ("general conditions") printed within so far as they are not varied by or inconsistent with these special conditions but general condition 8(5) shall apply in any event.

B. For the purposes of the following general conditions—
    1(*b*)   the contract rate is   % per annum above the base rate from time to time of

    1(c)   contractual completion date is   198
    21(2)(*b*) the specified bank is
    21(5)(a)   the latest time is   am/pm
    1(g)   the following are not working days

    5(3)   the retained land is

C. General condition 4 shall not apply. [For the purposes of general condition 4(2) the period shall be   from the date hereof and for the purposes of general condition 4(3)(*b*) the specified use is   .]

D. The Vendor shall convey as

E. The Vendor's title is registered with   title under Title No.
    in the   District Land Registry.
    The Vendor authorises the Purchaser's solicitors to inspect the register and to obtain office copies thereof.

(or) E. The abstract of title shall begin with

F. The property is sold with vacant possession on completion.

(or) F. The property is sold subject to the following leases or tenancies

G. The property is sold subject to

© 1984 *The Law Society, Law Society's Hall, 113 Chancery Lane, London WC2A 1PL*   GM. SET 803F   *Printed by Oyez Press Limited* **oyez**
27 Crimscott Street, London SE1 5TT   F3681 9-84
★ ★

Although mention of (3) and (4) should be made in the particulars, full details are usually given by special condition.

The vendor's solicitor normally describes unregistered land by reference to the title deeds, but "it is the duty of the conveyancer in framing a description upon sale not to take it for granted that he is to follow the exact terms of the description of the existing title but to make full enquiry into the facts in order that he may be able to describe correctly the subject intended to be disposed."[30] Where the whole of land comprised in a registered title is being sold reference to the title number is sufficient.[31] A sale of part only of the vendor's registered land necessitates a new description and plan.[32] In *Scarfe* v. *Adams*,[33] the Court of Appeal criticised the use of small scale plans in cases where boundaries have to be defined with precision.

Purchase money, deposit paid, chattels, etc.   If the purchase price is uncertain, there is no contract.[34]

Referential bids   The House of Lords recently decided the fate of the purported acceptance of a referential bid (C$2,100,000 "or C$101,000 in excess of any other offer which you may receive which is expressed as a fixed monetary amount, whichever is the higher"), which was made in response to an invitation for offers by sealed tender or confidential telex, and a promise to sell to the "highest bidder." *Harvela Investments Ltd.* v. *Royal Trust of Canada (C.I.) Ltd.*[35] involved the sale of shares, but the principle is equally applicable to the sale of land. Lord Templeman, in delivering the main judgment, said that where a vendor promises to sell to the "highest bidder," he may do so by fixed bidding, only inviting fixed bids, or by auction, permitting referential bids. The method he chooses depends on the terms of the invitation itself. Three provisions in this invitation pointed to a fixed bidding sale. First the vendors had undertaken to accept the highest offer that showed that they had been anxious to ensure that a sale should result. Secondly, they had extended the same invitation to both offerees. That showed that they had wished each to have equal opportunity of purchasing the shares. Thirdly, they had insisted that the offers must be confidential and remain confidential until the expiry of a specified time limit. That showed that they had wanted to provoke from each offeree the best price they were prepared to pay, in ignorance of the other's bid. The vendors had intended a fixed bidding sale and had not been entitled to accept a referential bid.

"normal" or reduced deposit   Law Society general condition 9(1) provides that the purchaser shall pay the "normal deposit" to the vendor's solicitors on or before the date of the contract, or such lesser sum as the vendor shall have agreed in writing. "Normal deposit" is defined by condition 1(f) as ten per cent. of the purchase price, excluding any separate price to be paid for chattels and fittings. The 10 per cent. includes any preliminary or pre-contract deposit

---

[30] *Gordon-Cumming* v. *Houldsworth* [1910] A.C. 537. at p. 574.
[31] Land Registration Rules 1925, r. 79.
[32] Land Registration Rules 1925, rr. 98 and 117. See r. 54 for flats and maisonettes.
[33] [1981] 1 All E.R. 843. See also *A.J. Dunning & Sons (Shopfitters) Ltd.* v. *Sykes & Son (Poole) Ltd.* [1987] 2 W.L.R. 167.
[34] See pp. 8 to 9, above.
[35] [1985] 3 W.L.R. 276 (H.L.), reversing [1985] Ch. 103 (C.A.).

paid by the purchaser. If the vendor has agreed to accept a reduced deposit, the lesser sum should be inserted here. The total value of chattels and fittings the vendor is leaving on the property is often agreed and stated separately, in order to reduce the purchase price and consequently the stamp duty (if any) the purchaser has to pay on conveyance. Duty at the rate of one per cent. of the purchase price is payable on purchases over £30,000.[36]

Space is left at the bottom of the front page for the names and addresses of the parties' solicitors and local authorities for making searches.

Special conditions

Excluding liability under implied covenants for breach of repair obligations under lease

Special condition A   This incorporates the Law Society's general conditions insofar as they are not inconsistent with the special conditions. It is stated that "general condition 8(5) shall apply in any event." General condition 8(5) limits the covenants which statute would otherwise imply on the assignment of a leasehold term. By section 76(1)(*a*) and (*b*) and Parts I and II of the Second Schedule to the Law of Property Act 1925, six covenants are implied in a conveyance of leasehold property for valuable consideration (other than a mortgage) by an assignor who conveys and is expressed to convey as beneficial owner, including one that the rent has been duly paid and the covenants and conditions have been duly observed and performed up to the time of conveyance. The same covenants are implied in an assignment of a leasehold term by section 24 of the Land Registration Act 1925. General condition 8(5) states that the implied covenants shall not operate so as to make the vendor liable for any breach of covenant concerning the state and condition of the property and the assignment shall so provide.

In 1974 it was suggested[37] that any modification of the implied covenants where there are breaches of repairing obligations might be precluded where the vendor sells as beneficial owner. Accordingly the phrase "general condition 8(5) shall apply in any event," was added to special condition A to bolster[38] the concluding sentence of that sub-condition: "This sub-condition applies notwithstanding that a special condition provides for the vendor to convey as beneficial owner." The words "in any event" do not mean that the parties cannot alter general condition 8(5) by special condition if they so wish.

It has since been said[39] that this exercise was unnecessary in view of the decision in *Butler* v. *Mountview Estates Ltd.*[40] In that case the purchaser failed to get damages from the vendor for breaches of repairing covenants because the contract, made under the Law Society general conditions (1934 edition), stated that the

---

[36] Finance Act 1984. No duty is payable where the consideration does not exceed £30,000 provided a certificate of value is duly given.
[37] [1974] Conv. 312.
[38] [1981] Conv. 2.
[39] H.W. Wilkinson, *Standard Conditions of Sale of Land* (3rd ed.), p. 78.
[40] [1951] 2 K.B. 563.

purchaser bought the property with full knowledge of its state and condition and took it as it stood. The stipulation was effective even though the vendor assigned as beneficial owner. Nevertheless the authors of the 1984 Revision obviously preferred to err on the safe side: general condition 8(5) and special condition A were not altered by them.

It might usefully be added that neither condition will protect a vendor from a claim for damages for misrepresentation, if he fraudulently conceals a breach of repairing obligation.[41]

Special condition B   This expands on some of the terms used in the general conditions.

(I) CONTRACT RATE   If no contract rate of interest is agreed between the parties and specified here, the fall back rate of interest under general condition 1(*b*) will be the rate payable by an acquiring authority on entry under compulsory powers. The rate is prescribed by the Treasury by statutory instrument[42]—the Acquisition of Land (Rate of Interest after Entry) Regulations—and whenever it is changed, the new rate is published in the *Solicitors' Journal.*

Importance of the contract rate   The contract rate is important to vendor and purchaser for, *inter alia,* two reasons. First, under general condition 22, where there is a delay in completion the party in default (if any) has to pay the other compensation for late completion. The party entitled to compensation can choose to take interest at the contract rate on the balance of the purchase price for the period of default instead of suing for damages at common law. And secondly, under general condition 18, the contract rate governs the amount of interest payable by the buyer on the balance of the purchase price if he is allowed to go into occupation of the property before completion.

(II) COMPLETION DATE, SPECIFIED BANK, LATEST TIME   The open contract rule is that completion shall take place within a reasonable time. This is a question of fact, to be measured by the legal business outstanding.[43] The rule is supplanted where a completion date is set by special condition B, or, if no date is specified, by general condition 21(1), which states that it shall be the twenty-fifth working day after the date of the contract.[44]

Time for completion   The contract should not provide for completion to take place when possession of the property is given if no date is fixed for the giving of possession. It was held on these facts in *Johnson* v. *Humphrey*[45] that the implication of common law that completion was to take place within a reasonable time was excluded by the express term that completion was to be determined by reference to possession and in turn had excluded any implied term as to when possession should be given. The contract was unenforceable.

---

[41] *Gordon* v. *Selico Co. Ltd.* (1986) 278 E.G. 53.
[42] Under the Land Compensation Act 1961, s.32.
[43] *Johnson* v. *Humphrey* [1946] 1 All E.R. 460.
[44] *Marks* v. *Lilley* [1959] 1 W.L.R. 749, *Smith* v. *Mansi* [1963] 1 W.L.R. 26.
[45] *Ibid.*

Completion date to be agreed in the future

There is some controversy as to the effect of the stipulation: "the date fixed for completion is to be agreed between the parties." In *Gavaghan* v. *Edwards*[46] the county court held that no concluded and binding contract could be found in an agreement to agree, and that the special condition eliminated the general condition that otherwise completion should take place within seven weeks. The Court of Appeal upheld the appeal on other grounds and unfortunately did not comment on this point. Two earlier cases[47] had favoured the view that even though the parties specified a completion date to be agreed in the future, the court would imply a term that completion should take place within a reasonable time, thus validating the contract.

Walters v. Roberts

In the latest case, *Walters* v. *Roberts*,[48] a contract for the sale of a sheep farm, a flock of sheep and additional farm land, was made under the National Conditions of Sale (19th edition). The contractual date for completion passed and the parties agreed that: "a completion date . . . will have to be agreed." Nourse J. in fact held that the evidence showed parties had not made an agreement to agree: they had agreed that completion should take place after the lambing season. However he said that if the parties had left the date for future agreement, the court would have implied completion within a reasonable time, in default of agreement: "Both parties must be taken to intend that completion will take place sooner or later."

In view of the doubt surrounding this point, parties who wish to agree a completion date in the future should leave, "1(*c*) contractual completion date is . . . ," blank. The general "fall back" condition will be able to operate in default of agreement, and questions as to "reasonable implications" will not arise.

Completion moneys are normally paid by banker's draft and general condition 21(2)(*b*) limits the range of banks whose drafts

CHAPS settlement banks

are acceptable on completion to CHAPS (which stands for clearing house automated payments system) settlement banks. They are: Bank of England; Bank of Scotland; Barclays Bank plc; Central Trustee Savings Bank plc; Clydesdale Bank plc; Co-operative Bank plc; Coutts & Co.; Lloyds Bank plc; Midland Bank plc; National Girobank; National Westminster Bank plc; Royal Bank of Scotland plc; Williams & Glyn's Bank plc. But the

"specified bank"

sub-condition does allow the purchaser to include within the range an otherwise unauthorised bank, by inserting its name into special condition B, providing the vendor agrees.

Latest time for completion

Special condition B also allows for the fixing of a latest time for completion (to facilitate the banking arrangements of the parties). If the money due on completion is not paid by the "latest time" on the day set for completion, or if no time is specified, by 2.30 p.m. on that day, completion is deemed to be postponed, by reason of the purchaser's delay, until the next working day, for the purposes of calculating compensation for late completion under general condition 22. (General condition 21(5)(*a*) and (*b*)).

[46] [1961] 2 Q.B. 220.
[47] *Simpson* v. *Hughes* (1897) 76 L.T. 237; *Fowler* v. *Bratt* [1950] 2 K.B. 96.
[48] (1981) 258 E.G. 965; [1981] Conv. 168.

Non-working days

(III) WORKING DAYS   All the time limits in the Law Society's general conditions are expressed in working days except those in 23(5) which relate to resale of the property after breach of contract and the option to claim liquidated damages.[49] General condition 1(g) defines "working day" as any day from Monday to Friday (inclusive) other than, Christmas Day, Good Friday, and any other statutory bank holiday, and any other day specified in special condition B as not a working day.

(IV) RETAINED LAND   Law Society general condition 5(3)(b) states:

Implied easements and reservations

> "The conveyance of the property shall contain such reservations in favour of the retained land and the grant of such rights over the retained land as would have been implied had the vendor conveyed both the property and the retained land by simultaneous conveyances to different purchasers."[50]

The effect of this sub-condition is that both vendor and purchaser can take advantage of the operation of the rule in *Wheeldon* v. *Burrows* and of section 62 of the Law of Property Act 1925: the conveyance to the purchaser will impliedly reserve easements for the benefit of the land retained over the land sold, as well as impliedly grant them for the benefit of the land sold over the land retained. By 5(3)(a), "retained land" means "land retained by the vendor (i) adjoining the property, or (ii) near to the property and designated as retained land in a special condition." This wording suggests that land which adjoins the property sold does not have to be designated for the purposes of 5(3)(b), whereas nearby land does. For obvious reasons, the purchaser's solicitor should ascertain what land adjoins and the vendor's solicitor should state correctly in the contract what land is nearby.

Purchaser's opportunity to rescind

Special condition C   This refers to Law Society general condition 4 which only applies if a special condition so provides and which gives the purchaser a limited right to rescind the contract should any of the following matters come to his knowledge and he did not know about it when contracting. The matters are: a financial charge on the property which the vendor cannot or will not discharge; a statutory prohibition adversely affecting the continued use of the property for the pre-sale purpose or the purpose mentioned in a special condition; or "a matter which is likely materially to reduce the price which a willing purchaser could otherwise reasonably be expected to pay for the relevant interest in the property in the open market at the date of the contract"—general condition 4(3). The purchaser must serve notice on the vendor of his intention to rescind and his reason for so doing within 20 working days from the date of the contract or such other period as may be agreed, time being of the essence—general condition 4(2).

A vendor will rarely accept the inclusion of general condition 4 in the contract for he will not be able to rely on the sale until one month after contract and there might later be an issue as to

---

[49] Periods of one year and one month.
[50] Law Society general condition 5(3) is discussed in more detail at p. 99.

whether the matter was "likely materially to reduce the price" and also whether the purchaser knew of it before contract or not. General condition 4(4) states that the purchaser's knowledge "includes everything in writing received in the course of the transaction leading to the contract by a person acting on his behalf from the vendor, a person acting on the vendor's behalf, or a competent authority"[51] but "does not include anything solely because a statute deems that registration of a matter constitutes actual notice of it."

Capacity

Special condition D This invites the vendor to state the capacity in which he is selling, the alternatives being, "as beneficial owner," "settlor," "trustee," "mortgagee," "as personal representative" or "under an order of the court." The practical consequence of responding is that later the vendor will be expressed in the conveyance itself to convey as stated in the special condition. This in turn will lead to certain alternative covenants for title (set out in Parts I to VI of the Second Schedule to the Law of Property Act 1925) being incorporated[52] into the conveyance. Should a defect in title become apparent after completion, these covenants for title will be available to protect the purchaser by imposing liability on the vendor. No assistance can be sought from the contract for sale after completion because the intention is that it should merge with the conveyance as to matters covered by the implied covenants for title. Therefore the respective interests of vendor and purchaser should be considered before filling in the blank in special condition D: is sufficient protection provided for the purchaser or, on the other hand, is the liability imposed on the vendor too great? A solicitor will not however incur liability in negligence for failure in good faith to negotiate any of the implied covenants for title.[53]

Implied covenants for title

The maximum number of covenants for title are given by a vendor who "conveys and is expressed to convey" as beneficial owner. On a conveyance of freehold land for value, these are (in summary) that the vendor has full power to convey, that the purchaser will have quiet enjoyment, that the vendor will indemnify the purchaser against undisclosed incumbrances and for further assurance. On an assignment of leasehold land for value the vendor further covenants that the lease is valid and subsisting and is not void or voidable and that the rent has been duly paid and the covenants and conditions have been duly observed and performed.[54] On a conveyance or assignment (whether for value or not) by a trustee, mortgagee, personal representative, or under an order of the court, only one covenant is implied, which is that the vendor himself has not created any

---

[51] A local authority or other body exercising powers under statute or Royal Charter; general condition 3(1).

[52] By the Law of Property Act 1925, s.76(1) and the Land Registration Act 1925, s.38 plus the Land Registration Rules 1925, rr. 76 and 77.

[53] The Law of Property Act 1925, s.182(1).

[54] By the Land Registration Act 1925, s.24, the vendor does not covenant that the lease is valid and subsisting but merely that all covenants in the lease have been performed and the rent paid. However this implied covenant is not dependant on the transfer being for value nor on the vendor transferring as beneficial owner.

incumbrance over the land. Settlors just give a covenant for further assurance.[55]

Co-owners

Joint tenants and tenants in common normally sell as trustees,[56] which of course means that they only have to give one covenant for title. Some say[57] that where the trustees are the sole beneficiaries, as with the common example of a dwellinghouse owned by husband and wife, they should convey as beneficial owners and give the purchaser the full implied covenants. However unless the contract so provides the purchaser cannot insist on the trustees conveying as beneficial owners.[58]

Special condition E   This requires the vendor to state how he intends to prove his title.

Open contract rules—title

Under an open contract the vendor must deduce a good title.[59] He fulfills this obligation in the case of unregistered land by abstracting a good root of title at least 15 years old[60] and all subsequent dealings. A good root of title is an instrument which deals with or shows title to the whole legal and equitable interest, contains a recogniseable description of the property and does nothing to cast doubt on the title; conveyances on sale being the most common type of root offered by vendors. If the sale happens to be of leasehold property the 15 year rule is subject to the limitations placed by section 44(2) to (4) of the Law of Property Act 1925 on a lessee's right to investigate superior titles.

Land Registration Act 1925, s.110

A vendor deduces title to registered land by complying with the requirements of section 110(1) and (2) of the Land Registration Act 1925. He must supply the purchaser with: an authority to inspect the register, copies of the entries on the register and of the filed plan, and an abstract or other evidence of matters as to which the register is not conclusive or which are excepted from the effect of registration. Nothing in section 110 prevents the application of section 44(2) to (4) of the Law of Property Act 1925 to the sale of registered leaseholds.

The Law Society general conditions make two small amendments to the open contract rules. General condition 8(2) slightly improves the lot of purchasers of leaseholds. General condition 12(1)(*b*) says that copies of entries on the register, filed plan and documents noted on the register and filed at the registry (supplied under section 110) shall be office copies,[61] and that the vendor shall supply such additional authorities to inspect the register as the purchaser shall reasonably require for any sub-purchaser or prospective mortgagee or lessee. It is almost universal practice for office copies to be sent with the draft contract.[62]

Special condition E alternatives

Special condition E is in the alternative (the inappropriate alternative should be crossed out). The first for unregistered land will, where appropriate, specify the root. The second for

---

[55] Valuable consideration is not a requirement.
[56] See the Law of Property Act 1925, ss.34–36.
[57] See, *e.g.* Cambridge Law Society's conveyancing protocol 1986.
[58] *Cottrell* v. *Cottrell* (1866) L.R. 2 Eq. 330.
[59] *Lysaght* v. *Edwards* (1876) 2 Ch. D. 499 at p. 507.
[60] Law of Property Act 1969, s.23.
[61] Following a Law Society recommendation, see (1973) 70 L.S.Gaz. 1281.
[62] A wise course following the decision in *Faruqui* v. *English Real Estates Ltd.* [1979] 1 W.L.R. 963.

registered land will alternatively give details of the nature of the vendor's title, the title number and the district land registry. The second special condition E further incorporates an authority for the purchaser's solicitors to inspect the register and obtain office copies of it, conveniently recognising the fact that solicitors need no longer lodge an authority with the Land Registry when applying for an official search of the register or office copies, they must just certify that an authority is held.[63]

A full discussion of title appears later in the book.[64]

Vacant possession

Special condition F   This also is in the alternative, this time to allow for a sale with vacant possession on completion or for the disclosure of existing tenancies. If a contract is silent as to vacant possession there is an implication that the purchaser is entitled to vacant possession.[65] This is so even where the contract is silent as to any tenancy to which the property is subject.[66]

Breach of term for vacant possession

It is not only tenancies which will amount to breach of a term for vacant possession. In *Wroth* v. *Tyler*[67] the breach was a Class F land charge registered against the vendor in respect of the statutory right of occupation of the vendor's spouse.[68] If "squatters" enter the property the purchaser would be entitled to refuse to complete on the ground that vacant possession was not being given. In *Cumberland Consolidated Holdings Ltd.* v. *Ireland*[69] it was said that occupation by a person having no claim of right prevents the giving of "vacant possession," and it is the duty of the vendor to eject such a person before completion. In *Topfell Ltd.* v. *Galley Properties Ltd.*[70] a "closing" order on the untenanted part of property prevented vacant possession of the ground floor from being given. The purchaser successfully sought a reduction in the purchase price, from £3,850 to £2,050, despite a general condition of the contract that he took subject to all notices. It was held that the general condition could not contradict the vendor's contractual obligation to give vacant possession.[71]

It has been suggested[72] that *Topfell* might be relevant if, for example, a purchaser contracted to buy property with vacant possession under the Law Society general conditions when someone who later claimed an overriding interest under section 70 of the Land Registration Act 1925 (or presumably an interest binding under the doctrine of constructive notice: section 199 of the Law of Property Act 1925) was already living in the property. Attempts by the vendor to rely on general condition 3(2)(c) (the

---

[63] Official Searches Rules 1981.

[64] See pp. 76–86, below.

[65] *Cook* v. *Taylor* [1942] Ch. 349.

[66] *Farrell* v. *Green* (1974) 232 E.G. 587.

[67] [1974] Ch. 30.

[68] Where a dwelling-house is sold with vacant possession s.4(1) of the Matrimonial Homes Act 1983 implies a term into the contract that the vendor will secure the cancellation of any registration of rights of occupation against it.

[69] [1946] K.B. 264.

[70] (1976) 239 E.G. 650.

[71] But see the earlier decision of *Korogluyan* v. *Matheou* (1975) 30 P. & C.R. 309 which was not cited in *Topfell* and where the opposite result was arrived at on similar facts.

[72] H.W. Wilkinson, *Standard Conditions of Sale of Land* (3rd ed., 1982).

property is sold subject to all matters discoverable on inspection) or general condition 5(*b*) (the property is sold subject to all rights etc. affecting the same) could be overriden by the express provision for vacant possession.

Excessive rubbish   The duty to give vacant possession can be broken if the vendor leaves the property in a physically non-vacant state. In the *Cumberland Consolidated* case (above) the vendor, who had contracted to give vacant possession of a warehouse, left its cellars filled to about two-thirds of their height with hardened cement and empty drums. The Court of Appeal said that the term "vacant possession" included freedom from any physical "impediment which substantially prevents or interferes with the enjoyment of the right of possession of a substantial part of the property,"[73] and ordered the vendor to remove the rubbish.[73a]

As a result this type of special condition is sometimes encountered: "The purchaser shall accept that vacant possession is given of the whole notwithstanding that there may be furniture fittings or effects remaining therein and shall not be entitled to require the removal of any such furniture fittings and effects or object to taking the same on the ground that the presence thereof prevents the giving of vacant possession." Occasionally an indemnity for any claims to such chattels and a disclaimer of any implication of the vendor's title to any item, are added. Obviously it would be unwise for a purchaser's solicitor to accept these variants. Moreover it should not be forgotten that the presence of a third party's belongings might constitute actual occupation so as to produce an overriding interest in registered land, or constructive notice of an interest in unregistered land.

Freedom from incumbrances   *Special condition G*   This will contain a statement of interests subject to which the property is sold. This is to rebut the presumption at common law that the vendor is selling the property free from incumbrances.[74] "No such implication arises, however, if the purchaser knew at the time of the contract . . . that . . . some encumbered interest was to be the subject of the sale."[75] At common law the vendor need only disclose latent defects in his title (whether he knows about them or not), that is incumbrances and other matters of title which the purchaser could not discover for himself by inspecting the property with reasonable care. The purchaser is deemed to know about patent (visible) defects in title and about physical defects in the property **Law Society** latent or patent. By Law Society general condition 5(1) the **general condition** vendor warrants that he has disclosed, "the existence of all **5(1)** easements, rights, privileges, and liabilities affecting the property, of which the vendor knows or ought to know, other than the existence of those known to the purchaser at the date of the contract, or which a prudent purchaser would have discovered by that date." Breach of this warranty entitles the

---

[73] [1946] K.B. 264, *per* Lord Greene.
[73a] See also *Hynes* v. *Vaughan* (1985) 50 P. & C.R. 444.
[74] *Purvis* v. *Rayer* (1821) 9 Price 488, *Ogilvie* v. *Foljambe* (1817) 3 Mer. 53, *Doe d. Gray* v. *Stanion* (1836) 1 H & W 695, *Hughes* v. *Parker* (1841) 8 M. & W. 244.
[75] *Timmins* v. *Moreland Street Property Ltd.* [1958] Ch. 110.

purchaser to rescind the contract or claim damages depending on the gravity of the non-disclosure (general condition 7).[76]

Obvious examples of what must be fully disclosed in special condition G are easements,[77] restrictive covenants,[78] and some overriding interests. They will be noted by the vendor's solicitor on an examination of the title deeds or the register or from searches, and either be reproduced in the special condition or be referred to as being contained in a particular deed, a copy or abstract of which is sent with the draft contract. For registered land reference is usually to the Charges Register and accompanying office copies.[79] Any incumbrance that will be discharged on completion, such as the vendor's existing mortgage, should not be referred to.

Unusually onerous covenants

A vendor of leasehold property is under a duty to reveal unusually onerous covenants in the lease.[80] This is most conveniently done by referring generally to the covenants and conditions in the lease in the special condition, and accompanying the contract with a copy of the lease. Law Society general condition 8(3) provides: "A copy of the lease and . . . all superior leases, the contents of which are known to the vendor, having been supplied or made available to the purchaser, he shall be deemed to purchase with full notice of the contents thereof. . . ."

Indemnity

Law Society general condition 17(4) states that: "the purchaser shall in the conveyance covenant to *indemnify* the vendor and his estate (and any estate of which the vendor is a personal representative or trustee) against all actions, claims and liability, for any breach of any covenant, stipulation, provision or other matter subject to which the property is sold and in respect of which the vendor or any such estate will remain liable after completion." The common law implies a similar covenant on the part of the purchaser where property is stated to be sold subject to covenants, but only with the object of affording an indemnity to the vendor and his estate.[81] In *Re Poole & Clarke's Contract*[82]

Observe and perform

it was said that where there is a covenant to *perform* covenants and indemnify an injunction would be granted against the covenantor to restrain breaches of the covenants, because a covenant for indemnity alone would be of no use to the covenantee if the covenantor became insolvent. (The covenantor could not however be *ordered* to perform the covenants[83]). This suggests that where the covenant is one for indemnity only, as in general condition 17(4) or at common law, an injunction to restrain breaches would not be granted. The other drawback with covenants for indemnity, as opposed to covenants for *performance* and indemnity, is that the vendor must wait until he is sued for breach of covenant before he can take action against the

---

[76] A full discussion of the vendor's duty of disclosure and relevant standard conditions can be found at pp. 76–86.

[77] *e.g. Yandle & Sons* v. *Sutton* [1922] 2 Ch. 199.

[78] *e.g. Re Stone and Saville's Contract* [1963] 1 W.L.R. 163.

[79] But see *Faruqi* v. *English Real Estates* [1979] 1 W.L.R. 963.

[80] *Melzak* v. *Lilienfeld* [1926] Ch. 480 and see p. 84, below.

[81] *Re Poole & Clarke's Contract* [1904] 2 Ch. 173.

[82] *Ibid.*

[83] *Harris* v. *Boots Cash Chemists (Southern) Ltd.* [1904] 2 Ch. 376.

purchaser.[84] In view of the above vendors' solicitors may wish to extend general condition 17(4) so that the purchaser additionally covenants in the conveyance "to observe and perform" the covenants.

Land obligations   Performance and indemnity covenants will to a certain extent become redundant if the Law Commission's proposals[85] in its report on the Law of Positive and Restrictive Covenants are enacted. No new restrictive covenants will be capable of being created and there will no longer be any need to use artificial means to make the burden of positive covenants run with the land. Vendors will not remain liable for breach of "land obligations" they have given: the benefit and burden of the obligations, positive or negative, will only be enforceable between the current owners of the land. However, the Law Commission's proposals are not retrospective. Therefore Law Society general condition 17(4) will still be pertinent to many sales.

Leaseholds   Where a leasehold interest is sold, section 77 of the Law of Property Act 1925 and section 24 of the Land Registration Act 1925 imply into the assignment or transfer covenants that the assignee will henceforth duly pay the rent, perform the covenants and observe the conditions affecting the land and indemnify the vendor against any action arising out of his failure to perform and observe the covenants and conditions. Law Society general condition 17(4) states that the vendor may not insist on an express covenant from the assignee to cover the same matters as the implied statutory covenant does. However it is uncertain[86] whether section 77 and section 24 allow the vendor to sue on the implied covenant unless he himself is sued by the person he is responsible to. It may be thought desirable to cure this uncertainty by special condition.

The National Contract of Sale (20th Edition) (reproduced at pp. 59–60)

Two forms of National Contract (both pale green) are published, differing only as regards what is printed on the back page under the heading "Special Conditions of Sale." The one form of back page simply leaves space for special conditions, starting with the letter "A," to indicate that the special conditions should be lettered, not numbered, so as to avoid confusion with the National conditions. The other form of back page offers five standard special conditions, lettered A–F and leaves space for other special conditions.

Much of what has been said already in connection with the Law Society's Contract applies equally to the National Contract. Only the differences will be mentioned here.

"Contract of Sale"   **Front page**   The front page is headed "Contract of Sale" to accommodate National condition 1(6) with its reference to "a document . . . in the form of a contract of sale in writing."

Interest   The agreed rate of interest and completion date are dealt

---

[84] *Reckitt* v. *Cody* [1920] 2 Ch. 452.
[85] Law Com. No. 127.
[86] See H.W. Wilkinson, *Standard Conditions of Sale of Land* (3rd ed., 1982).

CONTRACT OF SALE
The National Conditions of Sale, Twentieth Edition

Vendor

Purchaser

Registered Land		Purchase price	£	
District Land Registry :		Deposit	£	
Title Number :		Balance payable	£	
Agreed rate of interest :		Price fixed for chattels or valuation money (if any)	£	
		Total	£	

Property and interest therein sold

Vendor sells as   Completion date :

AGREED that the Vendor sells and the Purchaser buys as above, subject to the Special Conditions endorsed hereon and to the National Conditions of Sale Twentieth Edition so far as the latter Conditions are not inconsistent with the Special Conditions.

    * *Signed*

Date   19

---

* This is a form of legal document. Neither the form nor the National Conditions of Sale which the form embodies, were produced or drafted for use, without technical assistance, by persons unfamiliar with the law and practice of conveyancing.

Re: :   to

SPECIAL CONDITIONS OF SALE

A. Condition 3 of the National Conditions of Sale shall [not] have effect [But it shall not apply to a matter or matters affecting the value of the property by less than £   or to the following:—

]

B. Title shall be deduced and shall commence as follows:—

C. The sale is with vacant possession/subject to the existing tenancy of which details have been supplied to the Purchaser/subject to the following tenancies:—

D. The property is sold on the footing that the authorised use thereof for the purposes of the Planning Acts is the use (if any) specified in the particulars of sale/use as

E. The sale includes the chattels fittings and separate items specified in the inventory annexed which are to be taken by the Purchaser for a sum (additional to the purchase price of the property) of £   / to be ascertained by a valuation to be made by
at the expense of

F. The property is sold subject so far as they are subsisting and capable of being enforced or of taking effect to the restrictions and stipulations

© 1981

oyez

THE SOLICITORS' LAW STATIONERY SOCIETY plc
Oyez House, 237 Long Lane, London SE1 4PU

F3419 BM35871 8/83

Form Con 14 —with special conditions

★ ★ ★

with on the front page rather than by special condition. The National's fall-back rate of interest is the same as the Law Society's, that is "the rate of interest prescribed from time to time under Land Compensation Act 1961, s.32"[87] (National construction condition (4)). Under National condition 7(1) it is only the purchaser who may have to pay interest at the prescribed rate on the balance of the purchase price for late completion.[88] (Law Society general condition 22 envisages payment of interest at the contract rate, as an alternative to compensation by the party "in default," be that vendor or purchaser). Under National condition 8 the prescribed rate governs the amount of interest a purchaser has to pay if he is let into occupation of the property before completion. National condition 7(iii) makes it clear that the vendor cannot receive interest twice on the balance of the purchase price, that is, under 8, if the purchaser goes into early occupation, and under 7, if there is also a delay in completion. Contrast the position under Law Society general condition 18(6): if the purchaser remains in occupation after the contractual completion date he must pay both the sum required for occupation under 18(4)(a) and compensation for late completion under general condition 22.

Completion date The fall-back completion date under National condition 5(1) is the twenty-sixth working day[89] after whichever is the later of the date of the contract or the date of delivery of the title.

Deposit The National conditions make no express provision for a deposit of less than 10 per cent. of the purchase price to be paid by the purchaser on exchange of contracts (National condition 2(1)). If a reduced deposit is agreed it should be provided for by special condition.[90]

Agreement The National contract is to be signed and dated at the foot of the front page immediately underneath the agreement that "the Vendor sells and the Purchaser buys as above, subject to the Special Conditions endorsed hereon and to the National Conditions of Sale Twentieth Edition so far as the latter Conditions are not inconsistent with the Special Conditions."

Special conditions

Special condition A This speaks of National condition 3 which,
Purchaser's short right to rescind like its Law Society counterpart general condition 4,[91] enables a contract for sale to be made subject to searches etc. When National condition 3 applies, and it will only do so if the special conditions so provide, the purchaser has 16 working days from the date of the contract (time being of the essence) in which to serve notice to rescind (National condition 3(3)). A "Condition 3 Notice" must expressly refer to that condition and to a matter to

---

[87] See the current Acquisition of Land (Rate of Interest after Entry) Regulations. The rate as it changes is published in the *Solicitors' Journal*.

[88] But see National condition 5(2)(ii) which preserves the purchaser's right to sue for damages at common law if there is a delay in completion.

[89] For definition see National construction condition (6) and pp. 50 to 51.

[90] See "Conditions as to payment of deposit" at pp. 93 to 99.

[91] See pp. 52 to 53, below.

which it applies (3(2)). It applies to "any matter materially affecting the value of the property" other than a matter not existing or subsisting at the date of the contract[92] or (essentially) a matter of which the purchaser on entering the contract had knowledge, excluding knowledge imputed by virtue of statute or the other National conditions (3(4)). This wide condition (it could, for example, relate to survey matters) was thought justified on the ground that practitioners would find it easier by special condition to reduce the scope of the condition, than to extend it, as they would have to think of doing, if it had a narrower basis.[93]

Additional to National condition 15

National condition 3 is additional to National condition 15. The latter condition gives the purchaser the right to rescind the contract if it appears before actual completion that the specified use of the property is not the authorised use for the purpose of the Planning Acts.[94] Recission under National conditions 3 and 15 is on the terms of condition 10(2): "the vendor shall return the deposit, but without interest, costs of investigating title or other compensation or payment, and the purchaser shall return the abstract and other papers furnished to him." "Abstract" includes the documents required to be furnished by section 110 of the Land Registration Act 1925 (National construction condition (11)).

Title

Special condition B "Title shall be deduced and shall commence as follows:–" The National conditions are silent as to the title to be shown, therefore the provisions of the common law apply.[95] National construction condition (11) confirms that a registered title (details of which should be inserted on the front page) shall be deduced in accordance with section 110 of the Land Registration Act 1925. The National conditions do not state that all documents supplied under a registered title must be office copies, but there is a Law Society recommendation to this effect.[96] An authority for the purchaser's solicitor to inspect the register of the vendor's title is not incorporated into the National contract and must be sent under separate cover.

Special condition C This is in the alternative: the sale is either with vacant possession or subject to tenancies.

Vacant possession or?

The National conditions, comprehending as the explanatory notes say, the legal problems arising out of *Williams & Glyn's Bank Ltd.* v. *Boland*,[97] very nearly allow purchasers to call for completion on the premises. According to National condition 5(4): "Provided that on a sale with vacant possession of the whole or part of the property, if the conveyance or transfer will not, by overreaching or otherwise, discharge the property from interests

---

[92] *e.g.* the purchaser would not be able to rescind if the property is greatly reduced in value by reason of being listed under the Planning Acts as occurred in *Amalgamated Investment & Property Co. Ltd.* v. *John Walker & Sons* [1977] 1 W.L.R. 164.

[93] Explanatory notes, issued December 1981.

[94] Defined by National Construction condition 1(8).

[95] See pp. 54 to 55 and pp. 76 to 86.

[96] Opinion 316(i).

[97] [1981] A.C. 487.

Occupational interests (if any) of persons in, or who may be in, actual occupation of the property or such part of it, then (subject always to the rights of the purchaser under the Law of Property Act 1925, s.42(1)), the purchaser may, by giving reasonable notice, require that on, or immediately before the time of, completion possession of the property or part be handed over to the purchaser or his representative at the property." It will be noted that the proviso is not confined to registered land, and assumes, wrongly according to *City of London Building Society* v. *Flegg*,[98] that the overriding can be overreached. Further the proviso should be read with National condition 9(2) which obliges the vendor to deal with requisitions concerning occupiers. The Law Society general conditions do not deal with occupational interests.

Planning *Special condition D*   National condition 15(2) gives the purchaser the right to raise requisitions concerning the authorised use of the property for the purposes of the Planning Acts.[99] But where a use is specified in special condition D the purchaser has to accept it as the authorised use. On the other hand, the use being specified here, means that the purchaser can rescind under National condition 15(3) if it appears before actual completion that this is not the authorised use.

Chattels, etc. *Special condition E*   This is for use where chattels, fittings or other items are to be sold separately from the property. A valuation is normally required only for the sale of stock in trade.

Incumbrances *Special condition F*   This will be used by the vendor to disclose to the purchaser all incumbrances affecting the property which will not be discharged on completion.

Purchaser's covenants National condition 19(5) and(6) provides:

> "(5) Where the property is sold subject to legal incumbrances, the purchaser shall covenant to indemnify the vendor against actions and claims in respect of them; and the purchaser will not make any claim on account of increased expense caused by the concurrence of any legal incumbrancer.
>
> (6) Where the property is sold subject to stipulations, or restrictive or other covenants and breach thereof would expose the vendor to liability, the purchaser shall covenant to observe and perform the same and to indemnify the vendor against actions and claims in respect thereof."

It will be noted that the covenant in condition 19(6) is for *performance and observance* as well as indemnity. An injunction will be granted against the purchaser to restrain his breaches of covenant,[1] at the suit of the vendor.[2] Contrast the position under Law Society general condition 17(4), where the purchaser gives a mere indemnity covenant.[3]

---

[98] [1986] 2 W.L.R. 616.
[99] Defined by National construction condition (8).
[1] *Re Poole & Clarke's Contract* [1904] 2 Ch. 173.
[2] *Butler Estates Co.* v. *Bean* [1942] 1 K.B.1.
[3] See pp. 57 to 58.

National condition 19(7) states that 19(5) and (6) operate without prejudice to section 77 of the Law of Property Act 1925 and section 24 of the Land Registration Act 1925 and that on the assignment or transfer of leasehold property the vendor may not insist on an express covenant from the purchaser to cover the same matters as the covenants implied by either of those sections do. For reasons stated earlier[4] where leasehold property is being sold the vendor's solicitor is advised to negotiate for the express right of the vendor to sue on the implied covenants regardless of whether he himself has been sued by the person he is responsible to.

Contracts with Unqualified Conveyancers

Note Before leaving the standard contract forms, attention is drawn to the following extract from the recent Law Society's Notes for the Guidance of Solicitors When Dealing with Unqualified Conveyancers[5]:

> *"Draft contracts*
> 8. Solicitors must decide in each case whether special provisions should be incorporated in the draft contract to take account of the problems which arise by reason of the other party having no solicitor, e.g., that the vendor should attend personally at completion if represented by an unqualified agent. All such matters must be considered prior to exchange of contracts since contractual conditions cannot, of course, be imposed subsequently.
> 9. The protection provided by s.69 of the Law of Property Act 1925 only applies when a document containing a receipt for purchase money is handed over by a solicitor or the vendor himself. Thus it should be considered whether a condition be incorporated in the contract providing either for the vendor to attend personally at completion or for an authority signed by the vendor, for the purchase money to be paid to his agent, to be handed over on completion."

---

[4] See p. 58 above.
[5] See (1986) 83 L.S.Gaz. 5.

5 CONDITIONS OF SALE

Introduction

Here we shall look in greater detail at the constituent parts of conveyancing contracts, where appropriate both under an open contract and at the modifications upon that position effected by the standard conditions. We shall also compare the position under the Law Society and the National conditions.

Description of the property

The contract must of course contain a description of the property which is to be sold. This description should be contained in the particulars of sale. As we have already seen in Chapter 4 the perfect particulars should give a physical description of the property but also describe the exact estate or interest sold and mention any adverse rights such as covenants, easements and profits to which it is subject.[1] Ideally any benefits which attach to the land should also be mentioned, although failure to do so will not matter. Where land is sold subject to incumbrances, these are often mentioned in the special conditions as well.

Drafting the particulars
　　Great care must be exercised when drafting the particulars of sale or any special condition describing adverse rights. The vendor has a duty to convey to the purchaser property which complies with the contractual description. Perfect accuracy is thus essential. If the vendor fails in this duty, various consequences may follow: he may be unable to obtain a decree of specific performance against a purchaser unwilling to proceed, while the purchaser may be able to rescind the contract or at any rate to claim an abatement of the purchase price. Remedies for misdescription will be looked at below.

Implied terms and duties
　　Apart from the necessity of avoiding misdescription, there is a further important point. In the absence of anything in the contract indicating the contrary, it will be assumed that the vendor is agreeing to sell the fee simple absolute in possession free from incumbrances.[2] The vendor has a duty to disclose any latent defects in his title to the purchaser, and will be liable to him for breach of contract if he fails to do so (see the next section). It is crucial therefore that the contract should not omit to mention such matters as restrictive covenants, easements or irregularities in the vendor's own title.

　　When describing the property, the contract must provide both a legal and a physical description.

The legal description
　　The contract should describe the estate owned by the vendor and any adverse rights affecting the property. The extent of the vendor's duty to disclose defects in title will be explained later: at

[1] See p. 40.
[2] See *Halsbury's Laws of England* (4th ed.), Vol. 42, para. 60.

this stage the important point is that the words actually used in the contract must be accurate if the purchaser is not to have remedies for misdescription. Decided cases afford various examples of legal misdescription. In *Russ and Brown's Contract*[3] the Court of Appeal upheld the decision of Clauson J. at first instance that there was a misdescription where the contract described various houses as *leasehold* properties when in fact they were held under underleases. However this case should be contrasted with *Becker* v. *Partridge*.[4] There the vendor entered into a contract to sell the underlease of a second-floor flat in a London house. In fact the vendor only had a sub-underlease. The Court of Appeal held that there was no misdescription since the document under which the vendor held was, in a sense, an underlease and the term sub-underlease, which might more appropriately have been used, was not actually a conveyancing expression in established use. Also of interest in this context is *Re Thompson and Cottrell's Contract*.[5] The vendor agreed to sell his underleasehold property to the purchaser, but the headlease had already been disclaimed by the underlessor's trustee in bankruptcy. Uthwatt J. held that, notwithstanding the disclaimer, it was still correct to describe the vendor's property as an underleasehold rather than a leasehold.[6]

Re Brine and Davies' Contract

A further example of legal misdescription is *Re Brine and Davies' Contract*.[7] There the vendor entered into an agreement to sell a "registered freehold house." In fact the property was registered with a possessory rather than an absolute title, and it was held that the purchaser was entitled to refuse to complete. When selling registered land, therefore, it is important to state what the nature of the vendor's title is—absolute, good leasehold, possessory or qualified. Failure to disclose that the title is less than absolute could lead to liability for non-disclosure, while a misleading statement such as that used in *Re Brine and Davies' Contract* may amount to misdescription. Indeed it is worth stressing that in that case the description was not positively wrong, but it was misleading enough to entitle the purchaser to pull out of the transaction. When selling registered land, the Law Society's standard form specifically provides in special condition E for insertion of the nature of the vendor's registered title. The National conditions do not specifically cater for this issue, though that form can easily be adapted accordingly.

Re Englefield Holdings Ltd. and Sinclair's Contract

One last example of legal misdescription is afforded by *Re Englefield Holdings Ltd and Sinclair's Contract*.[8] The vendor agreed to sell a flat to the purchaser which was already subject to a tenancy; the contract stated that the rent was £1.8s.3d. a week.

[3] [1934] 1 Ch. 34, C.A.; see similarly *Re Beyfus and Masters' Contract* (1888) 39 Ch.D. 110, C.A.

[4] [1966] 2 Q.B. 155, C.A.

[5] [1943] Ch. 97.

[6] Note that on a sale of an underlease of part only of the property comprised in the headlease, this fact must be disclosed to the purchaser as he could face forfeiture proceedings because of acts done by tenants of other parts of the property; see *Darlington* v. *Hamilton* (1854) Kay 550 at p. 558; *Cresswell* v. *Davidson* (1887) 56 L.T. 811 and *Re Lloyds Bank Ltd. and Lillington's Contract* [1912] 1 Ch. 601.

[7] [1935] Ch. 388.

[8] [1962] 1 W.L.R. 1119; see also *Pagebar Properties Ltd.* v. *Derby Investment Holdings Ltd.* [1972] 1 W.L.R. 1500.

In fact a certificate of disrepair had been served under the Rent
Act 1957, the effect of which was that the recoverable rent had
been abated to 15s.7d. a week. It could only go back to the
contractual level when the repairs had been effected. Pennycuick
J. held that the purchaser was entitled to complete at an
appropriately reduced purchase price. The failure to mention the
certificate of disrepair meant that the words used in the contract
misdescribed the actual legal situation.

**The physical
description**

The contract must also contain a clear and precise physical
description of the land to be sold. Particular care must be taken
over the physical description when dealing with unregistered
land.

**Unregistered land:
use of earlier
description**

It may well be sufficient when drafting a contract for the sale
of unregistered land simply to copy the description used in the
conveyance to the vendor. However it is by no means inevitable
that that description will be appropriate: it may be that it was
itself inaccurate or misleading,[9] or that the boundaries of the
property have since changed, or that part of the land originally
acquired by the vendor has since been sold off. New land may
have been bought.[10] This is why Lord Kinnear warned against
the slavish copying of descriptions contained in earlier title deeds
in *Gordon-Cumming* v. *Houldsworth*.[11]

New errors

Of course, misdescriptions do not come about only by
slavishly copying old documents. The draftsman may himself
make an original error. A not uncommon one is to misdescribe
the area of the land to be sold. In *Watson* v. *Burton*[12] the contract
stated that the vendor agreed to sell 3,920 square yards of land to
the purchaser. The actual extent of the land was 2,360 square
yards. The mistake was made entirely innocently, but it was held
that, as the error was a substantial one which had prejudiced the
purchaser, the vendor should not be granted a decree of specific
performance; instead the purchaser was given a declaration that
he was entitled to rescind the contract and to recover the deposit
which he had paid on exchange. This case shows how important
it is to take clear instructions from one's client. If there is any
uncertainty as to the precise area of a piece of land, particularly
large amounts of agricultural land, a qualified specialist should be
appointed to provide accurate measurements.

Plans

One way of surmounting any difficulty felt in adequately
describing a piece of land is of course to incorporate a plan in the
contract. In practice there tends to be a reluctance to use plans,
despite the advantages that can be obtained from doing so. As
Brightman J. (as he then was) said in *Lloyd* v. *Stanbury*[13]: "If
there is a moral to this unfortunate story it is the danger of
dispensing with a plan to a contract of sale, particularly where
natural boundaries are not obvious and the vendor is selling part
of his land."

[9] See *Spall* v. *Owen* (1982) 44 P. & C.R. 36 noted by Aldridge (1983) 127 S.J.
263.
[10] *Wallington* v. *Townsend* [1939] Ch. 588.
[11] [1910] A.C. 537 at p. 547: the relevant extract from his speech is reproduced at
p. 48 above.
[12] [1957] 1 W.L.R. 19; see similarly *Earl of Durham* v. *Legard* (1865) 34 Beav.
611, where the contract said the land comprised 21,750 acres when in fact it
was only 11,814.
[13] [1971] 1 W.L.R. 535 at p. 544.

Accuracy   If a plan is used in the contract, it is extremely important that it should be accurate: the vendor could be just as liable for a misleading plan as a verbal misdescription.[14] The legal adviser should specifically ask the client to approve any plan to be incorporated in the contract.[15] If the plan to be used is taken from an earlier conveyance, care should be exercised to ensure that it was itself correct and that the position has not changed since that conveyance, for example because the boundaries have been altered or part of the land has been sold off. One further point is that any plan that is used should be of an appropriate

Scale   scale. In *Scarfe* v. *Adams*[16] an estate was split into several lots which were then sold off. The individual conveyances described the lot in question partly by reference to a small-scale ordnance survey map. Cumming-Bruce L.J. was highly critical of the conveyancing. He said[17]:

> "The facts of the present case are really very simple, but I hope that this judgment will be understood by every conveyancing solicitor in the land as giving them warning, loud and clear, that a conveyancing technique which may have been effective in the old days to convey large property from one vendor to one purchaser will lead to nothing but trouble, disputes and expensive litigation if applied to the sale to separate purchasers of a single house and its curtilage divided into separate parts. For such purposes it is absolutely essential that each parcel conveyed shall be described in the conveyance or transfer deed with such particularity and precision that there is no room for doubt about the boundaries of each, *and for such purposes if a plan is intended to control the description, an ordnance map on a scale of 1:2500 is worse than useless.*" (italics added).

These comments would be of equal applicability where the plan is attached to the contract rather than the conveyance.

Registered land   When selling registered land, the draftsman's task is somewhat easier. Instead of having himself to frame a proper description of the land, it will suffice to quote simply the property's title number.[18] If for some reason it is necessary to incorporate a plan in the contract, it will be possible to obtain a copy of the filed plan from the appropriate Land Registry, although it is wise to check this document since it is not definitive.[19]

Where the owner of registered land sells off part, rule 79 of the Land Registration Rules[20] requires him to attach a plan. The comments of Cumming-Bruce L.J. in *Scarfe* v. *Adams*, above, would be equally applicable in this situation.

Establishing   Having described the property in the contract, the vendor
identity   must then convey land to the purchaser which conforms with that

---

[14] See, *e.g. Re Lindsay and Forder's Contract* (1895) 72 L.T. 832.
[15] See *Darby* v. *Thorner* [1983] C.A. Bound Transcript 490 for an excellent illustration of the need to check plans carefully.
[16] [1981] 1 All E.R. 843, C.A.
[17] *Ibid.* at p. 845.
[18] Registered Land Practice Notes 1982/83 ed. p. 15. Remember that the *legal* description must state what kind of title the vendor has.
[19] *Lee* v. *Barrey* [1957] Ch. 251.
[20] S.R. & O. 1925 No. 1093.

description. A potential problem is the purchaser or his legal adviser claiming that the title deeds fail to establish clearly that the land actually to be conveyed is identical to that described in the agreement. The important question in such circumstances is to decide what rights the purchaser has to insist upon further evidence as to the identity of the land.

Under an open contrat, the answer is that where the contract description materially differs from that in the title deeds, the purchaser has a right to call for further evidence of identity.[21] It is common for the vendor to attempt to restrict the purchaser's rights in this respect, and indeed both sets of standard conditions purport to do so. It may be helpful to quote the relevant standard conditions in full at this point, although they raise some other issues which will be dealt with below. Law Society general condition 13:

Law Society general condition 13

"13. Identity and Boundaries

(1) The vendor shall produce such evidence as may be reasonably necessary to establish the identity and extent of the property, but shall not be required to define exact boundaries, or the ownership of fences, ditches, hedges or walls, nor, beyond the evidence afforded by the information in his possession, separately to identify parts of the property held under different titles.

(2) If reasonably required by the purchaser because of the insufficiency of the evidence produced under sub-condition (1), the vendor shall at his own expense provide and hand over on completion a statutory declaration as to the relevant facts, in a form agreed by the purchaser, such agreement not to be unreasonably withheld."

National condition 13

"13. Identity: boundaries: condition of property

(1) The purchaser shall admit the identity of the property with that comprised in the muniments offered by the vendor as the title thereto upon the evidence afforded by the descriptions contained in such muniments, and of a statutory declaration, to be made (if required) at the purchaser's expense, that the property has been enjoyed according to the title for at least twelve years.

(2) The vendor shall not be bound to show any title to boundaries, fences, ditches, hedges or walls, or to distinguish parts of the property held under different titles further than he may be able to do from information in his possession.

(3) The purchaser shall be deemed to buy with full notice in all respects of the actual state and condition of the property and, save where it is to be constructed or converted by the vendor, shall take the property as it is."

---

[21] *Flower* v. *Hartopp* (1843) 6 Beav. 476.

National condition 13 more favourable to the vendor

Failure to establish identity

Four particular comments should be made about these standard conditions. The first is that the National condition is clearly drafted more favourably to the vendor than the Law Society condition.[21a] The second point is that, notwithstanding the language of National condition 13(1), it will not avail a purchaser in circumstances where the title deeds fail to establish identity between the land described in the contract and the land owned by the vendor at all. In *Re Bramwell's Contract*[22] Stamp J., dismissing the vendor's application for specific performance of an agreement made under the National conditions, said "If the root of title is not shown to comprise the land agreed to be sold, how can it be said that it affords any evidence of the identity of the property with that agreed to be sold? The contract that the deeds shall show identity is broken."

Statutory declaration from vendor

The third point about establishing identity under the standard conditions is that each condition entitles the purchaser to call for a statutory declaration if this is needed. Again however the Law Society condition is more favourable to the purchaser. It provides that the declaration shall be produced at the vendor's expense, that it shall be in a form agreed by the purchaser, and there is nothing to indicate that it should be limited to a particular number of years. Instead, by inference from the wording of condition 13(2), it must be of such a nature as is reasonably required by the purchaser because of the insufficiency of the evidence provided by the vendor. By contrast, under the National condition the statutory declaration is to be produced at the purchaser's expense and will simply state that the property has been enjoyed according to the title for at least 12 years.

Statutory declaration from third party

The last comment on establishing identity is that, at common law, the purchaser would be entitled to call upon the vendor to ask a third party to swear a statutory declaration where this is appropriate (*e.g.* because the vendor has only himself been owner for a couple of years).[23] Neither the Law Society nor the National conditions deal with this point explicitly, but there is nothing in either of them which would appear to alter the position at common law.

Separate titles

Where the land to be sold is held under two or more separate titles, the common law obliges the vendor to show which bit of land is sold under which title.[24] Both Law Society and National conditions 13 absolve the vendor from this duty except to the extent that it can be discharged by using information in his possession.

Boundaries

Importance of definition

If it often extremely difficult to be certain where the boundaries between two properties lie and who owns any relevant walls, ditches, fences and hedges.[25] Disputes between neighbours break out regretably frequently over this issue, for

---

[21a] Compare the National condition ("The purchaser shall admit . . . " with the Law Society "The vendor shall produce such evidence as may be reasonably necessary . . . ").

[22] [1969] 1 W.L.R. 659 applying *Flower* v. *Hartopp* (1843) 6 Beav. 476 and *Curling* v. *Austin* (1862) 2 Dr. and Sm. 129.

[23] *Hobson* v. *Bell* (1839) 2 Beav. 17.

[24] See, *e.g. Dawson* v. *Brinckman* (1850) 3 Mac. & G 53; *Monro* v. *Taylor* (1852) 3 Mac. & G. 713.

[25] See generally Powell-Smith, *Boundaries and Fences* (2nd ed., 1975); Aldridge, *Boundaries, Walls and Fences* (5th ed., 1982).

example where one is claiming that the other is encroaching on his land or where a wall or fence is in poor condition and the question of responsibility for maintenance is raised. It is important therefore that the purchaser should obtain as much information as he can about the boundaries before he completes, so that he has some idea as to his position. It has never been entirely clear whether a purchaser under an open contract can insist upon the vendor defining the boundaries of the property.[26] Both Law Society condition 13(1) and National condition 13(2) absolve the vendor from responsibility for so doing. Note however that the Law Society condition is slightly less favourable to the vendor ("The vendor . . . shall not be required to define exact boundaries . . . ") than the National condition ("The vendor shall not be bound to show any title to boundaries . . . ").

In practice the issue of boundaries is dealt with in the purchaser's preliminary enquiries.[27] At that point the vendor must be careful not to make any false or misleading statement when making his replies, since he might otherwise be liable for misrepresentation.

Remedies for misdescription

Having considered what constitutes a misdescription, it is necessary to look at the remedies available to a purchaser. Before doing so, a few preliminary points might usefully be made. The

Difference between misdescription and misrepresentation

first is that misdescription and misrepresentation are not one and the same thing. Liability for misrepresentation arises where a misleading statement is made which *induces* a purchaser to enter into a contract. Misrepresentation does not involve a breach of contract, and at common law there is no *right* to damages. The position is now governed by the Misrepresentation Act 1967.[28] On the other hand, a misdescription actually involves a breach of a term of the contract itself. It may well be that a statement which would be actionable as a misrepresentation also becomes incorporated in the contract, thus giving rise to liability for misdescription as well, but it is still necessary to recognise the conceptual distinction between the two ideas. In conveyancing transactions, liability for misrepresentation is most likely to arise from statements made by the vendor when replying to preliminary enquiries.[29]

Latent defects

A second point is that there is a close relationship between misdescription and the vendor's duty to disclose latent defects in title. Of course a misdescription is a positive statement while a non-disclosure is necessarily negative, but the two do shade into one another. In *Re Englefield Holdings Ltd and Sinclair's Contract*[30] there is little more than a hair's breadth between saying that the vendor misdescribed the rent and that he failed to disclose the certificate of disrepair. A failure to disclose a latent

---

[26] *Dawson* v. *Brinckman* (1850) 3 Mac. & G. 53.
[27] See Annand and Cain, *Enquiries Before Contract* (1986).
[28] See Treitel, *The Law of Contract* (6th ed., 1983) Chap. 9; Cheshire, Fifoot and Furmston's, *Law of Contract* (11th ed., 1986), Chap. 9.
[29] See Annand and Cain, *Enquiries Before Contract* (1986) pp. 6–15.
[30] [1962] 1 W.L.R. 1119; and see pp. 66–67 above.

defect in title is treated as a breach of contract and, as we shall see, the remedies for misdescription and non-disclosure are much the same.

Fact and opinion

One final preliminary point that should be made is that liability for misdescription only arises from misstatements of *fact*; statements of opinion, even if mistaken, do not give rise to liability. In *Watson* v. *Burton*[31] the particulars of sale described the property as "valuable and extensive" "in a first-class position" and "suitable for development" but these expressions were dismissed as being "typical auctioneer's 'puff,' not to be regarded as part of the contract".

Remedies under an open contract

It is helpful in the first place to consider the consequences of misdescription where land is sold under an open contract and then to look at the way in which the standard conditions affect the position. Under an open contract, it is necessary to distinguish between substantial, material and immaterial misdescriptions.

Substantial misdescription

Where the misdescription is substantial, the vendor will be unable to obtain a decree of specific performance against the purchaser, even if he is willing to accept an abatement of the purchase price.[32] The converse of this is that the purchaser will be entitled to rescind the contract and to insist upon the return of any deposit he may have paid.[33] If however he wishes to go ahead with the purchase subject to an abatement of the price, he may do so.[34]

It can be a difficult matter to advise on what qualifies as a "substantial" misdescription. In *Flight* v. *Booth*[35] Tindal C.J. said that a misdescription would be substantial if it related to a matter "so far affecting the subject-matter of the contract that it may reasonably be supposed that, but for the misdescription, the purchaser might never have entered into the contract at all." Some indication of what qualifies can be gleaned from the cases in which errors were held to be substantial. In *Watson* v. *Burton*[36] the area of land to be sold was described as 3,920 square yards but in fact it was only 2,360 square yards; in *Stanton* v. *Tattersall*[37] a house was described as 58 Pall Mall when in fact it had no frontage on Pall Mall at all; in *Fisher* v. *Andrews*[38] a property was said to be connected to the mains water supply and water rates were said to be payable when in fact it was supplied by a private water company; and in *Mustafa* v. *Baptist Union Corporation Ltd.*[39] a freehold house was sold with "entire vacant possession" when in fact part of the first floor was blocked off and rented as a storeroom by the owners of adjoining property.

---

[31] [1957] 1 W.L.R. 19.
[32] *Flight* v. *Booth* (1834) 1 Bing. N.C. 370.
[33] *Watson* v. *Burton* [1957] 1 W.L.R. 19.
[34] *Rutherford* v. *Acton-Adams* [1915] A.C. 866.
[35] (1834) 1 Bing. N.C. 370.
[36] [1957] 1 W.L.R. 19.
[37] (1853) 1 Sm. & Griff. 529.
[38] [1955] J.P.L. 452.
[39] (1983) 266 E.G. 812.

What amounts to a substantial misdescription is a question of fact to be decided by the court in the circumstances of each case.[40]

Material misdescription

If the misdescription is not substantial, it may be classified either as material or as immaterial. If it is a material misdescription, the vendor will be able to obtain specific performance of the contract but will have to allow the purchaser an abatement of the purchase price. Put the other way round, this means that the purchaser will not be allowed to rescind the contract, but that he will be entitled to compensation for the misdescription. An example is *Re Englefield Holdings Ltd. and Sinclair's Contract*[41] where the court reduced the purchase price of the property from £550 to £520 to compensate the purchaser for the reduced rent he would receive. An exception to the rule just stated is that, if it is impossible to give a monetary value to the error that has been made, then the purchaser will not be entitled to compensation: instead the contract will have to be rescinded.[42] Also if he wishes to claim compensation because of a material misdescription, he must do so before completion[43] unless he only became aware of the problem after completion.[44] However, it is important to appreciate that after completion he may have other remedies available to him; in particular he may be able to sue the vendor on his implied covenants for title.[45]

Re Englefield Holdings Ltd. and Sinclair's Contract

Immaterial misdescription

If a misdescription is immaterial, that is to say if the purchaser obtains almost exactly what he paid for, the vendor will be able to obtain specific performance and the purchaser will be unable to rescind or to claim an abatement of the price. At the most he can claim nominal damages for the technical breach of contract. An example of an immaterial breach is afforded by *Vartoukian* v. *Daejan Properties Ltd.*[46] The vendor agreed to sell a number of flats which he described as being let to tenants on long leases. In fact one of the flats was only held on a short lease. Before completion the landlord granted a long lease of that particular flat. As the purchaser obtained all that he had agreed to buy, he received nominal damages only.

Vendor's position

It may of course happen that the misdescription prejudices the vendor rather than the purchaser, for example where he understates the size of the plot of land which he intends to convey. Under an open contract the vendor in such circumstances has no right to compensation: the responsibility is his to ensure that the property is adequately described.[47] However, if the misdescription by the vendor could inflict serious hardship on him, the court may take this into account when exercising its discretion as to whether a purchaser should be granted the equitable remedy of specific performance. For example in *Manser* v. *Beck*[48] the vendor sold property at auction, but the particulars omitted to mention that the vendor intended

---

[40] *Watson* v. *Burton* [1957] 1 W.L.R. 19.
[41] [1962] 1 W.L.R. 1119; see also *Re Fawcett and Holmes' Contract* (1889) 42 Ch.D 150.
[42] *Rudd* v. *Lascelles* [1900] 1 Ch. 815.
[43] *Joliffe* v. *Baker* (1883) 11 Q.B.D. 255.
[44] *Clayton* v. *Leech* (1889) 41 Ch.D. 103.
[45] See Annand and Cain, *Modern Conveyancing* (1984), pp. 375–379.
[46] (1969) 20 P. & C.R. 983.
[47] *Re Lindsay and Forder's Contract* (1895) 72 L.T. 832; see also *Lloyd* v. *Stanbury* [1971] 1 W.L.R. 535 at p. 544.
[48] (1848) 6 Hare 443.

to reserve a right of way for himself across the land in question. The purchaser claimed specific performance free from any right of way; the court gave him a choice: he could either be granted specific performance subject to the right of way, or be left with an action against the vendor for damages for breach of contract.

Remedies and the standard conditions of sale

Having looked at the position at common law, we shall have to consider how the standard conditions of sale affect the remedies available for misdescription. At common law, the vendor's position is weak, and it is not surprising to find that the standard conditions attempt to alter the balance as between vendor and purchaser. The relevant conditions are:

Law Society general condition 7:

"7. Errors, Omissions and Misstatements
(1) No error, omission or misstatement herein or in any plan furnished or any statement made in the course of the negotiations leading to the contract shall annul the sale or entitle the purchaser to be discharged from the purchase.
(2) Any such error, omission or mis-statement shown to be material shall entitle the purchaser or the vendor, as the case may be, to proper compensation, provided that the purchaser shall not in any event be entitled to compensation for matters falling within conditions 5(2) or 6(3).
(3) No immaterial error, omission or misstatement (including a mistake in any plan furnished for identification only) shall entitle either party to compensation.
(4) Sub-condition (1) shall not apply where compensation for any error, omission or misstatement shown to be material cannot be assessed nor enable either party to compel the other to accept or convey property differing substantially (in quantity, quality, tenure or otherwise) from the property agreed to be sold if the other party would be prejudiced by the difference.
(5) The purchaser acknowledges that in making the contract he has not relied on any statement made to him save one made or confirmed in writing."

National condition 17:

"17. Errors, mis-statements or omissions
(1) Without prejudice to any express right of either party, or to any right of the purchaser in reliance on Law of Property Act 1969, s.24, to rescind the contract before completion and subject to the provisions of paragraph (2) of this condition, no error, mis-statement or omission in any preliminary answer concerning the property, or in the sale plan or the Special Conditions, shall annul the sale, nor (save where the error, mis-statement

or omission relates to a matter materially affecting the description or value of the property) shall any damages be payable, or compensation allowed by either party, in respect thereof.

(2) Paragraph (1) of this condition shall not apply to any error, mis-statement or omission which is recklessly or fraudulently made, or to any matter or thing by which the purchaser is prevented from getting substantially what he contracted to buy.

(3) In this condition a "preliminary answer" means and includes any statement made by or on behalf of the vendor to the purchaser or his agents or advisers, whether in answer to formal preliminary enquiries or otherwise, before the purchaser entered into the contract."

Substantial misdescription   At common law, the courts were unsympathetic to conditions purporting to prevent a purchaser rescinding where there was a substantial misdescription. In *Flight* v. *Booth*[49] there was a term in the contract saying that errors contained in it could not vitiate the sale, and yet, when the purchaser found that there were covenants affecting the property which prevented him using it for the purpose he intended, it was held that he could rescind and recover his deposit. Both standard conditions appear to prevent the purchaser rescinding at first glance (Law Society condition 7(1) "No error . . . shall annul the sale"; National condition 17(1) " . . . no error . . . shall annul the sale.") On closer inspection, however, one finds that the position is much the same as under *Flight* v. *Booth*. Law Society condition 7(4) provides that neither party shall be able to compel the other to acquire or convey "property differing *substantially* (in quantity, quality, tenure or otherwise) from the property agreed to be sold. . . ." Note however that it then adds the gloss that 7(4) only applies where the other party would be prejudiced by the difference. This was not actually a requirement under *Flight* v. *Booth*, but it is hard to see how a *substantial* misdescription could fail to prejudice the person seeking to rescind the contract.

National condition 17(2) specifically provides that 17(1) shall not apply to any error, mis-statement or omission "by which the purchaser is presented from getting substantially what he contracted to buy."

Material misdescription[50]   Under both standard conditions, the purchaser is entitled to compensation, but not to rescind (Law Society condition 7(1), National condition 17(1)). Two points should be noted. First, the Law Society condition 7(4) expressly repeats the rule in *Rudd* v. *Lascelles*[51] where the error cannot be given a value; the National condition is silent on the matter, so that the common law would presumably apply anyway. Secondly, the standard conditions remain effective even after completion, reversing the position at common law.[52]

---

[49] (1834) 1 Bing. N.C. 370.
[50] On the distinction between substantial and material misdescriptions, see (1984) Conv. 333.
[51] See p. 73.
[52] *Palmer* v. *Johnson* (1884) 13 Q.B.D. 351.

Immaterial misdescription

Law Society condition 7(3) and (by implication) National condition 17(1) provide that no compensation shall be payable in respect of immaterial misdescriptions.

Vendor's position

As we have seen, a vendor prejudiced by a misdescription has no right to compensation at common law. Law Society condition 7(2) provides however that a vendor as well as a purchaser shall be entitled to compensation where there is a material misdescription and condition 7(4) provides that the vendor cannot be compelled to convey property where there has been a substantial misdescription.

National condition 17(1) is not so clear as this. It does not specifically allow the vendor to claim compensation, though there is a reference to "compensation allowed by either party." Since there is no common law right to compensation for the vendor and the condition itself does not confer one, it is not obvious that this phrase achieves anything.

Vendor's duty of disclosure

We shall here consider the extent to which a failure by the vendor to disclose important information about the property to the purchaser can lead to liability.

Disclosure under an open contract

Caveat emptor

The general rule of contract is *caveat emptor*—let the buyer beware. A vendor is not generally responsible if he fails to bring the purchaser's attention to defects in the property. Only where a contract is of the utmost good faith (uberrimae fidei) is there a duty of disclosure.[53] This is particularly important in the case of insurance contracts. The position with contracts for the sale of land lies somewhere between these two extremes: there is no general duty of disclosure on the vendor, but he is required to disclose irremovable, latent defects in title of which the purchaser is unaware. Failure to do so may mean that the vendor will be unable to obtain a grant of specific performance against the purchaser, and that the purchaser will be able to rescind the contract or claim an abatement in the purchase price. Remedies will be dealt with below.

Latent and patent defects

The vendor's duty relates to *latent* defects as to *title*. This means that he does not have to disclose *patent* defects (that is to say defects visible to the eye) nor defects affecting the *quality* of the property (although he may be liable for the condition of the property in other ways: see below). Because the vendor's duty of disclosure is a fairly limited one, the purchaser must satisfy himself that the property is suitable for his purposes, and this is of course why so many matters (local searches, surveys, preliminary enquiries) must be sorted out before exchange of contracts.

---

[53] See Treitel, *The Law of Contract* (6th ed., 1983), pp. 300–308; Cheshire, Fifoot and Furmston's, *Law of Contract* (11th ed., 1986), pp. 290–294.

Rationale for the vendor's duty of disclosure

Why does the law impose a duty of disclosure, albeit a limited one, on the vendor at all? Fry L.J. gave a succinct explanation in *Reeve* v. *Berridge*[54]:

> "There is great practical convenience in requiring the vendor, who knows his own title, to disclose all that is necessary to protect himself, rather than in requiring the purchaser to demand an inspection of the vendor's title deeds before entering into a contract, a demand which the owners of property would in some cases be unwilling to concede, and which is not, in our opinion, in accordance with the usual course of business in sales by private contract."

Given established conveyancing practice, therefore, the vendor must disclose latent defects in title to the purchaser in the contract: if he does not, there will be a breach of contract and the purchaser will have various remedies; if he does, so that the purchaser knows of the defect, he cannot complain.[55]

Difference between latent and patent defects

The crucial distinction is that between a latent and a patent defect. A classic case on this is *Yandle & Sons* v. *Sutton*.[56] There the vendor agreed to sell a piece of land to the purchaser across which there was an unmetalled and somewhat irregular track. After exchanging contracts, the purchaser discovered that there was a public right of way across the land and refused to complete. The vendor sought specific performance, and all turned on whether the defect was latent or patent. Sarjant J. held that the defect was latent and that the contract was unenforceable. He said[57]: "in considering what is a latent defect and what a patent defect, one ought to take the general view, that a patent defect, which can be thrust upon the purchaser, must be a defect which arises either to the eye, or by necessary implication from something which is visible to the eye." On the facts of this case, it was plausible that the track across the land was used simply for the accommodation of the property itself. Of course an easement could be a patent defect, for example where a metalled road crosses one piece of land clearly in order to give access to another one.[58] But the test is quite strict from the vendor's point of view:

What is "patent"?

to be patent, the defect must be visible or be a necessary implication from something that is visible. For the conveyancer, the answer must be that if there is anything which could possibly be considered a defect in title, disclose it to the purchaser in the contract.

The distinction between latent and patent defects may become clearer with the help of some illustrations.

Examples of latent defects A defect in the vendor's own title would be latent. For example this would be the case where there had been a conveyance by trustees to one of themselves[59] or where the root of title is a voluntary deed.[60]

---

[54] (1888) 20 Q.B.D. 523 at p. 528.
[55] *Timmins* v. *Moreland Street Property Co. Ltd.* [1958] Ch. 110, C.A.
[56] [1922] 2 Ch. 199.
[57] *Ibid.* at p. 210.
[58] See *Bowles* v. *Round* (1800) 5 Ves. 508; *Ashburner* v. *Sewell* [1891] 3 Ch. 405.
[59] *Pilkington* v. *Wood* [1953] Ch. 770.
[60] *Re Marsh and The Earl of Grenville* (1882) 24 Ch.D. 11.

Adverse rights   More often the defect relates to some kind of adverse right which a third party has in relation to the land in question. The following defects have been held to be latent: unusually onerous covenants in a lease[61]; a party wall structure notice under the London building legislation[62]; an easement invisible to the eye[63]; a restrictive covenant[64]; service of a notice to increase the rent of a property under a rent review clause from £4,650 per annum to £13,000 per annum[65]; the fact that a lease is liable to forfeiture for arrears of rent.[66] Many more examples could be given (for example licences by estoppel, some overriding interests, rentcharges and the exception and reservation of the mines and minerals beneath land).[67] One interesting recent example may be given. In *Peyman* v. *Lanjani*[68] the defendant wished to purchase the lease of a restaurant. Consent was needed to the assignment from the landlord. As the defendant himself was a scruffy and unpresentable character, a third party impersonated him in an interview with the landlord. Consent was forthcoming and the defendant completed. Later he agreed to sell his lease to the plaintiff. When the plaintiff discovered what had taken place, he refused to complete. The Court of Appeal held that the deception of the landlord had given rise to a latent defect of title which was irremovable, and that the plaintiff was entitled to rescind and recover his deposit.[69]

Unenforceable interests   A defect which was once latent may cease to be a defect where the interest in question has become unenforceable. For example a pre-1926 restrictive covenant which has already been defeated by a bona fide purchaser for value without notice would no longer be a latent defect[70]; nor would an unregistered estate contract once the legal estate had passed to a third party[71]; nor a 60-year old contract which is no longer enforceable.[72]

Statute   In some situations, statute may remedy an apparent defect in the vendor's title. For example, if a mortgagee enters into a contract to sell the mortgaged property, he can convey the fee simple although it is actually in the vendor[73]; and an equitable owner in some circumstances has the power to convey the legal estate.[74]

Defect incidental   A defect is not latent if it is incidental to the tenure of the property or necessarily incidental to some interest affecting it. For example where property is subject to a tenancy, it is not necessary for the vendor to disclose that the tenancy is protected under the Rent Act 1977 or the Landlord and Tenant Act 1954.

---

[61] *Re White and Smith's Contract* [1896] 1 Ch. 637.
[62] *Carlish* v. *Salt* [1906] 1 Ch. 335.
[63] *Heywood* v. *Mallalieu* (1883) 25 Ch.D. 347; *Yandle & Sons* v. *Sutton* [1922] 2 Ch. 199.
[64] *Re Stone and Saville's Contract* [1963] 1 All E.R. 535, C.A.
[65] *F. & H. Entertainments Ltd.* v. *Leisure Enterprises* (1976) 120 S.J. 331.
[66] *Pips (Leisure Productions) Ltd.* v. *Walton* (1982) 43 P. & C.R. 415.
[67] See *Halsbury's Laws of England* (4th ed.), Vol. 42, para. 63.
[68] [1984] 3 All E.R. 703.
[69] A separate issue was whether the purchaser had waived his rights by going into possession before completion: see Wilkinson (1985) 135 New L.J. 247.
[70] *Wilkes* v. *Spooner* [1911] 2 K.B. 473.
[71] *Hollington Brothers Ltd.* v. *Rhodes* [1951] W.N. 437.
[72] *MEPC Ltd.* v. *Christian-Edwards* [1981] A.C. 205, H.L.
[73] Law of Property Act 1925, s.42(4)(i).
[74] *Ibid.* s.42(4)(ii).

At the end of this section (see pp. 81–85) we shall consider how the contract should disclose particular types of latent defects, and how the standard conditions affect the situation.

Examples of patent defects A defect will be patent rather than latent where it is possible to tell by looking at the land that some adverse right exists. The most obvious example is an easement evidenced by a metalled road.[75] In *Re Leyland and Taylor's Contract*[76] it was held that a notice to carry out private street works was a patent defect, since an inspection of the property would have made it obvious that such a notice might be served. In *Spooner v. Eustace*[77] it was held in New Zealand that the fact that a house encroaches over the boundary of an adjoining property is a patent defect.

Person in occupation
It could be argued that a person in actual occupation of property and with an equitable interest in it constitutes a patent rather than a latent defect in title; as between that person and a third party the former would be protected, in the case of unregistered land by the doctrine of constructive notice[78] and in the case of registered land by virtue of section 70(1)(g) of the Land Registration Act 1925.[79] If the person's occupation is capable of binding a purchaser, it might seem quite logical to argue that, in a contractual dispute between vendor and purchaser, the fact of occupation makes the defect in title patent. Some cases have dabbled with this suggestion[80] though there is also authority to the contrary.[81] As a matter of principle there seems no reason why the occupier's protection as against a purchaser should be equated with that of the purchaser's as against the vendor. However, the position under the Matrimonial Homes Act 1983 should be noted (see p. 801).

Concealing patent defects
It is important to point out that, while there is no duty to disclose patent defects to the purchaser, the vendor may be liable for fraudulent misrepresentation if he takes active steps to

Active concealment
conceal a defect from him. This is well illustrated by a recent case, *Gordon v. Selico Ltd.*[82] Before granting a lease to the plaintiff, active steps were taken to conceal dry rot in the flat to be demised; damages were awarded against the defendants. In this case the defect was as to quality, in respect of which there is no general duty of disclosure anyway; however the principle would have equal applicability where the vendor actively tried to hide a patent defect in title.

Removable and irremovable defects
The vendor is only bound to disclose to the purchaser *irremovable* defects in title. If a defect is removable, then the vendor can have it removed and insist upon the purchaser accepting the title; equally, a purchaser is entitled to insist that the defect is removed before he takes a conveyance, even if he

---

[75] *Bowles v. Round* (1800) 5 Ves. 508.

[76] [1900] 2 Ch. 625.

[77] [1963] N.Z.L.R. 913.

[78] See *Hunt v. Luck* [1902] 1 Ch. 428 and *City of London Building Society v. Flegg* [1986] 1 All E.R. 989 (C.A.); the latter case breathed new life into s.14 of the Law of Property Act 1925.

[79] See, *e.g. Williams and Glyn's Bank Ltd. v. Boland* [1981] A.C. 487 (H.L.).

[80] See, *e.g. James v. Lichfield* (1869) L.R. 9 Eq. 51.

[81] *Caballero v. Henty* (1874) L.R. 9 Ch. 447 (C.A.).

[82] (1986) 278 E.G. 53.

"removable"

knew of the defect when he entered into the contract.[83] A defect is removable if the vendor himself is able to remove it or if he is in a position to insist upon its removal. For example, if he owns the freehold but it is mortgaged, it may be that he is entitled to redeem the mortgage at any time so that there is no defect in the title.[84] In practice, of course, this is common. However it may be that the right to redeem has been postponed for a considerable period[85]; in that case the mortgage would be an irremovable defect which should be disclosed in the contract. Another example of a removable defect would be the breach of a positive covenant in a lease, since by performing the necessary obligation (for example repairing the demised property) the breach would be terminated.

Special position under the Matrimonial Homes Act 1983

Where a spouse registers rights of occupation under the Matrimonial Homes Act 1983, this constitutes a latent rather than a patent defect in title.[86] If the vendor enters into a contract to sell the property in question with vacant possession,[87] section 4(1) provides that it shall be a term of the contract that, before completion, the vendor will procure the cancellation of the registration of the rights of occupation at his own expense. The parties may express a contrary intention in the contract.[88] If the vendor fails to persuade the spouse to remove the registration, the consequences may be dire.[89]

Express agreement to make good title

On rare occasions the vendor may expressly agree to confer a good title on the purchaser. Where this happens, the vendor would be in breach of contract if there are any latent defects in his title, even if the purchaser was aware of them when he entered into the contract. In *McGrory* v. *Alderdale Estate Co. Ltd.*[90] Lord Finlay said[91]: "The law is clear that, if there is a written agreement of sale which expressly provides that a good title is to be made it is not open to the vendor to prove that at the time of the contract the purchaser knew of the defect in the

Cato v. Thompson

title . . . ." An example of this rule is afforded by *Cato* v. *Thompson*.[92] The defendant agreed to sell land to the plaintiff on the basis that he would "make a good marketable title." In fact there was a restrictive covenant affecting the land of which the plaintiff was aware at the time of the contract and which made the land unmarketable. It was held that the plaintiff was entitled to rescind the contract and recover his deposit. Jessel M.R. said that the contract really meant that the purchaser was telling the vendor "I know that there is a serious defect in your title, but I will buy if you can make it marketable."

Vendor's ignorance of the defect is no defence

The vendor has a duty to disclose any latent defect in title; however it may be that he himself is unaware of the defect in question. It would be quite possible not to realise that a neighbour has a right to light or a right to come onto one's land to

---

[83] *Re Gloag and Miller's Contract* (1883) 23 Ch.D. 320.
[84] *Brickles* v. *Snell* [1916] A.C. 599 (P.C.).
[85] See, *e.g. Knightsbridge Estates Trust Ltd.* v. *Byrne* [1939] Ch. 441. and [1940] A.C. 613.
[86] *Wroth* v. *Tyler* [1974] Ch. 30.
[87] Or to grant a lease or underlease: Matrimonial Homes Act 1983, s.4(6).
[88] *Ibid.* s.4(4).
[89] See *Wroth* v. *Tyler* [1974] Ch. 30.
[90] [1918] A.C. 503.
[91] *Ibid.* at p. 508.
[92] (1882) 9 Q.B.D. 616.

effect repairs to adjoining property.[93] However at common law, the ignorance of the vendor does not affect his duty to disclose all latent defects to the purchaser: his liability is absolute.[94] As we shall see below, the standard conditions do attempt to redress the balance in favour of the vendor.

Disclosing the defect

The duty of disclosure imposes a considerable risk upon the vendor. Obviously if there is any doubt as to whether a defect is latent or patent or whether it is removable or irremovable, the sensible course of action is to disclose it to the purchaser in the contract. If the purchaser knows of the defect, he will be unable to rescind. The defect may be disclosed in either the particulars or the special conditions: the overriding principle is that there should be full and frank disclosure. The disclosure must not be vague or couched in terms which only a "trained equity conveyancer"[95] can understand. If the defect is not specifically described in the contract, it is permissible to refer to some other document which accompanies the contract (for example office copy entries in the case of registered land or a copy of an earlier conveyance containing restrictive covenants in the case of unregistered land). However in this case the reference must be a clear and unequivocal one.

Full and frank disclosure

The Land Charges Act 1972

One particular problem which requires brief mention is the notorious one of knowledge and the land charges system. Until 1969, registration of a land charge constituted notice of that charge to all the world[96] and it was suggested at first instance in *Re Forsey and Hollebone's Contract*[97] that this would mean that a purchaser could not rescind for non-disclosure. The suggestion was *obiter*, and the Court of Appeal did not comment on it; if correct, it would have been a nonsense, since the purchaser would be deprived of a remedy simply through a statutory fiction. However, section 24 of the Law of Property Act 1969 provides that a purchaser's knowledge of a registered land charge at the time of the contract should be determined by reference to his *actual knowledge* and that for these purposes section 198 Law of Property Act 1925 should be disregarded. It is possible that the suggestion in *Re Forsey and Hollebone's Contract* may still be applicable in the case of *local* land charges, since the 1969 Act does not apply to them. The purchaser conducts his local search before exchanging contracts, however, so that the same problem does not arise.

Disclosure and the standard conditions

Here we shall consider how the vendor should proceed when disclosing particular common defects in title, and how the common law situation is affected by the Law Society and National conditions.

---

[93] As in *Ward* v. *Kirkland* [1967] Ch. 194.
[94] *Re Brewer and Hankin's Contract* (1899) 80 L.T. 127.
[95] See *Faruqi* v. *English Real Estates* [1979] 1 W.L.R. 963 at p. 967.
[96] Law of Property Act 1925, s.198; the same problem does not arise in the case of registered land, as the Land Registration Act 1925 does not contain a provision equivalent to s.198 of the Law of Property Act.
[97] [1927] 2 Ch. 379.

Easements

At common law the vendor must disclose to the purchaser all easements and analogous rights which are latent and of which the purchaser is unaware. It is important to recognise how varied the categories of easements and profits may be: there are many easements besides the more obvious ones such as rights of way and rights of drainage.[98] Law Society condition 5(1) provides that:

Law Society condition 5(1)

> "The vendor warrants that he has disclosed the existence of all easements, rights, privileges and liabilities affecting the property, of which the vendor knows or ought to know, other than the existence of those known to the purchaser at the date of the contract, or which a prudent purchaser would have discovered by that date."

Two points should be made about this condition. First, the vendor's warranty is *not* limited to *latent* defects: he could be liable even in respect of a patent defect of which he knows or ought to know provided that it is not one which a prudent purchaser should have discovered. Secondly, whereas at common law the vendor's liability is absolute (that is he can be liable though ignorant of the defect), this condition slightly limits his liability by providing that he should only disclose defects of which he knows or ought to know. Law Society condition 5(2)(*b*) provides that, without prejudice to condition 5(1),

Law Society condition 5(2)(*b*)

> "the property is sold, and will if the vendor so requires be conveyed, subject to all rights of way, water, light, drainage and other easements, rights, privileges and liabilities affecting the same."

National condition 14

National condition 14 provides:

> "Without prejudice to the duty of the vendor to disclose all latent easements and latent liabilities known to the vendor to affect the property, the property is sold subject to any rights of way and water, rights of common, and other rights, easements, quasi-easements, liabilities and public rights affecting the same."

This condition slightly varies the position at common law, where the vendor is absolutely liable; under condition 14 he is only liable in respect of latent easements of which he knows.

Existing leases

Unless the contract contains a term to the contrary, the purchaser is entitled to vacant possession. It follows that all existing tenancies should be revealed to the purchaser and the recoverable rent should be accurately stated.[99] If the vendor has received a notice to quit, it should be disclosed.[1] There is no need to disclose the fact that a tenant has suggested he might soon serve a notice to quit.[2]

Under both sets of standard conditions, provision is specifically made for disclosing existing tenancies. Under the Law Society's conditions, special condition F should be adapted appropriately and copies of all leases or tenancies sent to the purchaser. Condition 6 then provides:

---

[98] See Megarry and Wade, *The Law of Real Property* (5th ed., 1984), p. 834–912.
[99] *Re Englefield Holdings and Sinclair's Contract* [1962] 3 All E.R. 503.
[1] *Dimmock* v. *Hallett* (1866) 2 Ch. App. 21.
[2] *Davenport* v. *Charsley* (1886) 54 L.T. 372.

"6. Tenancies

(1) This condition applies if the property is sold subject to any lease or tenancy and shall have effect notwithstanding any partial, incomplete or inaccurate reference to any lease or tenancy in the special conditions or the particulars of the property.

(2) Copies or full particulars of all leases or tenancies not vested in the purchaser having been furnished to him, he shall be deemed to purchase with full knowledge thereof and shall take the property subject to the rights of the tenants thereunder or by reason thereof. The purchaser shall indemnify the vendor against all claims, demands and liability in respect of such rights, notwithstanding that they may be void against a purchaser for want of registration.

(3) The vendor gives no warranty as to the amount of rent lawfully recoverable from any tenant, as to the effect of any legislation in relation to any lease or tenancy or as to the compliance with any legislation affecting the same.

(4) The vendor shall inform the purchaser of any change in the disclosed terms and conditions of any lease or tenancy.

(5) If a lease or tenancy subject to which the property is sold terminates for any reason, the vendor shall inform the purchaser and, on being indemnified by the purchaser against all consequential loss, expenditure or liability, shall act as the purchaser may direct."

Under the National conditions, special condition C must be adapted and general condition 18 then provides:

"18. Leases and Tenancies

(1) Abstracts or copies of the leases or agreements (if in writing) under which the tenants hold having been made available, the purchaser (whether he has inspected the same or not) shall be deemed to have notice of and shall take subject to the terms of all the existing tenancies and the rights of the tenants, whether arising during the continuance or after the expiration thereof, and such notice shall not be affected by any partial or incomplete statement in the Special Conditions with reference to the tenancies, and no objection shall be taken on account of there not being an agreement in writing with any tenant.

(2) Where a lease or tenancy affects the property sold and other property, the property sold will be conveyed with the benefit of the apportioned rent (if any) mentioned in the Special Conditions or (if not so mentioned) fixed by the auctioneer, and no objection shall be taken on the ground that the consent of the tenant has not been obtained to the

apportionment and the purchaser shall not require the rent to be legally apportioned.

(3) The purchaser shall keep the vendor indemnified against all claims by the tenant for compensation or otherwise, except in respect of a tenancy which expires or is determined on or before the completion date or in respect of an obligation which ought to have been discharged before the date of the contract.

(4) Land in the occupation of the vendor is sold subject to the right (hereby reserved to him) to be paid a fair price for tillages, off-going and other allowances as if he were an outgoing tenant who had entered into occupation of the land after 1st March 1948, and as if the purchaser were the landlord, and in case of dispute such price shall be fixed by the valuation of a valuer, to be nominated in case the parties differ by the President of the Royal Institution of Chartered Surveyors."

Restrictive covenants

Restrictive covenants must be disclosed in the contract, unless for some reason they have ceased to be enforceable.[3] In practice the contract will disclose the existence of the covenant, but its actual terms will be contained in a copy of the deed creating it which will also be sent to the purchaser. Provided that the disclosure is full and frank, this will suffice. The Law Society conditions do not make any specific provision for the disclosure of restrictive covenants. Under National condition 12(2) it is provided that:

(2) "If the property is sold subject to restrictive covenants, the deed imposing those covenants or a copy thereof having been made available, the purchaser (whether he has inspected the same or not) shall be deemed to have purchased with full knowledge thereof."

Selling leaseholds

We have already seen that when selling leasehold interests the vendor must take care to avoid any misdescription.[4] As far as non-disclosure is concerned, he must disclose any unusually onerous covenants.[5] It is not easy to say with confidence whether a covenant is unusual or not, since the court has to take into account many factors such as the nature of the premises, the locality, the purpose of the letting and current conveyancing practice.[6]

Unusual covenants may be set out in full in the contract. More commonly, however, the vendor will send a copy of the lease to the purchaser for him to inspect. Both sets of conditions make special provision for this:

---

[3] As in *Wilkes* v. *Spooner* [1911] 2 K.B. 473.

[4] See pp. 65–67.

[5] See, *e.g. Melzak* v. *Lilienfeld* [1926] Ch. 480; *Flexman* v. *Corbett* [1930] 1 Ch. 672.

[6] For a recent discussion of the issue, see *Chester* v. *Buckingham Travel Ltd.* [1981] 1 W.L.R. 96, noted by Annand [1981] Conv. 233.

Law Society condition 8(3):

> (3) "A copy of the lease and a copy of, sufficient extract from, or abstract of, all superior leases, the contents of which are known to the vendor, having been supplied or made available to the purchaser, he shall be deemed to purchase with full notice of the contents thereof, whether or not he has inspected the same."

National condition 11(2):

> (2) "The lease or underlease or a copy thereof having been made available, the purchaser (whether he has inspected the same or not) shall be deemed to have bought with full notice of the contents thereof."

However, clauses such as this will not avail the vendor when there is a positive misdescription in the contract. In *Charles Hunt Ltd.* v. *Palmer*[7] the property was subject to a covenant not to use the premises otherwise than for carrying on the business of a ladies outfitter. In the particulars in the contract, the premises were misdescribed as "valuable business premises." It was held that the purchaser should not be required to complete, notwithstanding a term in the contract that deemed him to have purchased with full notice of the contents of the lease.

Local land charges Local land charges may constitute latent defects in title, although it is highly likely that the purchaser will have discovered their existence before exchanging contracts by carrying out a local search. However it is important to appreciate that both Law Society condition 3 and National condition 15 impose a wide duty of disclosure on the vendor in respect of notices, communications and similar matters which he has received and which affect the property.[8] At common law there is no duty to disclose breaches of planning control, since this is not a matter relating to title in the strict sense.[9] However the vendor's duty is extended by the standard conditions above, and he must also avoid making pre-contract misrepresentations or contractual misdescriptions.[10]

Remedies for non-disclosure

Where the vendor fails to disclose a latent defect in title to the purchaser, the position is much the same as in the case of misdescription.[11] Apart from the standard conditions, if the defect is substantial the purchaser may rescind the contract or, if he prefers, complete but with an abatement of the purchase price.[12] The vendor will not be able to obtain specific performance.[13] If the defect is material rather than substantial,

---

[7] [1931] 2 Ch. 387.

[8] See *Sakkas* v. *Donford Ltd.* (1982) 46 P. & C.R. 290, noted [1984] Conv. 85.

[9] See Gibson, *Conveyancing* (21st ed., 1980) pp. 135–136; Farrand, *Contract and Conveyancing* (4th ed., 1983), p. 68; Barnsley's *Conveyancing Law and Practice* (2nd ed., 1982), p. 234.

[10] *Sinclair-Hill* v. *Southcott* (1973) P. & C.R. 490; *Laurence* v. *Lexcourt Holdings Ltd.* [1978] 1 W.L.R. 1128.

[11] See pp. 71–76 above.

[12] *Rudd* v. *Lascelles* [1900] 1 Ch. 815.

[13] *Phillips* v. *Caldcleugh* (1868) L.R. 4 Q.B. 159.

the purchaser cannot rescind, but he can obtain compensation.[14] Only nominal damages would be available in the case of an immaterial misdescription. The effect of the Law Society's and National conditions would be the same as in the case of misdescription.

Defects in quality

Having seen that the vendor must disclose latent defects in title, the final issue is whether he also has any responsibility to disclose latent defects as to the quality of the property. On some occasions, the courts have appeared to suggest that there is such a duty.[15] These cases should be treated with scepticism. There may be liability in contract for misdescription, and any false or misleading statement may also be actionable as a misrepresentation. There is a big step from these propositions to saying that the vendor is also under a duty of disclosure. The better view is that, as regards the quality of the property, the general principle remains *caveat emptor*.[16]

However it is important to bear in mind that tortious liability in this area has increased considerably in recent years,[17] and that important rights may be exercised by home-owners under the National House-Building Council scheme.[18]

Definition conditions

Law Society general condition 1

"1. Definitions.
In these conditions—
  (a) 'completion notice' means a notice served under condition 23(2)
  (b) 'the contract rate' means the rate specified in a special condition or, if none is so specified, the rate prescribed from time to time under section 32 of the Land Compensation Act 1961 for interest payable thereunder
  (c) 'contractual completion date' has the meaning given in condition 21
  (d) 'conveyance' includes an assignment and a transfer under the Land Registration Acts
  (e) 'lease' includes underlease
  (f) 'normal deposit' means the sum which, together with any preliminary deposit paid by the purchaser, amounts to ten per centum of the purchase money (excluding any separate price to be paid for any chattels, fixtures or fittings)

[14] *Re Belcham and Gawley's Contract* [1930] 1 Ch. 56.
[15] See, *e.g. Re Puckett and Smith's Contract* [1902] 2 Ch. 258; *Shepherd* v. *Croft* [1911] 1 Ch. 521.
[16] See, *e.g.* Atkinson J. in *Otto* v. *Bolton and Harris* [1936] 2 K.B. 46 at p. 52.
[17] See, *e.g.* Barnsley's *Conveyancing Law and Practice* (2nd ed., 1982), pp. 168–177; Annand and Cain, *Modern Conveyancing* (1984), pp. 210–213.
[18] See, Barnsley, *Conveyancing Law and Practice* (2nd ed., 1982), pp. 177–181.

(g) 'working day' means any day from Monday to Friday (inclusive) other than—
   (i) Christmas Day, Good Friday and any statutory bank holiday, and
   (ii) any other day specified in a special condition as not a working day
(h) a reference to a statute includes any amendment or re-enactment thereof."

National construction conditions

"Construction of the conditions
In these conditions where the context admits—
(1) The 'vendor' and the 'purchaser' include the persons deriving title under them respectively
(2) 'Purchase money' includes any sum to be paid for chattels, fittings or other separate items
(3) References to the 'special conditions' include references to the particulars of sale and to the provisions of the contract which is made by reference to the conditions
(4) The 'prescribed rate' means the agreed rate of interest or, if none, then the rate of interest prescribed from time to time under Land Compensation Act 1961, s.32
(5) 'Solicitor' includes a barrister who is employed by a body corporate to carry out conveyancing on its behalf and is acting in the course of his employment
(6) 'Working day' means a day on which clearing banks in the City of London are (or would be but for a strike, lock-out, or other stoppage, affecting particular banks or banks generally) open during banking hours, except in condition 19(4), in which 'working day' means a day when the Land Registry is open to the public
(7) 'Designated bank' means a bank designated by the Chief Registrar under the Building Societies Act 1962, s.59
(8) The 'Planning Acts' means the enactments from time to time in force relating to town and country planning
(9) On a sale by private treaty references to the 'auctioneer' shall be read as references to the vendor's agent
(10) On a sale in lots, the conditions apply to each lot
(11) 'Abstract of title' means in relation to registered land such documents as the vendor is required by Land Registration Act 1925, s.110, to furnish."

We have already encountered some of the definitions in Law Society general condition 1 and the National construction condition, for example "the contract rate" (Law Society) and "prescribed rate" (National). Others, like National construction (1), need no explanation. The following are however deserving of specific mention:

"solicitor" (i) "*solicitor*" is defined to include a barrister who is employed by a corporate body to carry out conveyancing on its behalf and is acting in the course of his employment. Note in particular that such barristers are permitted to exchange contracts by telephone or telex[19] (National condition 1(6)). The definition should be amended by special condition to include a reference to licensed conveyancers, where appropriate. The Law Society general conditions do not define "solicitor."

Payment of completion moneys

(ii) "Designated bank" Both sets of standard conditions specify how completion moneys should be paid. Authorised modes of payment under the National condition include bankers' drafts and guaranteed cheques drawn on a "designated bank" (5(3)(ii) and (iii)). "Designated bank" means, by National construction (7), a bank authorised to hold funds of building societies under section 59 of the Building Societies Act 1962.[19a] However, there is every indication that these "designated banks" will cease to exist after October 1987.[20] Instead building societies will be permitted (by regulations brought out under the Building Societies Act 1986) to deposit funds with any institution authorised under the Banking Act 1979, or its successor. Should this happen, the authorised modes of payment for completion monies in National condition 5(3)(ii) and (iii) will be ineffective. This can be overcome by amending National construction (7) by special condition, as follows: "Designated bank" means a bank authorised from time to time to hold the funds of building societies under the Building Societies Act 1986 and any regulation made there under. The equivalent provision in the Law Society conditions is found not in the definitions but in general condition 21(2)(*b*). This restricts the range of "authorised" banks whose drafts are acceptable for the purposes of completion to CHAPS (Clearing House Automated Payments System) settlement banks, which were listed earlier at page 51.[21]

Interest

National condition 7(1)(ii) allows the purchaser to place the balance of the purchase money on deposit in a "designated bank" where delay in completion is not the purchaser's fault. Provided the purchaser gives written notice to the vendor or his solicitor, the vendor is only entitled to receive the income earned on deposit, not interest at the "prescribed rate." The Law Society conditions contain no such provision.

Working day

(iii) "Working day" Law Society general condition 1(g) defines working day as any day from Monday to Friday inclusive except Christmas Day, Good Friday, any statutory bank holiday and any other day specified in a special condition. All the time-limits in the Law Society general conditions are expressed in working days, with the one exception of those time-limits mentioned in general condition 23(5) dealing with the vendor's right of re-sale, where the purchaser has not complied with a completion notice. Exactly the same is true of the time-limits in the National conditions: National condition 22(3) corresponds to Law Society general condition 23(5). National construction (6) defines working days in terms of the working days of the London clearing banks . The effect of strikes, lock-outs, and other stoppages is excepted. Where National condition 19(4) applies

---

[19] See pp. 119 to 120.
[19a] The current list of "designated banks" is reproduced at Appendix B.
[20] See "Liquid Assets," Building Societies Commission, 1987.
[21] The reasons for the restriction appear at (1984) 81 L.S.Gaz. 2270.

(priority notices) working day means a day on which the Land Registry is open to the public.

Saturday

It will be noted that both definitions follow Walton J.'s observation in *Rightside Properties Ltd.* v. *Gray*[22] that "Saturday is not now a working day for most solicitors."

Oakdown Ltd. v. Bernstein

Any other day the parties wish to make a non-working day must be expressly stated in the contract. This point was recently illustrated by the case of *Oakdown Ltd.* v. *Bernstein*.[23] The solicitors representing both sides were Jewish. The purchasers, Oakdown, failed to complete the purchase of a block of flats in March 1982. Mr. Bernstein, acting for the vendors, served a notice to complete under the National Conditions of Sale (19th ed.). The notice was due to expire on April 9, Good Friday, so Mr. Saunders, Oakdown's solicitor offered to complete on the 8th. The 8th was the first day of the Jewish festival of Passover and neither Bernstein nor the vendors were willing to do business on this date. Saunders then suggested that Bernstein should deliver the deeds to him on the 7th; he would hold the deeds to Bernstein's order and remit the purchase money on the 8th by telegraphic transfer (Saunders was not averse to working on the first day of Passover). Saunders thought that this arrangement had been agreed to; certainly he was told nothing to the contrary. However after consideration, Bernstein and his clients decided it was improper to be parties to Saunders working on Passover. No deeds were sent on the 7th. When the vendors offered to complete April 13 they were told by the purchasers that the contract was at an end. Both sides claimed the deposit.

Scott J. held that the vendors had repudiated the contract by not completing on the 8th, thereby entitling the purchasers to terminate the contract and to the return of the deposit. The purchasers had effectively selected the 8th for completion, since it was a working day under the contract and within the period for completion set by the notice to complete. If the vendors had wished Jewish holidays to be non-working days, they should have said so in the contract.

Time limits

Neither the Law Society or National conditions state when the time limits set by them should start. Therefore the common law rule applies. Where a person must do something within a certain period of days, the day from which the period starts to run is not counted against him.[24] So, for example by Law Society general condition 15(2) the purchaser must deliver his requisitions on title six working days from the receipt of the abstract or date of the contract whichever is the later. If the abstract is received on Tuesday, time starts to run against the purchaser on Wednesday and expires the following Wednesday.

Time limits set by reference to working days can only run out on a working day.

(iv) "Planning Acts" National condition 15 makes several references to the "Planning Acts." These are defined by National construction (8) as meaning the enactments from time to time in force *relating* to town and country planning. Clearly the Acts are not limited to those with "town and country planning" in the title

[22] [1975] 1 Ch. 72.
[23] (1984) 49 P. & C.R. 282; [1985] Conv. 309–311.
[24] *Blunt* v. *Heslop* (1838) 3 Ad. & El. 577.

(v) "Normal deposit"   Recognition was given for the first time in the 1984 Revision of the Law Society contract, to the practice of allowing the purchaser to pay a deposit of less than 10 per cent. in sales by private treaty. To emphasise that payment of a reduced deposit should be the exception rather than the rule, general condition 1(*f*) says that a "normal deposit" is the sum which, together with any preliminary or pre-contract deposit paid by the purchaser amounts to 10 per cent. of the purchase price. Any separate price to be paid for chattels or fittings etc. is excluded from the calculation. The National conditions do not cater for reduced deposits.

(vi) Statute   The reader is reminded here of two statutory

L.P.A. 1925, s.61 provisions. First, by section 61 of the Law of Property Act 1925 in all deeds, contracts, wills, orders and other instruments executed, made or coming into operation after the commencement of the Act, unless the context otherwise requires, "month" means a calendar month; "person" includes a corporation; the singular includes the plural and vice versa; and the masculine includes the feminine and vice versa. Secondly,

L.P.A. 1925, s.41 under section 41 of the same Act, time is not to be of the essence of the contract unless the contract itself so provides, or the surrounding circumstances show that the parties intended it to be so.

     Where time is of the essence under the contract for completion or something to be done towards it, then non-performance by either party of the act in question by the time specified will entitle the innocent party to treat the contract as at an end.

Conditions as to service and delivery

Law Society general condition 2

"2. Service and Delivery.

    (1) Section 196 of the Law of Property Act 1925 applies to any notice served under the contract, save that—

(*a*) a notice shall also be sufficiently served on a party if served on that party's solicitors

(*b*) a reference to a registered letter shall include a prepaid first class ordinary letter

(*c*) if the time at which a letter containing a notice would in the ordinary course be delivered is not on a working day, the notice shall be deemed to be served on the next following working day

(*d*) a notice shall also be sufficiently served if—

  (i) sent by telex or by telegraphic facsimile transmission to the party to be served, and that service shall be deemed to be made on the day of transmission if transmitted before 4 p.m. on a working day, but otherwise on the next following working day

  (ii) When the addressee is a member of a document exchange (as to which the inclusion of a reference thereto in the solicitors' letterhead shall be conclusive evidence) delivered to that or any other affiliated exchange, and that service shall be deemed to have been made on the first working day after that on which the document would, in the ordinary course, be available for collection by the addressee.

(2) Sub-condition (1) applies to the delivery of documents as it applies to the service of notices."

Document exchanges Law Society general condition 2(1)(*d*)(ii) now provides for the service of notices or delivery of documents under the contract by document exchange.[25] In the absence of express provision it is uncertain whether document exchanges can be used for this purpose.

Imprint (Print and Design) Ltd. v. Inkblot Studios Ltd. In *Imprint (Print and Design) Ltd.* v. *Inkblot Studios Ltd.*[26] the Court of Appeal held that a summons was not properly served via an exchange. Parker L.J. said that it was possible for parties to make a specific agreement to accept service of a document by a method other than that provided by the Rules of the Supreme Court (Ord. 65, r.5(1), for example, said that service of any document might be effected by leaving the document at the proper address of the person to be served, or sending it by post or in such other manner as the court might direct). But the mere fact that the solicitors of both parties were members of the same exchange, each firm having a contract with the company that ran the exchange, did not constitute such an agreement: "the leaving of a document in a document exchange box simpliciter was not proper service."

John Willmott Homes Ltd. v. Read On the other hand, in *Willmott (John) Homes Ltd.* v. *Read*[27] Whitford J. held in the alternative[28] that a notice to exercise an option was so sufficiently served. He said that: "if parties instruct solicitors to carry out certain transactions on their behalf, and if they enter into an agreement under which acts may be done by solicitors on their behalf, they are empowering those solicitors as their agents to transact the business in whatever manner may seem to them appropriate."[29] With respect, this does not deal with the points made by the Court of Appeal in *Imprint*, that is that there must be an express agreement between the parties (or their solicitors) to accept service through a document exchange and membership of an exchange alone does not signify such agreement. *Imprint* was referred to Whitford J. but he chose to distinguish that decision by confining it to methods of service under the Rules of the Supreme Court.

Law Society general condition 2(1)(*d*)(ii) Obviously no problem arises where Law Society general condition 2(1)(*d*)(ii) applies to the contract. If the addressee is a member of a document exchange[30] (as to which the inclusion of a reference thereto in the solicitors' letterhead shall be conclusive evidence) and the notice (or document) is delivered to "that or any other affiliated exchange," it will be sufficiently served, "and that service shall be deemed to have been made on the first

---

[25] For Britdoc's charges see (1985) 82 L.S.Gaz. 1306.

[26] (1985) 129 S.J. 132, and see [1985] Conv. 239.

[27] (1986) 49 P. & C.R. 90.

[28] For the main decision see p. 95 below.

[29] (1986) 49 P. & C.R. 90 at pp. 99 and see [1985] Conv. 239.

[30] See Council Statement as to membership of document exchanges (1984) 81 L.S.Gaz. 2823.

working day after that on which the document would, in the ordinary course, be available for collection by the addressee." Note that even though the rules of a particular exchange may produce "premature" deemed service, general condition 2(1)(*d*)(ii) will prevail.

The National conditions

The National conditions do not authorise the use of document exchanges. Since it may be unwise to rely on Whitford J.'s widely expressed dictum at first instance in the *Willmott (John) Homes* case, express provision for their use should be made in the contract, where appropriate.

Other methods of service under Law Society general condition 2

Other available methods of service under Law Society general condition 2 are, utilising and extending section 196 of the Law of Property Act 1925, personal service on the party's solicitor, registered or first class letter, and telex or telegraphic facsimile transmission. These methods are also available for the delivery of documents as well as for the service of notices. If the post is used, and "the time at which a letter containing a notice [or document] would in the ordinary course be delivered is not on a working day, the notice [or document] shall be deemed to be served [or delivered] on the next following working day." (2(1)(*c*)).

Practice Direction on use of post

Attention is drawn in this regard to a recent Practice Direction[31] to the effect that delivery in the ordinary course of the post shall be taken (subject to proof to the contrary) to be effected, (a) in the case of first class mail, on the second working day after posting, (b) in the case of second class mail, on the fourth working day after posting. "Working days" for this purpose are Monday to Friday, excluding any bank holiday.

Service or delivery by telex or telegraphic facsimile transmission is effective on that day, but if transmitted after 4 p.m. on the next working day (2(1)(*d*)(i)).

Law Society general condition 2 only applies to the service of notices and delivery of documents. It is suggested that other communications made pursuant to the conditions, like, for example, a letter authorising the purchaser to go into occupation of the property before completion under general condition 18, are "served" when received.[32]

No "authorised" method of service under National conditions

The National conditions do not deal with service and delivery. It is unlikely that any of the notices referred to in the National conditions fall within section 196 of the Law of Property Act 1925. Words like "Notice to . . ." show an intention contrary to the "deemed" service provisions of section 196(5).[33] Such words are also inconsistent with, and displace, the rule that the mere posting of a letter can be acceptance of an offer if the parties contemplate such a method of acceptance, acceptance taking place at the time of posting.[34] Therefore, in the absence of a special condition along the lines of Law Society general condition 2, the service of notices and delivery of documents and other communications under the National conditions takes place at the time of actual receipt.[35]

---

[31] [1985] 1 All E.R. 889.
[32] By analogy with *Rightside Properties Ltd.* v. *Gray* [1975] 1 Ch. 72.
[33] *Holywell Securities Ltd.* v. *Hughes* [1974] 1 W.L.R. 155.
[34] *Henthorn* v. *Fraser* [1892] 2 Ch. 27.
[35] *Sun Alliance and London Assurance Co. Ltd.* v *Hayman* [1975] 1 W.L.R. 177.

Deposit conditions

Law Society general condition 9

"9. Deposit
(1) The purchaser shall on or before the date of the contract pay by way of deposit to the vendor's solicitors as stakeholders the normal deposit, or such lesser sum as the vendor shall have agreed in writing. On a sale by private treaty, payment shall be made by banker's draft or by cheque drawn on a solicitors' bank account.
(2) Upon service by the vendor of a completion notice, the purchaser shall pay to the vendor any difference between the normal deposit and any amount actually paid (if less).
(3) If any draft, cheque or other instrument tendered in or towards payment of any sum payable under this condition is dishonoured when first presented the vendor shall have the right by notice to the purchaser within seven days thereafter to treat the contract as repudiated."

National condition 2

"2. Deposit
(1) Unless the Special conditions otherwise provide, the purchaser shall on the date of the contract pay a deposit of 10 per cent. of the purchase price, on a sale by auction to the auctioneer, or on a sale by private treaty, to the vendor's solicitor and, in either case, as stakeholder
(2) In case a cheque taken for the deposit (having been presented, and whether or not it has been re-presented) has not been honoured, then and on that account the vendor may elect—
either (i) to treat the contract as discharged by breach thereof on the purchaser's part or (ii) to enforce payment of the deposit as a deposit, by suing on the cheque or otherwise."

Is a deposit necessary?

One element in a conveyancing transaction which has frequently been challenged in recent years is the practice of requiring a purchaser of resdential property to pay a deposit of up to 10 per cent. of the purchase price on exchange of conracts.[36] It has been suggested that the deposit might be reduced to a few hundred pounds or even abandoned altogether.[37] At common law there is no implication that a deposit must be paid on the sale of land, still less that any particular percentage must be paid. The statutory conditions implied into contracts by correspondence[38] leave open the question of whether a deposit should be paid. Nevertheless in *Morris* v. *Duke-Cohan*[39] the court thought a

[36] See for example H.W. Wilkinson (1975) 72 L.S.Gaz. 184, H.W. Wilkinson (1981) 78 L.S.Gaz. 1128, J.E. Adams (1970) 120 New L.J. 28, J.E. Adams (1983) 80 L.S.Gaz. 2811, H.W. Wilkinson (1984) 81 L.S.Gaz. 347, H.W. Wilkinson (1984) 81 L.S.Gaz. 1268. For a response see P.H. Kenny (1984) 81 L.S.Gaz. 1964.
[37] The Second Report of the Conveyancing Committee (1985), paras. 6.30–6.31, 9.30.
[38] Prescribed by the Lord Chancellor under s.46 of the Law of Property Act 1925. As to contracts by correspondence, see pp. 126 to 127 below.
[39] (1962) 106 S.J. 512.

solicitor who failed to advise the vendor of the need for a deposit was negligent.

Reduced deposits   Law Society general condition 9 recognises the trend towards smaller deposits, although it still regards 10 per cent. as the norm (a 10 per cent. deposit must be paid on a sale by auction). To protect the vendor who accepts a reduced deposit, sub-condition 9(2) says that if he serves a notice to complete, then the purchaser is to pay him the balance of the 10 per cent. No time limit is stated for payment so the money will be due at once. In *Damon Cia Naviera S.A.* v. *Hapag-Lloyd International S.A.*[40] the Court of Appeal confirmed that the vendor can in any event sue for this balance at common law. National condition 2(1) stoically provides for the payment of a 10 per cent. deposit. ·

The deposit is calculated on the balance of the purchase price. Law Society general condition 1(*f*) says that any separate price to be paid by the purchaser for chattels etc. is to be excluded from the purchase price for the purpose of calculating the "normal" 10 per cent. deposit. The National conditions achieve the same result impliedly by separating "chattels or valuation money" from "purchase price" in the box on the front of the contract form.

Argument for   The argument against abolishing deposits is that the vendor
deposits   would be deprived of a most effective remedy, that is forfeiture of the deposit. When house prices are stable, a 10 per cent. deposit duly forfeited often does no more than cover the vendor's costs of reselling the property and obtaining bridging finance to complete on the property he is buying. Even if he does make a profit the court has power under section 49(2) of the Law of Property Act 1925 to order the return of all or part of the deposit to the purchaser.[41] On the other hand it is said that the overall cost to purchasers in withdrawing or obtaining finance for their deposits is unjustified, given that it is extremely rare for deposits actually to be forfeited in practice: in these few cases it would not be untoward to say that the vendors involved should have to rest content with their remedy in damages, even if they will not always be recovered.

However, many feel that some deterrent (other than the threat of litigation) is needed to stop purchasers from entering
Alternative to   into contracts willy-nilly. As an alternative to substantial
deposits—   deposits, the Conveyancing Committee recommend[42] for
"deposit   investigation a proposal that banks, building societies, or
guarantees"   insurance companies should sell through solicitors "a deposit guarantee," which for a single premium (cheaper than the cost of obtaining a bridging finance) would supply the function of a deposit. Quite simply the purchaser gives a guarantee instead of paying money. Obviously vendors would then have nothing to give for their deposits but they too could give a guarantee. And to cover everything the vendor's solicitor would be compensated for loss of stakeholder interest[43] by payment of "agency"

---

[40] [1985] 1 W.L.R. 435, noted at [1985] Conv. 286.

[41] *Universal Corporation* v. *Five Way Properties Ltd.* [1979] 1 All E.R. 552; *Dimsdale Developments* v. *De Haan* (1984) 47 P. & C.R. 1, noted at [1984] Conv. 311.

[42] The Second Report of the Conveyancing Committee (1985), paras. 6.32–6.34, 9.32, (1985) 82 L.S.Gaz. 1530.

[43] See p. 97 below.

commission. In Appendix C we include, by way of example, a "deposit guarantee scheme" launched by Legal and Professional Indemnity Ltd. and underwritten by Lombard Continental Insurance plc and Eagle Star Insurance Co. Ltd.[44] Vendors' arguments against "deposit guarantees" will include having to satisfy insurance companies, etc., that they have a claim and, more fundamentally, having to make a claim at all: they will no longer have ready money to forfeit.

Time for and method of payment

By Law Society general condition 9(1) the purchaser must pay the deposit on or before the date of the contract; by National condition 2(1), on the date of the contract. Time is not of the essence of payment.[45] If the vendor needs to receive the deposit by a certain date, he should say so by special condition. Law Society general condition 9(1) goes on to say that on a sale by private treaty, the deposit must be paid by banker's draft or solicitors' cheque. The National conditions do not specify how the deposit should be paid. Cash or banker's draft are the only really safe alternatives.

Status of a deposit

Is payment of a contractual deposit a condition precedent to the formation of a binding contract or merely a condition of it? With regard to this point there are conflicting decisions and dicta at first instance.[46] The difference is important. If the deposit is a condition precedent to the coming into being of a contract the purchaser who has yet to pay a deposit despite contracts having been exchanged has the unattractive choice of whether to pay the deposit and bring the contract into existence or withdraw. This of course does not accord with the expectations of parties who exchange parts of a formal contract which provides for a deposit to be paid.

Fundamental term

Generally preferred is the view of Warner J. in *Millichamp* v. *Jones*[47]: "that a requirement, in a contract for the sale of land, that a deposit should be paid by the purchaser does not constitute a condition precedent, failure to fulfil which prevents the contract from coming into existence, but is in general to be taken as a fundamental term of the contract, breach of which entitles the vendor, if he so elects to treat the contract as at an end and sue for damages including the amount of the unpaid deposit." His "fundamental term" approach was recently applied by the Court of Appeal in relation to the sale of a ship in *Damon Cia Naviera S.A.* v. *Hapag-Lloyd International S.A.*[48] Also applied in that case was the view[49] that having terminated the contract the vendor can sue for damages and the amount of the unpaid deposit. Furthermore the unpaid deposit is recoverable in full, even though (as in *Damon's* case), it exceeds the vendor's actual loss.

---

[44] See (1985) 129 S.J. 477 and (1985) 82 L.S.Gaz. 1004.
[45] *Willmott (John) Homes Ltd.* v. *Read* (1986) 51 P. & C.R. 90.
[46] *Dewar* v. *Mintoft* [1912] 2 K.B. 373, *Lowe* v. *Hope* [1970] Ch. 94, *Myton Ltd.* v. *Schwab-Morris* [1974] 1 W.L.R. 331, *Millichamp* v. *Jones* [1982] 1 W.L.R. 1422, *Portaria Shipping Co.* v. *Gulf Pacific Navigation Co. Ltd.*, *The Selene G* [1981] 2 Lloyd's Rep. 180. The point was also discussed by the Court of Appeal in *Pollway Ltd.* v. *Abdullah* [1974] 1 W.L.R. 493.
[47] [1982] 1 W.L.R. 1422 at p. 1430.
[48] [1985] 1 W.L.R. 435 noted [1985] Conv. 286.
[49] Supported by *Dewar* v. *Mintoft* [1912] 2 K.B. 373, *Johnson* v. *Agnew* [1979] 2 W.L.R. 487 and *Millichamp* v. *Jones* [1982] 1 W.L.R. 1422. The decision to the contrary is *Lowe* v *Hope* [1970] Ch. 94.

Both standard conditions treat non-payment of the deposit as breach of a fundamental term. Law Society general condition 9(3) states:

> "If any draft, cheque or other instrument tendered in or towards payment of any sum payable under this condition is dishonoured when first presented the vendor shall have the right by notice to the purchaser within seven working days thereafter to treat the contract as repudiated."

"bounced" cheques and the standard conditions

The revised sub-condition now contains no reference to fundamental breach in deference to the decision in *Millichamp* v. *Jones*. The vendor is not given the chance to represent the cheque or other instrument under 9(3). Should a represented cheque, etc., not be met the vendor probably has the right to terminate the contract at common law.

National condition 2(2) provides:

> "In case a cheque taken for the deposit (having been presented, and whether or not it has been re-presented) has not been honoured, then and on that account the vendor may elect—either (i) to treat the contract as discharged by breach thereof on the purchaser's part or (ii) to enforce payment of the deposit as a deposit by suing on the cheque or otherwise."

Trustbridge Ltd. v. Bhattessa

No limit is placed on the time within which the vendor must make his election. Presumably he will have a reasonable time to do so, and his conduct will be relevant. He may waive his right to insist on payment of the deposit if he proceeds with the sale in the normal way.[50] In *Trustbridge Ltd.* v. *Bhattessa*,[51] the Court of Appeal refused to accept the argument that National condition 2(2) only applies where one cheque is given for the whole of the deposit. In that case the defendant had paid the deposit by two cheques of £20,000 each, one of which was dishonoured. Fox J. said that the plaintiff had a right under National condition 2(2) to treat the contract as discharged. The dishonoured cheque was "a cheque taken for the deposit" within the terms of the clause.

Omission in the standard conditions

Both Law Society and general condition 9(3) and National condition 2(2) contemplate the tendering of a cheque or other instrument in or towards payment of the deposit, which is subsequently dishonoured. Neither expressly deals with the situation where contracts are exchanged and, either the purchaser duly pays part of the deposit and tenders nothing towards the rest, or the purchaser does not pay the deposit at all. Clearly the omission in the standard conditions is because in most cases if the deposit is not tendered in full then exchange simply does not take place. Should, however, such a case arise, the vendor would be forced back on his position at common law as expounded by Warner J. in *Millichamp* v. *Jones*[52] and approved by the Court of Appeal in *Damon Cia Naviera S.A.* v. *Hapag-Lloyd International S.A.*[53] The facts of *Millichamp* v. *Jones*[54] were unusual. The

Millichamp v. Jones

---

[50] *Johnson* v. *Agnew* [1979] 2 W.L.R. 487.
[51] (1985) 82 L.S.Gaz. 63.
[52] [1982] 1 W.L.R. 1422.
[53] [1985] 1 W.L.R. 435.
[54] Above.

plaintiffs had simply forgotten to pay the deposit required on the exercise of their option to buy certain farmland from their brother-in-law. We have already seen that Warner J. held that payment of the deposit was a fundamental term of the option. Logic should have led him to conclude that the plaintiffs were in breach of that term (because they had not paid the deposit at the due time) and the defendant could therefore terminate the contract. However on the facts of the case his Lordship found that non-payment of the deposit was a "mere oversight" and although this was a breach of contract it was not a "sufficient breach of the term to entitle the defendant to treat the contract as discharged." He went on to say that before the vendor could treat the plaintiffs' breach as a repudiatory breach of the contract, he should have given them notice saying that he would so regard the failure to pay the deposit and requiring the plaintiffs now to pay. Then he said a fundamental breach would only occur if the plaintiffs' conduct was such as to show they were unable or unwilling to pay the deposit.

Two problems   *Millichamp* v. *Jones* poses two problems to a vendor who is not covered by the standard conditions (that is under an open contract or in the rare situations mentioned above). First, how long must he wait for the purchaser to pay once he has served a notice requiring payment of the deposit? Secondly, he is put in the unenviable position of having to decide when the breach by the purchaser has become fundamental enough to entitle him to terminate the contract. In the *Damon* case, failure by the purchasers to pay the deposit on being given three days notice by telex within which to do so, was a sufficiently fundamental breach of their contract to buy three ships to entitle the vendor to terminate the deal.

Agent or   Both conditions provide for the deposit to be paid to the
stakeholder   vendor's solicitors as stakeholders. On a sale by auction governed by the National conditions the deposit is to be paid to the auctioneer, again as stakeholder. If there is no express provision the following rules apply. The vendor's solicitors hold a deposit as agent for the vendor[55]; an auctioneer holds a deposit as stakeholder[56]; and an estate agent does not take a deposit as agent for the vendor. In *Sorrell* v. *Finch*[57] the House of Lords stressed that where an estate agent is instructed to find a purchaser he has no implied or ostensible authority to receive a pre-contract deposit from a prospective purchaser. Accordingly if the deposit should disappear along with the estate agent, it is the prospective purchaser who must bear the loss, even if the vendor knows that he paid a deposit.

Stakeholder   A stakeholder is the agent of both parties. Unless and until the purchase is completed, when he must hand the deposit to the vendor, or the deposit becomes returnable to the purchaser, he may not pay it to either party without the other's consent.[58] A stakeholder is entitled to keep the interest earned by the deposit pending payment to the appropriate party.[59] In *Potters* v.

---

[55] *Edgell* v. *Day* (1865) L.R. 1 C.P. 80, *Tudor* v. *Hamid* (1987) 137 New L.J. 79.
[56] *Harrington* v. *Hoggart* (1830) 1 B. & Add. 577.
[57] [1977] A.C. 728.
[58] *Collins* v. *Stimson* (1883) 11 Q.B.D. 142, *Harrington* v. *Hoggart*, above.
[59] *Harrington* v. *Hoggart* (1830) 1 B. & Ad. 577 at pp. 586–587.

Loppert[60] this rule was extended to an estate agent who was expressed to hold a pre-contract deposit as stakeholder, even though the contract was never concluded. The Estate Agents (Accounts) Regulations 1981 now prescribe how such clients' money should be dealt with, and in particular the payment of interest. If for some reason a stakeholder deposit is lost, because for example the stakeholder has gone bankrupt, the vendor must bear the loss once contracts are exchanged.[61] If no concluded contract has been made, the purchaser bears the loss.[62] Under section 13 of the Estate Agents Act 1979 stake money held by an estate agent is trust money and not available to the agents' trustee in bankruptcy.

Agent for the vendor
Where after contract the deposit is held as agent for the vendor, the deposit-holder may hand it to the vendor.[63] Any action to recover the deposit must be brought against the vendor. The agent must account to the vendor for any interest the deposit has earned.[64] If the contract has not yet become binding the purchaser is entitled to repayment of the deposit on demand and cannot sue the vendor for it if the agent has defaulted.[65]

The "agents for the vendor" system is used in practice as a way of reducing the cost to a vendor-purchaser by allowing him to use the deposit from his sale to pay the deposit on his purchase. However, to protect himself, a purchaser's solicitor who is asked to agree to the deposit being held as agent for the vendor, should enquire as to the purpose for which it is to be used and attempt to negotiate an amendment to the contract so that the deposit is held by stakeholders. If the vendor will not agree to such an amendment, the solicitor should warn the purchaser of the risks involved in allowing the deposit to be held to the order of the vendor.[66] If the vendor should fail to complete or the purchaser justifiably rescinds the contract, he may have difficulty in recovering his money. He may have to sue the vendor (not the case where the deposit is stake money) and litigation costs time and money. To ensure that the purchaser does not lose his money altogether (he is an unsecured creditor), his lien for it should be registered as an equitable charge[67] against the property the vendor is buying. To be absolutely safe it has even been suggested[68] that a purchaser should take and register an equitable charge against both the vendor's present property and the one he is selling.

Dangers in "agents for vendor" system

We leave "deposits" with this extract from the Law Society's recent "Notes for the Guidance of Solicitors when Dealing with Unqualified Conveyancers"[69]:

---

[60] [1973] Ch. 399.
[61] *Rowe* v *May* (1854) 18 Beav. 613.
[62] *Sorrell* v. *Finch* [1977] A.C. 728.
[63] *Ellis* v. *Goulton* [1893] 1 Q.B. 350.
[64] *Harrington* v. *Hoggart* (1830) 1 B. & Ad. 577.
[65] *Sorrell* v. *Finch* [1977] A.C. 728.
[66] H.W. Wilkinson (1981) 78 L.S.Gaz. 1128.
[67] A class C(iii) land charge for unregistered land; notice or caution for registered land.
[68] By J.E. Adams (1970) 120 New L.J. 1128.
[69] (1986) 83 L.S.Gaz. 5.

"Acting for the Purchaser
Payment of Deposit

14. Difficulties may arise in connection with the payment of the usual 10 per cent. deposit where there is no estate agent involved who is a member of one of the recognised professional bodies and to whom the deposit may be paid as stakeholder in the ordinary way. It is of course possible for the deposit to be paid direct to the vendor himself, but this course of action cannot be recommended since it is equivalent to parting with a portion of the purchase money in advance of the investigation of the title and other matters.

15. Some unqualified agents are now insisting that the deposit be paid to them. The Council do not recommend that this be done. If a solicitor is obliged to pay the deposit to any unqualified agents, incorporated or otherwise, he should make certain to inform his client of the considerable dangers involved, and obtain the client's specific instructions before proceeding.

16. An alternative method is for the deposit to be paid to the purchaser's solicitors as stakeholders. The purchaser's solicitor should insist that where possible the deposit is paid to him as stakeholder. If the vendor will not agree to this course, then it may be possible to agree that the deposit be placed in a deposit account in the joint names of the purchaser's solicitors and the vendor, or for such an account to be in the vendor's name, with the deposit receipt to be retained by the purchaser's solicitor."

Conditions as to creation and reservation of easements

Law Society general condition 5(3)

"(a) In this sub-condition 'the retained land' means land retained by the vendor–
   (i) adjoining the property, or
   (ii) near to the property and designated as retained land in a special condition.
(b) The conveyance of the property shall contain such reservations in favour of the retained land and the grant of such rights over the retained land as would have been implied had the vendor conveyed both the property and the retained land by simultaneous conveyances to different purchasers."

National condition 20

"Where the property and any adjacent or neighbouring property have hitherto been in common ownership, the purchaser shall not become entitled to any right to light or air over or in respect of any adjacent or neighbouring property which is retained by the vendor and the conveyance shall, if the vendor so requires, reserve to him such easements and rights as would become appurtenant to such last-mentioned property by implication of law, if the vendor had sold it to another purchaser at the same time as he has sold the property to the purchaser."

These two conditions concern the situation where a vendor sells off part of his land, while retaining other land nearby. Two problems may arise as far as easements are concerned: does the purchaser acquire any easements over the vendor's retained land, and does the vendor have any rights over the land sold off? If the parties fail to deal with this issue explicitly, it may nonetheless be that certain rights will be deemed to have been created at common law. In particular, any intended or necessary easements will be deemed to have been granted[69a]; however, the courts will be much slower to imply such rights in favour of the vendor than the purchaser. Also easements may be created in a purchaser's favour under the rule in *Wheeldon* v. *Burrows*[69b] or through the operation of section 62 of the Law of Property Act 1925.[69c]

These two conditions modify the position at common law in the vendor's favour, the Law Society condition less so than the National.

In the case of the Law Society condition, it provides that the same rights will be created in favour of a vendor as would be created in favour of a purchaser. This overcomes the problem that the courts normally are unwilling to come to the vendor's assistance, and also means that the vendor can benefit both from the rule in *Wheeldon* v. *Burrows* and section 62 of the Law of Property Act 1925.

The National condition produces the same effect but also goes further, for it provides that the purchaser shall not acquire any right to light or air over the vendor's retained land.

Conditions as to licences to assign

Law Society general condition 8(4)

"(4) Where any consent to assign is necessary—
  (*a*) the vendor shall forthwith at his own cost apply for and use his best endeavours to obtain such consent.
  (*b*) the purchaser shall forthwith supply such information and references as may reasonably be required by the reversioner before granting such consent.

National condition 11(5)

  (*c*) if any such consent is not granted at least five working days before contractual completion date, or is subject to any condition to whch the purchaser reasonably objects either party may rescind the contract by notice to the other."

National condition 11(5)

"(5) The sale is subject to the reversioner's licence being obtained, where necessary. The purchaser supplying such information and references, if any, as may reasonably be required of him, the vendor will use his best endeavours to obtain such licence and will pay the fee for the same. But if the licence cannot be obtained, the vendor may rescind the contract on the same terms as if the purchaser had persisted in an objection to the title which the vendor was unable to remove."

[69a] See Megarry and Wade *The Law of Real Property* 5th edition, 1984, pp. 859–861.
[69b] *Ibid.*, pp. 861–864.
[69c] *Ibid.*, pp. 864–867.

These conditions concern an issue central to leasehold conveyancing, the obtaining of any requisite consents to the sale. The extent to which a tenant may assign lawfully depends on the terms of the lease. In advising a tenant-client whether he can assign, a helpful guideline may be obtained from the following classification[70]:

Assignability of lease

(i) The lease contains no restriction against assignment. In such a case the tenant may freely assign his interest without obtaining the licence or consent of the landlords. Note the special position of statutory tenants under the Rent Act 1977 and of secure tenants under the Housing Act 1985.

(ii) The lease contains an absolute covenant against assignment. At present there is no way round this unless the landlord consents expressly (in which case he may impose what conditions he likes on the proposed assignment) or impliedly, for example by accepting rent from the assignee.[71]

(iii) The lease contains a qualified covenant against assignment. Where a lease contains a covenant not to assign without obtaining the consent or licence of the landlord then section 19(1)(a) of the Landlord and Tenant Act 1927 applies. This provides that, notwithstanding any provision to the contrary, the covenant shall be deemed to be subject to the proviso that such consent shall not be unreasonably withheld.

(iv) The lease contains an express proviso that consent shall not be unreasonably withheld.

(v) The lease contains a qualified covenant against assignment (in form (iii) or (iv)) with an express proviso to the effect that if the tenant wishes to assign he must first make an irrevocable offer to the landlord to surrender the lease (which of course gives the landlord power to prevent the proposed assignment on whatever grounds). The validity of surrender clauses was confirmed by the Court of Appeal in *Bocardo S.A.* v. *S. & M. Hotels Ltd.*[72] However, practitioners should note that in the case of a business tenancy having the protection of Part II of the Landlord and Tenant Act 1954, such a clause is contrary to section 38(1) of that Act and will be struck out.[73]

"where necessary"— Bickel v. Courtenay Investments Ltd.

Law Society general condition 8(4) and National condition 11(5) oblige the vendor to obtain, at his own expense, consent to assign "where necessary." In *Bickel* v. *Courtenay Investments Ltd.*[74] the court was asked for the true construction of "where necessary" in National condition 11(5). The plaintiffs were the trustees of the Ancient Order of Foresters and had a lease of premises in Bury Street, London W1, which were formerly Quaglino's Hotel and Restaurant. Quaglino's were the Foresters

---

[70] See Partington, *Landlord and Tenant* (11th ed.). This classification may change in the future; "Covenants Restricting Dispositions, Alterations and change of User" Law Com. 141 (1985).

[71] *Hyde* v. *Pimley* [1952] 2 Q.B. 506.

[72] [1980] 1 W.L.R. 17.

[73] *Allnatt London Properties Ltd.* v. *Newton* [1984] 1 All E.R. 423.

[74] [1984] 1 W.L.R. 795; see H.W. Wilkinson (1984) 134 New L.J. 584.

tenants. The lease contained a covenant not to assign without the landlords' consent, such consent not to be unreasonably withheld in the case of a respectable responsible tenant. By a contract dated February 7, 1983 the plaintiffs contracted to sell the residue of their term to the defendants, who were a subsidiary of a substantial property company. At the date of the contract Joseph Rochford & Sons Ltd. were the plaintiffs' landlords but on the day before completion the reversion was bought by Quaglino's. From February to April 1983 the plaintiffs unsuccessfully tried to get consent to assign, first from Rochford's and then from Quaglino's. The defendants argued that the assignment should go ahead without consent, for since they were assignees of the nature demanded, the plaintiffs ran no risk in assigning to them. They commenced an action for a declaration to that effect and for specific performance or damages. The plaintiffs issued an originating summons for a declaration that in the events that happened and on the true construction of National condition 11(5) they were entitled to rescind the contract.

The present decision was on the plaintiffs' summons. Leave to consolidate the two actions was refused. Warner J. felt that on the submissions advanced by the plaintiffs and the defendants as to the true construction of National condition 11(5) it was unnecessary for him to decide whether either Rochford's or Quaglino's withholding of consent was reasonable or unreasonable.

It was conceded by counsel for the plaintiffs that, since the decision in *Treloar* v. *Bigge*,[75] where a lease contains a requirement for the landlord's consent to assign, if the landlord unreasonably withholds consent, then it becomes unnecessary to have that consent. The plaintiffs argued however that, under National condition 11(5), the question as to whether the landlords' consent was necessary had to be answered by reference only to the lease; "necessary" in that condition meant necessary under the lease and did not invite inquiry into whether at some stage between contract and completion the landlords had by their conduct rendered their consent unnecessary. They had shown that the landlords' consent was required, that they had used their best endeavours to obtain it, but had failed to gain it. They were entitled to rescind.

The defendants argued on the other hand that "where necessary" in condition 11(5) meant "where necessary as between landlord and tenant from time to time during the subsistence of the contract," so that if the landlords' consent ceased to be necessary because they unreasonably withheld it, the contract ceased to be subject to consent being obtained; thus so long as an issue remained as to the reasonableness of the landlords' withholding of consent the plaintiffs could not rescind.

Warner J. began by seeing what the position would be in the absence of an express requirement for consent to assign. The vendor would be obliged to obtain the reversioner's consent to assign. If he failed to obtain it he would be in breach of contract but the damages would be limited to the purchaser's expenses if

---

[75] (1874) L.R. 9 Exch. 151.

the vendor had used his best endeavours, under *Bain* v. *Fothergill*.[76] Then, in rejecting the defendants' approach he said:

"If the construction of condition 11(5) for which counsel for the defendant contends is right, its effect is to alter that position only to the extent of absolving the vendor from liability for damages if the landlord's consent is reasonably withheld and to give the vendor in that event a right to rescind the contract. It does not alter the position where the landlord's consent is unreasonably withheld. Nor does it do anything to solve the problems that arise where there is doubt whether the landlord is withholding his consent reasonably or unreasonably."

In his view[77] the object of National condition 11(5) was not to generate litigation but to afford the vendor a means of escape from litigation and delay. He therefore granted to the plaintiffs a declaration that they were entitled to rescind the contract for sale. Warner J.'s decision is equally applicable to Law Society general condition 8(4).

Specific performance Could the defendants in Bickel have successfully sought an order for specific performance of the contract on the ground that since they were assignees of the nature demanded, the plaintiffs ran no risk in assigning to them? Or to put it another way, can a purchaser waive the requirement for consent to assign in National condition 11(5) or Law Society general condition 8(4)? It is clear from the decision of Goff J. in *Lipman's Wallpaper Ltd.* v. *Mason & Hodghton Ltd.*[78] that a purchaser cannot demand that his vendor assign without licence even though damages for such a breach of covenant by the vendor might be nominal. The vendor would be "exposed to liability in costs and to the hazards of litigation." As to waiver of the standard conditions, Goff J. said of National condition 11(5) (or more exactly its predecessor in the National conditions, 17th edition), that it was "at least for the benefit of the vendors as well as for the purchaser, if not exclusively for that of the vendors and therefore in my judgement . . . cannot be waived by the [purchaser]."

On the reverse side of the coin the vendor cannot insist that a purchaser take an assignment without licence, even if in the vendor's view the licence has been unreasonably withheld.[79] The correct course, if the purchaser is willing to wait that long, is to

Declaration of suitability as assignee apply to the court for a declaration that the purchaser is a suitable assignee.[80] When advising parties desirous of going to these lengths to complete their sale, regard should be had to the recent case of *International Drilling Fluids Ltd.* v. *Louisville Investment*

---

[76] (1874) L.R. 7 H.L. 158.
[77] Guided by the decision of Goff J. in *Lipman's Wallpaper Ltd.* v. *Mason & Hodghton Ltd.* [1969] 1 Ch. 20. But see *29 Equities Ltd.* v. *Bank Leumi (U.K.) Ltd.* [1987] 1 All E.R. 108.
[78] [1968] 1 All E.R. 1123.
[79] *Re Marshall & Salt's Contract* [1900] 2 Ch. 202.
[80] *Young* v. *Ashley Garden Properties Ltd.* [1903] 2 Ch. 112. This is especially so since the landlord can rely on reasons for his withholding consent advanced by him for the first time at the hearing; see *Sonnenthal* v. *Newton* (1965) 109 S.J. 333, *Welch* v. *Birrane* (1974) 29 P. & C.R. 102 and Slade L.J. in *Bromley Park Garden Estates Ltd.* v. *Moss* [1982] 1 W.L.R. 1019. But the reason must have affected the landlord's mind at the time he refused his consent, *Lovelock* v. *Margo* [1963] 2 Q.B. 786.

(*Uxbridge*) *Ltd.*[81] in which the Court of Appeal gave an authoritative statement of the present law relating to the reasonableness or otherwise of a landlord's refusal of consent on an application by a tenant for licence to assign. This statement of law is reproduced in full at Appendix D.

Vendor to use best endeavours

The vendor cannot use his powers of rescission under either Law Society general condition 8(4) or National condition 11(5) unless he has used his best endeavours to obtain any requisite consent to assign. This means doing what all reasonable persons would do in the circumstances, or to quote Megarry V.-C. in *Pips (Leisure Productions) Ltd.* v. *Walton*[82]: "something less than efforts which go beyond the bounds of reason but are considerably more than casual and intermittent activities." In that case a tenant had contracted to sell his lease and use his best endeavours to obtain his landlord's consent to assign. After contract it was found that the landlords had obtained a court order for forfeiture against the tenant for non-payment of rent. Obviously the tenant could not obtain consent to assign but he could not enforce the contract since he was and had been before contract unable to make title and was liable to the purchaser in damages. The vendor's obligation does not extend to trying to persuade his landlord to change his mind, nor to allowing the purchaser time to approach the landlord himself, nor, where consent is refused on the ground that the proposed use is in breach of covenant in the head-lease, to approaching the freeholders for consent to the change of use or affording the purchaser opportunity to do so.[83]

Purchaser to supply reasonable information and references

Under the conditions the purchaser is to supply such information and references as may reasonably be required of him by the landlord. It has been suggested[84] that if the purchaser deliberately refuses to give any references asked for, he will be in breach of contract and the vendor can forfeit any deposit paid and sue for damages. But if the purchaser supplies the requisite references and some or all are unacceptable to the landlord, the contract can be rescinded by either party under Law Society general conditon 8(4) or by the vendor under National condition 11(5).[85] At common law there is an implied obligation on the part of a purchaser of leasehold property to use his best endeavours to satisfy the reasonable requirements of the landlord.[86] It was

Shires v. Brock

argued for the vendor in *Shires* v. *Brock*[87] that condition 10(5) of the National Conditions of Sale (18th ed.) (the predecessor to the current 11(5)) superseded that obligation and was an absolute covenant on the purchaser's part to satisfy the reasonable requirements of the landlord. The Court of Appeal refused to accept this argument. They held that the words "the purchaser supplying such information and references, if any, as may

---

[81] [1986] 1 All E.R. 321. See also most recently *Ponderosa International Development Inc.* v. *Pengap Securities (Bristol) Ltd.* (1986) 277 E.G. 1252 and *British Bakeries (Midlands) Ltd.* v *Michael Testler & Co. Ltd.* (1986) 277 E.G. 1245.
[82] 43 P. & C.R. 415. See also *Vasilou* v. *Metz* (1960) 176 E.G. 260 and *Wroth* v. *Tyler* [1974] Ch. 30.
[83] *Lipmans Wallpaper Ltd.* v *Mason Hodghton Ltd.* [1968] 1 All E.R. 1123.
[84] Wilkinson, *Standard Conditions of Sale of Land* (3rd ed.), p. 82.
[85] *Sheggia* v. *Gradwell* [1963] 1 W.L.R. 1049.
[86] *Ibid.*
[87] (1977) 247 E.G. 127.

reasonably be required of him" in condition 10(5), merely qualified the vendor's obligation to obtain a licence to assign. Thus if a purchaser was alleging a breach by the vendor of that obligation, it would be open to the vendor to say, if the facts warranted it, "But I was discharged from my obligation because you did not satisfy the condition upon which it depended." But if both parties meet their obligations and still no licence is granted, neither party is in breach of contract and the deposit must be returned to the purchaser, with no liability on him for damages. In *Elfer* v. *Beynon-Lewis*[88] it was held that the obligation on the purchaser to provide information and references did not extend to his having to attend for interview by the landlord's agent.

Timing   Both sets of standard conditions in substance make the sale of leaseholds subject to obtaining the reversioner's licence to assign, if necessary; the essential difference is one of timing. National condition 11(5) specifies no period. It was held in *29 Equities Ltd.* v. *Bank Leumi (U.K.) Ltd.*[88a] that condition 11(5) does *not* require the licence to be obtained by the contractual completion date. The vendor cannot rescind the contract until a situation has been reached when it can fairly be said that the landlord's licence "cannot be obtained." In some cases it may not be possible to say this until some time after the contractual date for completion has passed. Law Society general condition 8(4)(*c*) avoids this particular problem by saying that the vendor must have consent at least five working days prior to the contractual completion date, when either party may rescind by notice.[89] However, it has been pointed out[90] that, as drafted, the condition

Rescission allows the vendor to rescind even if the purchaser is willing to grant an extension of time.[91] No period of notice is required under 8(4)C. Rescission is in accordance with general condition 16(2). The vendor must repay the deposit within four working days; beyond that date he will become liable for interest on it at the contract rate. The purchaser must forthwith return any documents sent to him by the vendor and at his own expense procure the cancellation of any entry relating to the contract in any register.

Only the vendor may rescind under National condition 11(5). Rescission is governed by condition 10(2) in that any deposit must be returned to the purchaser, the abstract to the vendor and each side must bear their own expenses. However the provision in condition 10(1) that 10 working days notice must be given does not apply.[92] The vendor may rescind without giving notice. Presumably once the contractual completion date has passed, the purchaser can serve a notice to complete under condition 22, to prevent himself being bound to the contract for an indefinite period. He should be wary of ending the contract on the contractual completion date, because unless time is expressly or impliedly[93] of the essence for completion, his conduct may

[88] (1973) 222 E.G. 1955.
[88a] [1987] 1 All E.R. 108. This decision seems to go against the intention of condition 11(5).
[89] The serving of the notice will be governed by Law Society general condition 2.
[90] [1982] Conv. 89.
[91] Wilkinson, *Standard Conditions of Sale of Land* (3rd ed.), p. 84.
[92] *Lipmans Wallpaper Ltd.* v. *Mason & Hodghton Ltd.* [1968] 1 All E.R. 1123.
[93] Since a lease is a wasting asset time might impliedly be of the essence *c.f. Pips (Leisure Productions) Ltd.* v. *Walton* (1981) 260 E.G. 601.

amount to a repudiation of the contract rendering him liable in damages.

Conditions as to fixtures and chattels

National condition 4

"4. Chattels, etc. and separate items
    If the sale includes chattels, fittings, or other separate items, the vendor warrants that he is entitled to sell the same free from any charge, lien, burden, or adverse claim."

Law Society general condition 24

"24. CHATTELS
The property in any chattels agreed to be sold shall pass to the purchaser on actual completion."

Importance of distinction between fixtures and chattels

A fixture is an item so attached to land as to become part of it—"quicquid planatur solo, solo cedit."[94] A fixture will pass with the land to the purchaser without any express mention in the contract.[95] If the vendor wishes to retain or be paid separately for a fixture he must say so in the contract. Items that are not fixtures may be removed by the vendor at will and do not pass with the land without express agreement. Therefore any chattels included in the sale must be specifically mentioned in the conditions. The purchaser may also want the price to be apportioned between the property and the chattels to achieve a possible saving in stamp duty.[96]

Twofold test

The twofold test for determining what is a fixture—the degree and purpose of annexation—is easy to state, but often very difficult to apply in practice. Most of the illustrative cases date from a byegone age, when tapestries[97] and stone statues[98] were the vogue. And the more modern cases betray an eerie

Hamp v. Bygrave

preoccupation with garden ornaments.[99] In one such, *Hamp* v. *Bygrave*,[1] a vendor represented in estate agent's particulars and replies to preliminary enquiries that eight outside light fittings, six stone flower urns, a stone statue, a lead trough, and a stone ornament possibly of Chinese origin standing on a stone plinth in a goldfish pond, all prima facie chattels, were included in the sale. The contract made no mention of the items. It was held that they had become fixtures and had therefore passed to the purchaser on completion. Alternatively the vendor was estopped from denying that the ornaments were included in the sale. So— if in doubt, list in the contract any fixtures/chattels the vendor intends to take with him.

Warranty in National condition 4

Both sets of conditions contain provisions dealing with chattels. National condition 4 states that the vendor warrants that any chattels included in the sale are his to sell. The Law Society general conditions contain no such specific warranty but one is

---

[94] *Holland* v. *Hodgson* (1872) L.R. 7 C.P. 328 at p. 334, *per* Blackburn J.
[95] Law of Property Act 1925, s.62; *Phillips* v. *Lamdin* [1949] 2 K.B. 33—purchaser entitled to reinstatement of Adam door removed by vendor.
[96] See p. 49 above.
[97] *Leigh* v. *Taylor* [1902] A.C. 157, *Spyer* v. *Phillipson* [1931] 2 Ch. 183.
[98] *D'Eyncourt* v. *Gregory* (1866) L.R. 3 Eq. 382.
[99] *Berkeley* v. *Poulett* (1976) 241 E.G. 911 at p. 242. E.G. 39 (pictures, marble statue and sundial), *Hamp* v. *Bygrave* (1983) 266 E.G. 720 (stone garden ornaments), *Dean* v. *Andrews* (1985) 135 New L.J. 728 (prefabricated greenhouse). See generally M. Haley (1985) 135 New L.J. 539–540 and 588–589.
[1] H.W. Wilkinson (1983) 266 E.G. 720, (1983) 80 L.S.Gaz. 1773.

Sale of Goods Act 1979

implied anyway under the general law as follows. Where the price is apportioned between the property and the chattels, there are in effect two contracts: one for the sale of the land, the other for the sale of the chattels—"goods." Section 12 of the Sale of Goods Act 1979 implies into a contract for the sale of goods a condition that the vendor will have the right to sell the goods at completion and a warranty that the goods are and will remain free from any charge or incumbrance not disclosed or known to the purchaser at the date of the contract. The vendor further impliedly warrants that the purchaser will enjoy quiet possession of the chattels except for claims under incumbrances that were disclosed. If the purchase price is not apportioned the Sale of Goods Act cannot apply. However where the sale includes chattels the same statutory condition and warranties are implies into the contract by the Supply of Goods and Services Act 1982. The contract for the sale of the land includes a "contract for the transfer of goods" within section 1 of the Act. Liability under the implied terms of section 12 of the Sale of Goods Act and section 2 of the Supply of Goods and Services Act cannot be contracted out of (Unfair Contract Terms Act 1977, s.6).

Supply of Goods and Services Act 1982

No contracting out

Hire-purchase agreements

The vendor has no title to transfer chattels that are subject to a hire-purchase agreement, and the purchaser cannot stop the third party repossessing the goods. Should this happen after completion the purchaser must seek redress from the vendor under National condition 4 or the implied statutory terms. If the vendor pays off the outstanding balance under a hire-purchase agreement after completion he perfects the previously defective title of the purchaser and makes him the owner of the chattel.[2]

None of the above provisions applies to fixtures. Fixtures, being part of the land, are covered by the implied covenant for title in the conveyance for freedom from incumbrances.

When does the risk in chattels pass to the purchaser?

Law Society general condition 24 provides that the purchaser will only become the owner of the chattels on actual completion. Thus the chattels are at the vendor's risk until completion and the purchaser need not insure them until then, which is not the case for the property itself[3] (including fixtures). The National conditions are silent on the matter so the general law applies. Where the price is apportioned between the property and the chattels, section 20 of the Sale of Goods Act 1979 states that "the goods remain at the seller's risk until the property is transferred to the purchaser." Sections 17 and 18 of the Act lay down implied rules[4] for determining when the property is transferred. For present purposes the net effect of these implied rules is that if the chattels are itemised in the contract, title passes to the purchaser on exchange of contracts. Even if the chattels are not specifically mentioned, so that the Sale of Goods Act does not apply, it is probable that the court would follow the same principles. Therefore where the sale is governed by the National conditions chattels should be insured as from the date of the contract.

---

[2] *Butterworth* v. *Kingsway Motors* [1954] 1 W.L.R. 1286.

[3] The risk in the property, including fixtures, passes to the purchaser on exchange of contracts and he should insure accordingly.

[4] The implied rules give way to contrary intention, *e.g.* Law Society general condition 24.

Completion conditions

21. Completion

(1) Contractual completion date shall be as stated in the special conditions but if not so stated shall be the twenty-fifth working day after the date of the contract. Completion shall take place in England or Wales either at the office of the vendor's solicitors or if required by the vendor at least five working days prior to actual completion, at the office of the vendor's mortgagee or his solicitors.

(2) The vendor shall not be obliged to accept payment of the money due on completion otherwise than by one or more of the following methods—

(*a*) legal tender

(*b*) a banker's draft drawn by and upon a settlement bank for the purposes of the Clearing House Automated Payments System or any other bank specified in a special condition.

(*c*) an unconditional authority to release any deposit held by a stakeholder.

(*d*) otherwise as the vendor shall have agreed before actual completion.

(3) If completion is effected otherwise than by personal attendance the time for completion is when on a working day

(*a*) the money due on completion is paid to the vendor or his solicitors, and

(*b*) the vendor's solicitors hold to the order of the purchaser all the documents to which he is entitled on completion.

(4) For the purposes of this condition money is paid when the vendor receives payment by a method specified in sub-condition (2). Where the parties have agreed upon a direct credit to a bank account at a named branch, payment is made when the branch receives the credit.

(5)(*a*) This sub-condition applies if the money due on completion is not paid by 2.30 p.m. on the day of actual completion or by such other time on that day as is specified in a special condition

(*b*) For the purposes of condition 22 only, completion shall be deemed to be postponed by reason of the purchaser's delay from the day of actual completion until the next working day

(*c*) The purchaser shall not as a result of the deemed postponement of completion be liable to make any payment to the vendor unless the vendor claims such payment by giving notice at completion or within five working days thereafter (as to which period time shall be of the essence). Payment shall be due five working days after receipt of such notice."

"5. Date and manner of completion

(1) The completion date shall be the date specified for

the purpose in the contract or, if none, the 26th working day after the date of the contract or the date of delivery of the abstract of title whichever be the later.

(2) Unless the Special Conditions otherwise provide, in respect of the completion date time shall not be of the essence of the contract, but this provision shall operate subject and without prejudice to—

   (i) the provisions of condition 22 and

  (ii) the rights of either party to recover from the other damages for delay in fulfilling his obligations under the contract

(3) The purchaser's obligations to pay money due on completion shall be discharged by one or more of the following methods—

   (i) authorisation in writing to release a deposit held for the purposes of the contract by a stakeholder

  (ii) banker's draft issued by a designated bank

 (iii) cheque drawn on and guaranteed by a designated bank

 (iv) telegraphic or other direct transfer (as requested or agreed to by the vendor's solicitor) to a particular bank or branch for the credit of a specified account

  (v) legal tender

 (vi) any other method requested or agreed to by the vendor's solicitor

(4) Completion shall be carried out, either formally at such office or place as the vendor's solicitor shall reasonably require, or (if the parties' solicitors so arrange) by post, or by means of solicitors' undertakings concerning the holding of documents or otherwise. Provided that on a sale with vacant possession of the whole or part of the property, if the conveyance or transfer will not, by overreaching or otherwise, discharge the property from interests (if any) of persons in, or who may be in, actual occupation of the property or such part of it, then (subject always to the rights of the purchaser under the Law of Property Act 1925, s.42(1)), the purchaser may, by giving reasonable notice, require that on, or immediately before the time of, completion possession of the property or part be handed over to the purchaser or his representative at the property

(5) The date of actual completion shall be the day on which, the contract being completed in other respects, the purchaser has discharged consistently with the provisions of this condition the obligations of the purchaser to pay the money due on completion Provided that—

   (i) for the purposes only of conditions 6, 7 and 8, if but for this proviso the date of actual completion would be the last working day of a week (starting on Sunday) and the purchaser is unable or unwilling to complete before 2.15 p.m. on that day, then the date of actual completion shall be taken to be the first working day thereafter

  (ii) a remittance sent by post or delivered by hand shall

be treated as being made on the day on which it reaches the vendor's solicitor's office, unless that day is not a working day in which case the remittance shall be treated as being made on the first working day thereafter."

Completion date

Under an open contract it is implied that completion shall take place within a reasonable time, taking into account the legal business yet to be carried out.[5] By Law Society general condition 21(1) completion is to be on the date specified in the special conditions but if none is stated it is to be on the twenty-fifth working day after the date of the contract. By National condition 5(1) the date is to be that specified in the contract or if none the twenty-sixth working day after the date of the contract or the date of delivery of the abstract whichever is the later. The fall-back conditions will apply despite a special condition for completion included in the contract, being neither deleted nor filled in, but left blank.[6] The contract should not provide that completion shall take place when possession of the property is given, if no date is fixed for the giving of possession; this may result in the contract being unenforceable.[7] In *Walters* v. *Roberts*[8] the parties left the completion date to be agreed in the future; it was held that in the absence of such agreement, there was an implied term that completion would take place as under an open contract, within a reasonable time. If a completion date is written into the contract after exchange it should be initialled.[9]

Time not of the essence for completion

The date for completion will not normally be of the essence of the contract unless the nature of the property or the circumstances of the transaction make it so. Thus for example time would be of the essence for the purchase of a farm[10] or pub[11] or cafe[12] as a going concern, or for the purchase of a short lease.[13] In *Raineri* v. *Miles*,[14] Lord Edmund-Davies suggested (obiter) that time might impliedly be of the essence for completion of the purchase of a dwelling-house if the purchase is part of a chain transaction. Both sets of conditions state that time shall not be of the essence of the contract in respect of the completion date unless the special conditions otherwise provide (Law Society general condition 23(1), National condition 5(2)) and the parties rights in the event of a delay in completion are set out.[15] The conditions seemingly exclude time being of the essence because of the nature of the subject matter. In such a sale it should be expressly provided that time is, or is not, of the essence.

Time for completion

The conditions also set a time for completion. Law Society general condition 21(5)(*a*) and (*b*) say that if completion does not take place before 2.30 p.m. on the day of actual completion (or such other time as is stated by special condition) then completion

[5] *Johnson* v. *Humphrey* [1946] 1 All E.R. 460.
[6] *Smith* v. *Mansi* [1963] 1 W.L.R. 26.
[7] *Johnson* v. *Humphrey* [1946] 1 All E.R. 460.
[8] (1980) 41 P. & C.R. 210; [1981] Conv. 168.
[9] *New Hart Builders Ltd.* v. *Brindley* [1975] Ch. 342.
[10] *Stickney* v. *Keeble* [1915] A.C. 386.
[11] *Lock* v *Bell* [1931] 1 Ch. 35.
[12] *Vasilou* v. *Metz* (1960) 176 E.G. 260.
[13] *Pips (Leisure Productions) Ltd.* v. *Walton* (1981) 260 E.G. 601.
[14] [1980] 2 W.L.R. 847.
[15] These are considered in detail in the next book in this series.

is deemed to have taken place on the next working day, for the purposes of claiming compensation for late completion under general condition 22. However the purchaser is only liable to account to the vendor for a deemed late completion under 21(5)(*a*) and (*b*) if the vendor gives him notice within 5 working days after completion, time being of the essence for the notice. The purchaser must then pay the compensation within 5 working days of the receipt of the notice. National condition 5(5)(i) less stringently states that if completion day falls on a Friday, the purchaser must complete before 2.15 p.m.; otherwise for the purpose of calculating apportionments and interest under conditions 6, 7 and 8, actual completion is deemed to take place on the first working day thereafter.

Place for completion
By Law Society general condition 21(1) completion shall take place in England or Wales at the vendor's solicitors' office or at the office of the vendor's mortgagee or his solicitors, if notice to that effect is given to the purchaser. National condition 5(4) says that completion shall be carried out at any place the vendor's solicitors "shall reasonably require." To combat the problem of occupational interests[16] it additionally provides that where the sale is with vacant possession, the purchaser may require, on giving reasonable notice to the vendor, that possession of the property be handed over to the purchaser or his representative at the property. Where the standard conditions cannot apply (that is, under an open contract or where the vendor is acting for himself) the rule is that the person tendering the money, the purchaser, must seek out his tenderee, the vendor.[17] The vendor may choose to complete at his home, the property or anywhere else, provided that the place lies within England or Wales.[18]

Completion by post
Edward Wong Finance Co. Ltd. v. Johnson Stokes
Provision is made in both conditions for completion by post. In 1984 the Council of the Law Society published a new practice code for completion by post to ease concern felt amongst the profession following the decision of the Privy Council in *Edward Wong Finance Co. Ltd. v. Johnson Stokes and Master*.[19] The appeal from Hong Kong concerned what their Lordships described as a "Hong Kong-style completion"; remitting the whole of the purchase money, advanced on mortgage to the purchaser, to the vendor's solicitor against the latter's undertaking to forward the documents of title which would include discharge of the vendor's mortgage. In other words a procedure closely resembling our's on a postal completion. The vendor's solicitor absconded with the purchase money leaving the vendor in possession of the property and his mortgagees in possession of the deeds. The Privy Council held that the loss of the money must be borne by the purchaser's solicitors for failing to take the necessary steps to protect their client's interests. Their Lordships said that the purchaser's solicitors should have insisted on a normal "proper English-style completion" by which they meant the purchaser's solicitors handing over a banker's draft in exchange for all the necessary documents including where

---

[16] *Williams & Glyn's Bank Ltd. v. Boland* [1981] A.C. 487 etc. See Annand and Cain, *Enquiries before Contract*, (1986), pp. 30–42.
[17] *Reading Trust Ltd. v. Spero* [1930] 1 K.B. 492.
[18] *Re Young and Harston's Contract* (1885) 31 Ch.D. 168.
[19] [1984] A.C. 1296.

appropriate a discharge of the vendor's mortgage. Their Lordships seemed totally unaware of the common practice in this country of completing by post and also of the standard procedure (adopted on formal and postal completions) of accepting the vendor's solicitor's undertaking that the purchase money will be used to pay off any mortgage debt.

Law Society's Code for Completion by Post (1984 ed.)

The Law Society's Code for Completion by Post (1984 ed.) (reproduced in App. E) provides a procedure for completion by post on an agency basis: the vendor's solicitor agrees to act as an unpaid agent for the purchaser's solicitor on completion. The purchaser's solicitor is protected against a *Wong* type occurrence because by virtue of clause 3 of the Code the vendor's solicitor undertakes that he has the express authority of the vendor, and, if need be, the vendor's mortgagee, to receive the purchase money on their behalf. Adoption of the Code must be agreed by all the solicitors concerned and preferably in writing. Enquiry 12(B) on Oyez's standard form of preliminary enquiries (Con 29) asks: "The Purchaser's solicitors wish to complete by adopting the Law Society's Code for Completion by Post (1984 edition)."[20]

By Law Society general condition 21(3) if completion is effected by a means other than personal attendance, completion shall take place when the money due on completion is paid to the vendor and the vendor's solicitors hold to the order of the purchaser all the documents to which he is entitled on completion. Apparently the decision to effect completion lies with the vendor once he has the purchaser's money. The sub-condition does not say that the vendor holds the documents to the purchaser's order when the money is paid. However if the new code for postal completion is used clause 5 requires the vendor's solicitor to complete "forthwith" on receiving the purchase money. By National condition 5(ii) a remittance sent by post is treated as made when it is delivered if that day is a working day, otherwise it is deemed made the following working day.

Remittance committed to document exchange

What if both parties' solicitors belong to the same document exchange and the remittance is delivered by the purchaser's solicitors to that exchange? Neither of the conditions nor the Law Society's Code for Completion by Post specifically cover this eventuality. According to the decision of Whitford J. in *Willmott (John) Homes Ltd.* v. *Read*[21] this would be an appropriate means of delivery and the remittance would be made when "deemed delivered" under the exchange's rules. But it will be remembered that there is doubt surrounding the question of whether document exchanges can be used in the absence of specific agreement between the parties following the Court of Appeal decision in *Imprint (Print and Design) Ltd.* v. *Inkblot Studios Ltd.*[22] The Law Society general conditions authorise the use of document exchanges for effecting the service of notices and the delivery of documents and the exchange of contracts and general condition 21(3) itself refers to completion by a means other than personal attendance. The Code speaks of document exchanges for the dispatch of the documents to the purchaser's solicitor after

[20] See Annand and Cain, *Enquiries before Contract*, (1986) pp 52–54.
[21] (1986) 49 P. & C.R. 90.
[22] (1985) 129 S.J. 132.

completion. The National conditions do not mention document exchanges at all.

Method of payment

As regards payment on completion both sets of conditions prescribe modes. Law Society general condition 21(2) specifies one or more of the following methods: legal tender, a CHAPS settlement banker's draft,[23] an unconditional authority to release stake money, and otherwise as the vendor shall have agreed. National condition 5(3) similarly lists an authorisation in writing to release stake money, a banker's draft issued by a designated bank, legal tender and any other method requested or agreed to by the vendor's solicitor, and in addition a cheque drawn on and guaranteed by a designated bank and telegraphic or other direct transfer (as requested or agreed to by the vendor's solicitor). If (as expected) the present arrangements under the Building Societies Act 1962 for the authorisation of banks to hold funds of building societies are replaced by regulations issued under the Building Societies Act 1986 the definition of "designated bank" will have to be amended by special condition, as explained earlier.[24] Under an open contract the vendor can technically insist on being paid in cash.[25]

Dealing with Unqualified Conveyancers

The following extracts are from the Council of the Law Society's "Notes for the Guidance of Solicitors when Dealing with Unqualified Conveyancers" ((1986) 83 L.S.Gaz. 5).

> "*General*
> Completions by Post
>> 6. Solicitors are under no duty to undertake agency work by way of completions by post on behalf of unqualified persons, or to attend to other formalities on behalf of third parties who are not clients, even where such third parties offer to pay the agent's charges."
>
> "*Acting for the Purchaser*
> Payment of Purchase Money
>> 17. . . . the purchaser's solicitor should ensure that all the purchase money, including any deposit, is paid either to the vendor or to his properly authorised agent."
>
> "*Acting for the Mortgagee*
> —Borrower not Represented by a Solicitor
>
> Advances
>> 22. Payment of mortgage advances—the importance of paying advances only to those properly entitled to receive them—is an additional reason for insisting either that the borrower attends personally on completion or that a signed authority from the borrower in favour of his agent be received on completion. S.69 of the Law of Property Act 1925 is a relevant consideration in this context.
>
> Redemptions
>> 23. On completion, cheques or drafts should be drawn in favour of solicitors or their clients, and not endorsed over to some intermediate party. The deeds should

---

[23] For a list of CHAPS settlement banks see p. 51 above.
[24] See p. 88.
[25] *Johnston* v. *Boyes* [1899] 2 Ch. 73.

normally be handed over to the borrower personally, unless he provides a valid authority for them to be handed over to a third party."

Auction conditions

Law Society general condition 25

"25. Auctions

(1) This condition applies if the property is sold by auction

(2) The sale is subject to a reserve price for the property and, when the property is sold in lots, for each lot

(3) The vendor reserves the right—

(*a*) to divide the property into lots and to sub-divide, re-arrange or consolidate any lots

(*b*) to bid personally or by his agent up to any reserve price

(*c*) without disclosing any reserve price, to withdraw from the sale any property or lot at any time before it has been sold, whether or not the sale has begun

(4) The auctioneer may—

(*a*) refuse to accept a bid

(*b*) in the case of a dispute as to any bid, forthwith determine the dispute or again put up the property or lot at the last undisputed bid

(5) The purchaser shall forthwith complete and sign the contract and pay, but not necessarily by the means specified in condition 9(1), the normal deposit."

National condition 1

"1. The sale: by Auction . . .

(2) Unless otherwise provided in the Special Conditions, the sale of the property and each lot is subject to a reserve price and to a right for the vendor or anyone person on behalf of the vendor to bid up to that price

(3) The auctioneer may refuse any bid and no person shall at any bid advance less than the amount fixed for that purpose by the auctioneer

(4) If any dispute arises respecting a bid, the auctioneer may determine the dispute or the property may, at the vendor's option, either be put up again at the last undisputed bid, or be withdrawn

(5) Subject to the foregoing provisions of this condition, the highest bidder shall be the purchaser and shall forthwith complete and sign the contract, the date of which shall be the date of the auction."

At an auction the contract is made when the auctioneer accepts the final bid.[26] However in order to satisfy the requirements of section 40 of the Law of Property Act 1925,[27] a formal contract will be prepared in advance by the vendor's solicitor in consultation with the auctioneer (usually incorporating either the Law Society's General or National Conditions of Sale) and will be made available to prospective

---

[26] Auctions subject to a reserve price, *Payne* v. *Cave* (1789) 3 T.R. 148 and *Harris* v. *Nickerson* (1872–73) L.R. 8 Q.B. 286; auctions without reserve, see *obiter dicta* in *Warlow* v. *Harrison* (1859) 1 E. & E. 309 at pp. 314 and 318 and *Harris* v. *Nickerson*, above.

[27] See Chapter 2.

purchasers for inspection for some time before the actual auction
(often the formal contract will be attached to the auctioneer's sale
particulars). The formal contract will normally be exchanged
immediately after the auction.

Both sets of conditions contain provisions governing the
conduct of auctions. Since these provisions are (at least until the
hammer falls) really terms of a non-existent contract, it is
difficult to see how they can be binding, unless they are viewed as
an expression of the intention of the parties, in which case the
provisions are effective.

Reserve price   The Sale of Land by Auction Act 1867 provides that the
particulars or conditions of sale must state whether the property
is sold without reserve or subject to a reserve price or whether a
right to bid is reserved.[28] If the sale is at a reserve price (but not
otherwise) and the vendor reserves a right to bid, the vendor or
any person acting on his behalf may bid.[29] Law Society general
condition 25(2) and National condition 1(2) accordingly state that
the property and each lot, where the property is sold in lots, is
subject to a reserve price, unless the contract provides otherwise.
A right for the vendor or his agent to bid up to the reserve price is
expressly reserved.[30] Should the auctioneer accept a bid lower
than the reserve then there is no binding contract.[31] Similarly if
he wrongly states that there is no reserve there can be no binding
contract for sale at a price less than the reserve.[32]

Right to withdraw   A right to withdraw any property or lot before sale is
reserved to the vendor by Law Society general condition 25(3)(c).
The National conditions do not specifically give the vendor a
right to withdraw, but he has one anyway at common law.[33] Law
Society general condition 25(3)(a), again otiosely, gives the
vendor the right to divide the property into lots and to rearrange
the lots.

Refusing bids   Law Society general condition 25(4)(a) and National
condition 1(3) provide that the auctioneer may refuse to accept
any bid. This probably merely restates the general law.[34] The
National sub-condition additionally provides that no person shall
at any bid advance less than the amount fixed for that purpose by
the auctioneer.

Determining   The auctioneer is given power to determine any dispute.[35]
disputes   Under Law Society general condition 25(4)(b) he can either
decide the dispute in favour of one party against the other or put
the property up for sale again at the last undisputed bid. National
condition 1(4) says that he must either determine the dispute or
the property may *at the vendor's option* either be put up again at
the last undisputed bid or be withdrawn. If the vendor is not
present at the sale it is suggested that the auctioneer has implied
authority to decide whether to put the property up again for sale
or withdraw it.

---

[28] s. 5. A reserve price is a price below which the property will not be sold. The
reserve price itself need not be disclosed.
[29] Sale of Land by Auction Act 1867, s.6.
[30] Law Society general condition 25(3)(b), National condition 1(2).
[31] *McManus* v. *Fortescue* [1907] 2 K.B.1.
[32] *Rainbow* v. *Howkins* [1904] 2 K.B. 332.
[33] *Harris* v. *Nickerson* (1872–3) L.R. 8 Q.B. 286, *Payne* v. *Cave* (1789) 3 T.R.
148.
[34] *Payne* v. *Cave* above.
[35] See for example *Richards* v. *Phillips* [1969] 1 Ch. 39.

Highest bidder

National condition 1(5) says that the highest bidder shall be the purchaser. Condition 1(5) must be read subject to 1(3), so that the "highest bidder" is the one who bids the highest in the amounts fixed by the auctioneer.[36] In *Johnston* v. *Boyes*[37] property was auctioned on terms that the highest bidder would be the purchaser and should pay a deposit immediately after the auction. The plaintiff's husband offered the highest bid, which was accepted by the auctioneer. His cheque for the deposit was however refused because he was known by the auctioneer to be insolvent. In fact the husband was buying the property on behalf of the plaintiff who had ample funds to cover the purchase. She sued for breach of contract. It was held that the contract would have been specifically enforceable had all the conditions of sale been complied with. Here they had not because of the implied requirement that at auctions deposits should be paid in cash (but see below). The Law Society general conditions do not specifically state that the highest bidder shall be the purchaser, though this is obviously a necessary inference.

Deposit

Both conditions state that the purchaser shall forthwith complete and sign the contract and pay a 10 per cent. deposit.[38] "Forthwith" is not defined by the conditions but probably means immediately or a short time after the auction. No method is prescribed for payment of the deposit, so the general law applies. We have already seen that in *Johnston* v. *Boyes* it was said that auction deposits should be paid in cash. However in the earlier case of *Farrer* v. *Lacy, Hartland & Co.*[39] payment by cheque was held to be acceptable.

Signing the contract

An auctioneer has implied authority to sign the contract for both parties. His authority to sign for the vendor lasts for as long as he has authority to sell and is not dependent on his receiving a deposit.[40] His authority to sign on behalf of the purchaser is limited to the time of sale,[41] which is a question of fact in each case. In *Chaney* v. *Maclow*[42] signature two hours after the auction was effective to bind the purchaser. An auctioneer's clerk has no authority to sign the contract on behalf of the purchaser[43] nor presumably on behalf of the vendor. Failure by the auctioneer to obtain the purchaser's signature to the contract is not necessarily negligent.[44]

---

[36] National condition 1(5) begins: "Subject to the foregoing provisions of this condition."

[37] [1899] 2 Ch. 73.

[38] Although Law Society general condition 9(1) allows for a reduced deposit to be paid on a sale by private treaty, the "normal" 10 per cent. deposit must be paid on a sale by auction.

[39] (1886) 31 Ch.D. 42.

[40] *Leeman* v. *Stocks* [1951] Ch. 941, *Phillips* v. *Butler* [1945] Ch. 358.

[41] *Ibid.*

[42] [1929] 1 Ch. 461.

[43] *Bell* v. *Balls* [1897] 1 Ch. 663.

[44] *Hardial Singh* v. *Hillyer & Hillyer* (1979) 251 E.G. 951 (purchaser disappeared unobserved after auction).

Conditions as to exchange of contracts

Law Society general condition 10

"10. Optional Methods of Exchange

(1) Exchange of contracts may be effected by a method authorised by condition 2 for the service of notices. If so effected the contract shall be made when the last part is, as the case may be, posted or delivered to a document exchange.

(2) Where contracts have not been exchanged, the parties' solicitors may agree by telephone or telex that the contract be immediately effective and thereupon the solicitors holding a part of the contract signed by their client shall hold it irrevocably to the order of the other party."

National condition 1

"1. The Sale: . . . by Private Treaty

(6) Where there is a draft contract, or an arrangement subject to contract, or a negotiation in which there are one or more outstanding items or suspensory matters (which prevent there being yet a concluded agreement of a contractual nature) a solicitor who holds a document signed by his client in the form of a contract of sale in writing and embodying this condition, shall (unless the other party or his solicitor is informed to the contrary) have the authority of his client to conclude, by formal exchange of contracts, or by post, or by telex or other telegraphic means, or by telephone, and in any case with or without involving solicitors' undertakings, a binding contract in the terms of the document which his client has signed.

(7) The date of the contract shall be—

(i) the date, if any, which is agreed and put on the contract, but if none, then

(ii) on an exchange of contracts by post (unless the parties' solicitors otherwise agree), the date on which the last part of the contract is posted, or

(iii) in any other case, the date on which, consistently with this condition, a binding contract is concluded."

Here we must return momentarily to the question considered earlier in Chapter 3—has a contract been concluded?

Intention to exchange

Lord Greene M.R. said, in *Eccles* v. *Bryant*[45-46]: "When parties are proposing to enter into a contract, the manner in which the contract is to be created so as to bind them must be gathered from the intentions of the parties express or implied." In that case the terms of a proposed sale, set out in correspondence, were expressed to be "subject to contract." The vendor's solicitors wrote to the purchaser's solicitors: "Our clients have now signed their part of the contract herein and we are ready to exchange." The purchaser's solicitors sent their client's part of the contract to the vendor's solicitors. The vendor decided not to go ahead with the sale and the vendor's solicitors never sent his part in exchange. The Court of Appeal held that no decree of specific performance should be granted as no contract

[45-46] [1948] 1 Ch. 93 at p.99.

had been formed. In the words of Lord Greene M.R. "Anyone . . . would have understood from the language of the earlier correspondence and the words 'subject to contract' that the contract would be brought about by an exchange of the two parts signed by the parties." He continued: "In such a contract as this, there is a well-known, common and customary method of dealing; namely by exchange and anyone who contemplates that method of dealing cannot contemplate the coming into existence of a binding contract before exchange takes place. It was argued that exchange is a mere matter of machinery, having in itself no particular importance and no particular significance. So far as significance is concerned, it appears to me that not only is it not right to say of exchange that it has no significance, but it is the crucial and vital fact which brings the contract into existence." The Master of the Rolls said that exchange was important because each party should have a document of title, which would settle any dispute as to whether a contract had been formed and the terms of it: "and that is why in past ages this procedure came to be recognised by everybody to be the proper procedure and was adopted." Cohen and Asquith L.JJ. agreed with this analysis. The Master of the Rolls explained that there could be more than one method of exchange: "the ceremonial form of exchange, namely the meeting of solicitors in the office of one of them—the vendor's solicitors' office as a rule—and the passing of the two signed engrossments over the table," or more commonly nowadays when solicitors are often in different parts of the country, exchange by post.

Law Society general condition 10 and National condition 1(6) clearly contemplate an exchange of signed parts before the contract is to become binding on the parties. Where the post is used, both conditions state that, unless otherwise agreed, the contract is made when the last part is posted (Law Society general condition 10(1), National condition 1(7)ii)). The Law Society condition also provides for exchange by document exchange, in which case the contract is made when the last part is delivered to the document exchange. (Contrast the rule in general condition 2(1)(d) for the service of notices and delivery of documents.) For the effectiveness of using a document exchange for making the contract under the National conditions (in the absence of a special condition) see the cases discussed earlier at page 91. Another problem here is, when is the contract made?[47]

Exchange by post or document exchange

Time of contract exchanged by post

At common law it is uncertain[48] when the contract would be formed in the event of an exchange by post. Is it when the last part is posted[49] or is it only when both parties or their solicitors have actually received from their opposite numbers their parts of the contract duly signed?[50] Mr. Barnsley[51] and Professor Farrand[52] prefer the latter view, whereas the authors of the

---

[47] Presumably the question is plagued by the same uncertainties as relate to postal exchanges at common law (see below) although according to *Willmott (John) Homes Ltd.* v. *Read* (1986) 51 P. & C.R. 90 the contract would be made when, according to the rules of the exchange, the last part is deemed to have been delivered to the other party.

[48] *Eccles* v. *Bryant* [1948] 1 Ch. 93.

[49] The normal rule laid down in *Adams* v. *Lindsell*(1818) 1 B. & Ald. 681.

[50] *Holwell Securities Ltd.* v. *Hughes* [1974] 1 W.L.R. 155.

[51] Barnsley, *Conveyancing Law and Practice*, p. 208.

[52] *Contract and Conveyance* (4th ed.) p. 17.

standard conditions obviously plumped for the former—the normal rule relating to acceptance by post of an offer. But since conditions 10(1) and 1(6) could be viewed as terms of a non-existent contract it might be better to agree and insert the date of the contract.

Telephonic exchange Domb v. Isoz

The efficacy of another method of exchanging contracts, this time by telephone, was tested in *Domb* v. *Isoz*.[53] There the purchasers' solicitor sent the purchasers' signed part of the contract and a cheque for the deposit to the vendor's solicitor pending simultaneous exchange of contracts by telephone—the transaction was one of several in a chain. About six weeks later the respective solicitors agreed by phone that contracts should be treated as immediately and irrevocably exchanged. The vendor's part of the contract was not sent to the purchasers' solicitor. On the purchasers' claim for specific performance and/or damages Mr. Brian Dillon Q.C.[54] held that no contract had been formed as the solicitors had purported to dispense with an exchange of contracts without their clients' authority. He considered that exchanging by phone was a bad conveyancing practice although it was adopted by experienced solicitors in the London area in a significant number of cases. On appeal, all three judges (Buckley, Templeman and Bridge L.JJ.) agreed that telephonic exchanges were both authorised and effective. The practice did not dispense with exchange. Lord Templeman said: "The client confers power to exchange but is not interested in the machinery or method of exchange which are matters for the solicitor and the general law." Although in *Domb* v. *Isoz* the two parts of the contract were in the vendor's solicitor's possession when the telephonic exchange was made, the decision is equally applicable to the case where each solicitor retains his client's part and gives an undertaking on the telephone to hold it to the other's order. In either case the contract becomes binding at the time of the telephone conversation and the process is completed in the normal way by sending (by post or document exchange) the relevant part or parts to the other side. The Court of Appeal recognised the

Inherent dangers

inherent dangers in constructive exchanges, notably the difficulty in proving what is said over the telephone.[55] Buckley L.J. said that solicitors are members of a professional body and people of integrity and officers of the court so there would not be many errors (but see the conflict of evidence from solicitors in *Griffiths* v. *Young*[56]). Templeman L.J. suggested that telephonic exchanges should only be made by partners and that a short formula for attendance notes should be used. The Council of the Law Society reacted promptly to the latter suggestion and produced two alternative formulae for exchanging contracts by telephone or telex.[57] The formulae were amended in 1984 to authorise the use of document exchanges as an alternative means of forwarding the contracts (remember that inclusion of a reference to a document exchange in a solicitors' letterhead is conclusive evidence of membership of that exchange), and again

The Law Society's formulae for exchanging contracts by telephone/telex

[53] [1980] Ch. 548; H.W. Wilkinson (1980) 130 New L.J. 295.
[54] (1978) 248 E.G. 783.
[55] Another difficulty is inability to check the signature and contents of the contract.
[56] [1970] Ch. 675.
[57] (1980) 77 L.S.Gaz. 144.

in 1986 to accommodate some slight changes. The 1986 version of the formulae (which takes effect from July 31, 1986) is reproduced in Appendix F with accompanying notes. The notes recommend that after the exchange there should be recorded: the date and time of exchange, the formula used and the exact wording of agreed variations, the completion date, the deposit or balance of deposit to be paid, and the identities of those involved in the conversation.

Exchange of contracts by telephone or telex is provided for in Law Society general condition 10(2) and National condition 1(6). Certain barristers may make constructive exchanges under the National conditions (see the definition of "solicitor" in National construction condition (5)).[58]

Telex exchanges

Although the effectiveness of an exchange by telex was accepted without doubt by Russell L.J. in *Aquis Estates Ltd.* v. *Minton*,[59] there is the problem of whether "telex" contracts also produce sufficient evidence by signed writing to satisfy section 40(1) of the Law of Property Act 1925.[60] And technical hitches were foreseen by the House of Lords in *Brinkibon Ltd.* v. *Stahag Stahl GmbH*.[61] Their Lordships confirmed in that case that where a contract is made by instantaneous communication, such as telex, the genral rule applies that the contract is made when and where the acceptance was received. However this general rule may only be applicable where the vendor and purchaser themselves, rather than their solicitors, make the contract by telex and the application of the rule may be affected by other factors. As Lord Wilberforce said[62]:

Brinkibon Ltd. v. Stahag Stahl GmbH

> "Since 1955 the use of telex communication has been greatly expanded, and there are many variants on it. The senders and recipients may not be the principals to the contemplated contract. They may be servants or agents with limited authority. The message may not reach, or be intended to reach, the designated recipient immediately: messages may be sent out of office hours, or at night, with the intention or upon the assumption, that they will be read at a later time. There may be some error or default at the recipient's end which prevents receipt at the time contemplated and believed in by the sender. The message may have been sent and/or received through machines operated by third persons. And many other variations may occur. No universal rule can cover all such cases: they must be resolved by reference to the intentions of the parties, by sound business practice and in some cases by a judgement where the risks should lie."

It will be noted that neither set of conditions of sale directs itself to the question of when exchange is effected by telex.

Solicitor's authority

A vital issue in both *Eccles* v. *Bryant*[63] and *Domb* v. *Isoz*[64] was whether the solicitor had authority from his client to effect

[58] See pp. 87–88 above.
[59] [1975] 1 W.L.R. 1452.
[60] See Chap. 2, p. 2.
[61] [1982] 2 W.L.R. 265, [1982] 46 Conv. 245.
[62] *Ibid.* at p. 267.
[63] [1948] 1 Ch. 93.
[64] [1980] 1 All E.R. 942.

the contract in that particular manner. In *Eccles* v. *Bryant*, Lord Greene M.R. said[65] that the principals, in instructing solicitors, must be "assumed to have given them authority to carry the business through in the ordinary way recognised as customary for dealing with conveyancing matters of this kind in the absence of any evidence to the contrary," that is by exchange. But he went on to say: "If the vendor's solicitors in this case had taken on themselves without authority to agree to a method of making the contract other than the customary method, by dispensing with exchange, they would have been committing a breach of duty to their client and might have found themselves liable for heavy damages for negligence." It is now clear that what Lord Greene meant was that a solicitor (or licensed conveyancer) needs the express authority of his client to conclude the contract in any way other than by exchange. In *Domb* v. *Isoz*[66] the Court of Appeal said that once a solicitor has his client's signed the purchasers part of the contract he has implied or ostensible authority to exchange contracts. Furthermore he may exchange by any method recognised by law as being effective to make an exchange. Law Society general condition 10 and National condition 1(6) in effect follow the ruling in *Domb* v. *Isoz*.

Identical parts On occasions a purported exchange may fail to bring a binding contract into existence. Subject to rectification, the parts exchanged must be identical. In *Harrison* v. *Battye*[67] the vendor agreed "subject to contract" to sell his house to the purchasers for £8,250. The draft contract stated that the deposit was £825. The parties' solicitors later agreed to reduce the deposit to £100. The purchasers' solicitor amended the purchasers' part of the contract accordingly and sent the amended part signed by the purchasers to the vendor's solicitor. The vendor's solicitor forgot to amend the vendor's part and by mistake sent back to the purchasers' solicitor the purchasers' own signed part, with a covering letter: "We enclose part contract signed by our client to complete the exchange." The vendor refused to proceed. The Court of Appeal thought that if the vendor's part had been amended there might well have been a binding contract. Sir Erich Sachs was "much impressed with the view that on the posting (of the letter sent with the wrong part of the contract) there was communicated to the purchasers an unequivocal appropriation of the counterpart signed by the vendor . . . (the purchasers) became entitled to possession of that document and an effective exchange . . . occurred despite the clerical error in the vendor's solicitor's office."[68] The point was left open. The case was decided on the ground that the two parts could not be exchanged because they differed from each other in a material respect. Lord Denning said: "When two people sell a house 'subject to contract' the contract is not concluded until the two parts are exchanged. These two parts must be in identical terms. If they differ in any material respect there is no contract."[69] A similar decision was arrived at in *Earl* v. *Mawson*.[70]

[65] *Ibid.* at p. 102.
[66] [1980] Ch. 548.
[67] [1975] 1 W.L.R. 58.
[68] *Ibid.* at p. 61.
[69] *Ibid.* at p. 60.
[70] (1974) 232 E.G. 1315.

In *Domb* v. *Isoz*[71] the two parts of the contract were also not identical; the vendor's part contained a clause about the apportionment of part of the purchase price between the property and fixtures, the purchasers' part did not. The Court of Appeal held that this did not affect the purchasers' right to enforce the contract: "[There] could . . . be no doubt whatever that the remedy of rectification would be available, for it is common ground that both parties intended that the sale should include the fixtures and fittings referred to and the apportionment of the price was purely a matter of conveyancing and not of contract and would be of no significance."[72] *Harrison*'s case was distinguished on the ground that there rectification was not available because the discrepancy was due to the amount of the deposit and resulted from the vendor's solicitor, without authority, accepting a reduced deposit.

Intention to make the contract by other means   It will be remembered that the manner of creating a binding contract is to be gathered from the intentions of the parties.[73] One example of when the parties will not intend an exchange of contracts is where the same solicitor acts for both parties.[74] This happened in *Smith* v. *Mansi*[75] where Danckwerts L.J. said: "Where there is only one document as the contract and only one solicitor, acting for both parties the idea of exchange, in my opinion, can only be described as artificial nonsense. It is impossible to carry out. Once a complete contract has been signed by both parties there is nothing more to be done."[76] Evidence that the vendor did not intend to be bound at the time of signing was held to be inadmissible, although Russell L.J. suggested that evidence that neither party intended to be bound would have been admissible.

Sale of council houses by Manchester City Council   Two cases involving the sale of council houses by Manchester City Council afford another example of the parties' intention to exclude the exchange procedure. In *Storer* v. *Manchester City Council*,[77] the council had instructed the town clerk to devise a simple form of agreement for the sale of council houses to sitting tenants, aimed at dispensing with legal formalities (to encourage quick sales). Mr. Storer applied to buy his council house with the aid of a council mortgage. The town clerk wrote to him: "I understand you wish to purchase your council house and enclose the Agreement for Sale. If you will sign the Agreement and return it to me I will send you the Agreement signed on behalf of the council in exchange." Mr. Storer signed the agreement and returned it. Before the town clerk could sign on behalf of the council, political control of the council changed and it was resolved to discontinue the sale of council houses. Mr. Storer was informed that the council would not proceed with the sale and he brought an action for specific performance. The Court of Appeal held that a binding contract had been created. The town clerk's letter comprised the offer, and acceptance was

---

[71] [1980] 1 All E.R. 942.

[72] *Ibid.* at p. 968, *per* Buckley L.J.

[73] *Eccles* v. *Bryant* [1948] 1 Ch. 93.

[74] This will be rate. The general rule is that the same solicitor should not act for vendor and purchaser, see *Practice Rule* (1972) 69 L.S.Gaz. 1117.

[75] [1963] 1 W.L.R. 294.

[76] *Ibid.* at p. 32.

[77] [1974] 1 W.L.R. 1403.

made by Mr. Storer signing and returning the agreement. The council's instructions to the town clerk to devise a simple form of agreement and the clerk's letter were evidence of the council's intention to dispense with exchange. The background to *Gibson* v. *Manchester City Council*[78] was the same, but Mr. Gibson had only got as far as applying for details of the purchase price of his house and of a mortgage. The council sent him an application form which he completed and signed. The House of Lords analysed the correspondence in terms of offer and acceptance and were of the opinion that the parties had never made a binding contract. The council had merely stated that they might be prepared to sell and had invited Mr. Gibson to make an application. The invitation was not an offer capable of acceptance.

Synchronisation   If a client is selling one property and buying another, a conveyancer may have to synchronise exchange on both contracts. If a conveyancer is instructed to act on the basis that the sale and purchase are to be simultaneous, he is liable in damages to his client if he fails to synchronise the transactions and loss results. Even in the absence of express instructions, a conveyancer should still try to synchronise the exchange of interdependent sale and purchase contracts, unless he has been told to make a unilateral exchange after he has explained the risks to the client. The Council of the Law Society in its evidence to the Royal Commission on Legal Services (1977) said it was part of a solicitor's duty to his client (vendor or purchaser) to ensure the synchronisation of exchange of contracts and completion dates.

The Conveyancing Committee thought that two suggestions addressing the problem of synchronisation in chain transactions might be of interest to conveyancers.[79] The second, from the Society of Public Teachers of Law was specifically directed to synchronising exchanges of contracts in a chain:

> " . . . it might be worth investigating the usefulness of adopting the American system of escrow agents to assist easier synchronisation. Solicitors could well undertake this role, both because reliance on solicitors' undertakings is a well-established feature of present practice and also because they are aware of the advantages of simultaneous exchange of a series of contracts. Either one solicitor already involved in a chain or, preferably, one independent of all parties, would gather in all the contracts and deposits and then, when the last item arrived, effect the simultaneous exchange of contracts for each link."

Contract races   The Council of the Law Society has issued the following ruling on the sending out of more than one draft contract[80]:

> "*Vendor's solicitor submitting forms of contract to more than one prospective purchaser.*
>   1. The Council recognise that a solicitor acting for a vendor may sometimes be instructed by his client to deal with more than one prospective purchaser at the same time.

[78] [1979] 1 W.L.R. 294.
[79] The Second Report (1985), paras. 5.20–5.21.
[80] (1977) 74 L.S.Gaz. 834.

2. The Council have accordingly directed that where a vendor instructs his solicitor to submit (whether simultaneously or otherwise) forms of contract to more than one prospective purchaser, the following steps by the solicitor are obligatory:

(A) WHERE SOLICITOR IS ACTING FOR VENDOR
The solicitor (with his client's authority) must at once disclose the vendor's decision direct to the solicitor acting for each prospective purchaser or (where no solicitor is acting) to the prospective purchaser(s) in person and such disclosure, if made orally, must at once be confirmed in writing if the vendor refuses to authorise disclosure, the solicitor must cease acting for the vendor forthwith.

(B) WHERE SOLICITOR IS ENTITLED TO ACT FOR BOTH VENDOR AND PURCHASER
Notwithstanding the exceptions contained in para (2) of Rule 2 of the Solicitors' Practice Rules 1936–72, a solicitor cannot act for both vendor and purchaser if a conflict of interest arises. Where there is more than one prospective purchaser, the Council consider that the danger of conflict of interest is greatly increased. The Council are reluctant to issue a general prohibition against acting in such cases and they therefore warn all solicitors concerned to consider most carefully whether, and if so to what extent, they can properly act in these cases. If in an exceptional case a solicitor decides that he can properly act for both vendor and one of the prospective purchasers, then (in addition to the steps he must take under paragraph A above) the solicitor must at once disclose his decision direct to those two clients and also to the solicitor acting for every other prospective purchaser or (where no solicitor is acting) to the prospective purchaser(s) in person and such disclosure, if made orally, must at once be confirmed in writing.

(C) WHERE SOLICITOR IS ASKED TO ACT FOR MORE THAN ONE PURCHASER
Where forms of contract are submitted to more than one prospective purchaser, a solicitor must not accept instructions to act for more than one prospective purchaser."

In 1979 the Council's ruling was republished with the following important notes[81]:

"3. For the avoidance of doubt the Council wish to emphasise that the Direction applies to all sales and purchases of freehold and leasehold property.
4. The Council also wish to emphasise to the profession that the Direction is mandatory upon all solicitors and that any solicitor who is found to be in breach of the Direction in future is liable to face proceedings before the Solicitor's Disciplinary Tribunal."

[81] (1979) 76 L.S.Gaz. 1117.

Unilateral contract

It has been suggested[82] that in sending out several copies of the draft contract the vendor makes an implied agreement to enter into a contract for sale with the first person to tender the deposit with his part of the contract signed. If so, paragraph 2(A) of the Council's ruling may create a trap for the unwary vendor's solicitor. In *Daulia* v. *Four Millbank Nominees Ltd.*[83] the vendor orally agreed with the purchaser, that if the purchaser attended his offices before 10.00 a.m. the following day with a banker's draft for the deposit and a signed copy of the contract then he, the vendor, would enter into a formal written contract for the sale of his property. The Court of Appeal held that the oral agreement (referred to as a "unilateral contract") was a contract for the disposition of an interest in land (it would result in the purchaser acquiring an equitable interest in the property) and unenforceable for non-compliance with section 40 of the Law of Property Act 1925. The decision suggests that if the vendor's oral agreement had been evidenced in writing, then it would have been enforceable. Paragraph 2(A) of the Council's ruling requires the vendor's solicitor to inform each prospective purchaser in writing that several contracts have been sent out. Might this writing not provide a memorandum (signed on behalf of the party to be charged) sufficient to enable the first purchaser who tenders the deposit and a signed contract, to force the vendor to enter into a contract for the sale of the land to him? Accordingly *Emmet on Title*[84] advises: "[S]olicitors complying with the Direction should also expressly make it clear that their client's position is reserved as to entering into any contract." The vendor does not impliedly contract to keep any offer made confidential *vis à vis* other potential purchasers.[85]

---

[82] [1978] Conv. 87.
[83] [1978] Ch. 231.
[84] (19th ed.), 2/20.
[85] *Trees Ltd.* v. *Cripps* (1983) 267 E.G. 596.

6 CONTRACTS BY CORRESPONDENCE

Section 46 of the Law of Property Act 1925 reads as follows:

L.P.A. 1925, s.46

"The Lord Chancellor may from time to time prescribe and publish forms of contracts and conditions of sale of land, and the forms so prescribed shall, subject to any modification, or any stipulation or intention to the contrary, expressed in the correspondence, apply to contracts by correspondence, and may, but only by express reference thereto, be made to apply to any other cases for which the forms are made available."

The Lord Chancellor's Statutory Form of Conditions of Sale

The Lord Chancellor's Statutory Form of Conditions of Sale was prescribed under that section on August 7, 1925.[1] The form badly needs updating (for example, the rate of interest it provides for in the event of a delay in completion is only 5 per cent.) and is rarely, if ever, expressly incorporated. Nevertheless where parties make a contract by correspondence without expressly incorporating one of the standard sets of conditions, they are on balance better off under the statutory conditions than they would be under an entirely open contract. The statutory form at least provides a timetable for the steps leading from the contract to completion and gives the vendor contractual remedies of rescission and re-sale.

Stearn v. Twitchell

Contracts by correspondence are not defined by the Act. Such contracts were however narrowly defined in *Stearn* v. *Twitchell*.[2] Warner J. held that correspondence involved an exchange of letters[3] ("I do not think that a single letter can constitute 'correspondence' "): a written acceptance of an oral offer or vice versa would be insufficient, even if the oral offer, or as the case might be, acceptance, referred to an existing document[4] (here it was an acceptance by letter of an oral offer referring to an option agreement). As Warner J. pointed out: "There is . . . a difference between correspondence that brings a contract into existence and correspondence that merely evidences a contract made by other means."[5] His Lordship did not agree that the phrase "contracts by correspondence" in section 46 should be given a wide meaning, for fear of leaving vendors without the shelter of conditions.[6] He said: "The section itself provides that the statutory form of conditions of sale may be made to apply to contracts other than those made by correspondence 'but only by express reference thereto,' which does not seem to me consistent with an intention that those

---

[1] S.R. & O. 1925 No. 779.
[2] [1985] 1 All E.R. 631.
[3] Warner J. preferred not to include or to comment on cases where the telegrams or telexes are used. *Quare* the use of telex or telephone.
[4] Warner J. disagreed with the suggestion to the contrary in *Emmet on Title* (18th ed., 1983), p. 83.
[5] *Ibid.* at p. 634.
[6] See Farrand, *Contract and Conveyance* (4th ed., 1983), p. 81.

conditions should be given the widest possible application. The section also refers, in the case of a contract by correspondence, to 'any modification, or any stipulation or intention to the contrary, expressed in the correspondence' which suggests that the authors of the section envisaged that, in the case of such a contract, all its terms would be found in the correspondence, or at all events would be ascertainable from it."[7]

The statutory form itself is reproduced in *Emmet on Title*.[8]

---

[7] *Ibid.* at p. 634.
[8] (19th ed.) 2/021–2/022.

APPENDICES

Appendix A is reproduced by kind permission of the Controller of Her Majesty's Stationery Office. The form of pre-contract deposit agreement is that published by Fourmat Publishing 27/28 St. Albans Place, London N1 0NX, from whom copies may be obtained.

Appendix C is reproduced by kind permission of Legal and Professional Indemnity Ltd., 3 Clanricarde Gdns., Tunbridge Wells, Kent TN1 1PE, from whom copies may be obtained.

Appendices E and F and G are reproduced by kind permission of the Law Society and of the Solicitors' Law Stationery Society plc.

Appendix H is reproduced by kind permission of the Solicitors' Law Stationery Society plc.

Appendix A

Pre-contract deposits: a practice recommendation by the conveyancing standing committee

1.   This report recommends a new procedure for dealing with some of the delays and uncertainties involved in buying and selling houses and flats. Complaints are often made about the delay and uncertainty between the time a vendor and purchaser agree a price "subject to contract" and the exchange of contracts. The scheme we are proposing aims to help in reducing both the delay and the uncertainty, without sacrificing the safeguards which the conveyancing procedure affords to both vendors and purchasers. We recognise that some people may seek to find fault with the scheme and to avoid its use. Nevertheless, we remain convinced that buyers and sellers will welcome any solution designed to reduce the delay and uncertainty before there is a binding contract. We believe that our proposals should make a significant contribution to this end.

2.   The "subject to contract" stage allows a number of valuable and often essential tasks to be performed by the parties or their professional advisers, before either party is irrevocably committed to the sale. A purchaser, for example, will usually require an inspection of the property, whether a valuation, a home buyer's report or a full structural survey. His solicitor (or, shortly, licensed conveyancer) makes searches and enquiries of the local authority to ensure that nothing adversely affects the property, now or in the foreseeable future; for example, a road widening scheme or proposed development for which planning permission has been obtained. Most purchasers also have to arrange a mortgage loan. On the other hand, the vendor's solicitor needs to prepare the contract; to do this he must inspect the title documents to make sure that the vendor only contracts to sell what he in fact owns.

3.   Both parties may also have to arrange related transactions: the seller has to find another house to buy, the buyer has to dispose of his present one. Chains of linked sales and purchases cause many of the current conveyancing frustrations. Realistically, there seems no generally accepted way to avoid them at present. The "subject to contract" period permits all these necessary arrangements to be made.

4.   Whilst we recognise the importance of the "subject to contract" period to prevent the parties being legally bound before they are ready, we are concerned that over the last 10 to 15 years this period has gradually lengthened. This has justifiably increased people's discontent with the system. We are therefore seeking ways to shorten this period of uncertainty for the benefit of both purchasers and vendors. As a primary contribution, we recommend the use of *pre-contract deposits*: each side guarantees his good faith and commitment to the other, a time limit is placed

on the uncertainty, and there is some small compensation for anyone who is let down. Our proposal will not solve all the problems and uncertainties that exist prior to exchange of contracts, but we consider that it makes a positive contribution towards alleviating them. It is a suggestion to help, to be adopted voluntarily by purchasers and vendors. The fact that there is no compulsion not only means that only those who recognise its advantages need adopt it, but also that, because legislation is not required, it is available immediately.

How do pre-contract deposits work?

5.   As soon as the vendor and purchaser have agreed a price "subject to contract," each of them puts down a deposit of $\frac{1}{2}$ per cent. of the purchase price. This confirms that they seriously intend to go ahead with the sale, and fixes a period within which binding contracts should be exchanged. The money is held by the vendor's solicitor as stakeholder. So the money is held safely, ready to pay out later in accordance with the terms of the scheme.

6.   When they put down their pre-contract deposits, the parties sign the standard form of agreement printed at the end of this report. Copies of the agreement will usually be supplied by the vendor's estate agent at an early stage in the transaction, generally as soon as an offer has been made and accepted "subject to contract."

7.   The agreement gives four weeks for contracts to be exchanged. (There is an exception: see paragraph 10). A party who withdraws or refuses to exchange within that time forfeits his pre-contract deposit to the other. The agreement we recommend has been carefully prepared to hold a fair balance between vendor and purchaser. Variations can easily be made to it, but we hope that they will not, because the parties may well not have legal advice at that stage. We have incorporated the words "as recommended by the Conveyancing Standing Committee" into our form so that everyone is clear whether they are signing the form we suggest.

8.   Of course, there are circumstances in which a party should be able to withdraw without losing his deposit. The agreement sets these out:

(a) If the purchaser discovers something reducing the property's open market value by more than the preliminary deposit, *i.e.* if the survey or searches reveal nasty surprises, the purchaser can back out. Trivial complaints are ruled out because the value must fall by at least $\frac{1}{2}$ per cent. On the other hand, there can be no complaint about anything of which the purchaser already knew.

(b) If the purchaser fails to obtain a satisfactory mortgage offer. Details of the offer he needs are written into the agreement, so he cannot later change his mind.

(c) If either party insists on a contract term which the other finds unacceptable. They must be acting in good faith and reasonably.

(d) Either party has not been able to make a contract for his linked transaction. We discuss this futher in the next paragraph.

9.   We gave careful consideration to whether a party should be able to recover his deposit simply because he has not exchanged contracts for the purchase or sale of another property. This could allow an unscrupulous party to avoid the agreement. However, we accept the majority of people would not be willing to contract to buy or sell without at the same time finalising their dependent transaction. We have therefore reluctantly included provision in clause 4(a) and in clause 4(b) to deal with the "chain" situation. These should be deleted where the parties do not require them. There is an advantage in having a deletable provision. A purchaser who falsely claims to be a cash buyer with no house to sell will have to give up the pretence in order to keep the option of relying on this escape clause.

10.   We also considered the period to be allowed for exchange of contracts. The longer the period, the less likely one of the parties will agree to enter into the agreement, particularly in a rapidly rising or falling market. But the shorter the period, the less likely that all the preliminary work would have been completed. We were also concerned that a period in excess of four weeks would encourage people to consider this longer period as unexceptional. That could actually extend the "pre-contract" period and slow down conveyancing. On the other hand, we note with concern that some local authorities take considerably longer than four weeks to reply to local authority searches and enquiries. We have therefore, felt it necessary to word clause 5 so that the purchaser can extend the four-week period until one week after the local authority has replied to the searches and enquiries. In some areas, however, the vendor submits the searches and enquiries in advance and supplies them to the purchaser with the draft contract. This practice is generally helpful, and should reduce the number of cases where the time has to be extended.

The purpose of pre-contract deposits

11.   We should emphasise that use of pre-contract deposits will not always prevent "gazumping." If a vendor is offered an increase in the price of substantially more than the $\frac{1}{2}$ per cent. preliminary deposit by a subsequent purchaser, the risk of losing his preliminary deposit will not deter him from "gazumping." A purchaser who sees house prices falling rapidly will not be put off withdrawing. However, the $\frac{1}{2}$ per cent. deposit will at least provide some compensation to the person who is let down for his wasted expenditure on professional fees. On the other hand, if someone refuses to pay a pre-contract deposit, the other party is put on his guard at the outset. He should consider carefully whether to continue with the deal.

12. It is essential that everyone paying a pre-contract deposit, and signing the agreement, understands what they are doing. For this reason, our form incorporates Guidance Notes. The form is not complete without them.

13. The form printed overleaf may be freely reproduced provided it is accompanied by the Guidance Notes and no alterations are made to the text of either document.

Please read the notes overleaf before completing this form

Pre-Contract Deposit Agreement
as recommended by the Conveyancing Standing Committee

1. We have agreed "subject to contract" on the sale and purchase of

   _____

   _____

   for £ _____.

   Insert address of house or flat

   Insert price

2. Each of us has paid a pre-contract deposit of $\frac{1}{2}$% of the price to

   _____

   as stakeholder.

   Insert Vendor's Solicitor or Licensed Conveyancer

3. If contracts are exchanged within four weeks both deposits shall be repaid.

4. If contracts are **not** exchanged within four weeks because one of us withdraws or is unwilling to exchange, both deposits shall be paid to the other.

   But both deposits will be repaid **if**

   a) the Purchaser withdraws or is unwilling to exchange because:
   - he has discovered something reducing the open market value of the property by more than his deposit;

   or • he has been refused a reasonably acceptable offer of a

   mortgage loan of £ _____ by _____

   _____

   or • any condition of sale proposed in good faith is not reasonably acceptable;

   †[or • contracts cannot be exchanged for the sale of his present dwelling];

   or b) the Vendor withdraws or is unwilling to exchange because:
   - any amendment made in good faith to the proposed conditions of sale is not reasonably acceptable;

   †[or • contracts cannot be exchanged for the purchase by him of another dwelling];

   or c) both the Vendor and the purchaser withdraw or neither is willing to exchange.

   Insert amount
   Insert name of bank or building society to which applying

   Delete † if no "chain" needed by purchaser

   Delete † if no "chain" needed by vendor

   Delete † if Vendor to supply with draft contract

5. The four weeks period for exchange must be complied with strictly †[but this period may be extended at any time by the Purchaser until one week after replies to local authority searches and enquiries have been received].

6. Date of Agreement _____

   Insert

Signed: Vendor[s]:   Purchaser[s]:

   _____   _____

   _____   _____

Guidance Notes

A. Before signing
Read the Agreement and these Notes carefully. Fill in all the blanks. Consult a solicitor or licensed conveyancer if the form has been altered or if anything seems unclear.

B. Purposes
Each of you guarantees his genuine interest in the sale of this dwelling by putting down a sum of money which will be lost on backing out. The amount lost should ordinarily be compensation for the other's wasted expenditure, such as valuation fees and legal costs. No additional legal liability is intended.

C. Exchange
This Agreement does **not** make the sale legally binding before your solicitor or licensed conveyancer has exchanged contracts. Then the purchaser's pre-contract deposit may be used in part payment of the full deposit.

D. Conditions
The pre-contract deposit should not be lost if there is a good enough reason for backing out. For example, if a survey or search reveals to the purchaser a defect or other matter costing more than the amount of the $1/2$ % deposit to put right, then normally he need not go on. Remember that the price agreed is not necessarily the same as the open market value, which may not be affected by the defect or other matter, and that the Vendor can avoid this risk by disclosing any known defect or other matter at the outset.

Similarly, if the purchaser duly applies for a mortgage loan of the amount mentioned (usually financial credit should be already ascertained, eg by obtaining a "mortgage certificate") but the loan is either refused or made subject to unreasonably onerous conditions, then he can get back his deposit.

Again the precise terms and conditions of the sale may still have to be negotiated and, if agreement as to these cannot reasonably be reached both sides will be entitled to back out without loss of their deposits. A solicitor or licensed conveyancer will be able to advise you about what is "reasonably acceptable" here. However, if the condition of sale or amendment is not put forward in good faith, this may be taken to show an unwillingness to exchange.

E. Deletions
The form caters for two situations which may not always apply. First, it recognises that the vendor may not want to sell the property until he has actually bought somewhere else to live and that the purchaser may not want to buy this property until he has sold his present house or flat. If exchanging contracts must depend on this sort of "chain" of transactions, then the relevant parts of Clause 4 should be left in. Otherwise, they should be deleted. Second, in some areas is still takes longer than 4 weeks to get replies to local searches and enquiries. This difficulty can be overcome if the vendor has got the replies ready for the purchaser, but otherwise the whole of clause 5 should be left in.

Although the 4 weeks period should be complied with strictly, (ie time is of the essence), it may be extended by agreement (or by the purchaser where clause 5 applies without any deletion).

F. Definitions
The expression "as stakeholder" means that the person concerned holds the deposit on behalf of both sides, unable to pay the money to either without the other's consent except in accordance with the provisions of the Agreement.

Generally in the Agreement, singular words include the plural (eg "Purchaser" also covers joint purchasers) and the masculine includes the feminine).

© Crown copyright
Form F500 Fourmat Publishing 27 & 28 St Albans Place Islington Green London N1 ONX   February 1987

Appendix B

List of Authorised Banks Designated by the Chief Registrar of Friendly Societies, with the Consent of the Treasury, to hold Funds of Building Societies under section 59 of the Building Societies Act 1962 as at October 13, 1986

Alexanders Discount plc
Algemene Bank Nederland N.V.
Allied Arab Bank Ltd.
Allied Irish Investment Bank plc
American Express Bank Ltd.
Amsterdam-Rotterdam Bank N.V.
Ansbacher & Company Ltd., Henry
A.N.Z Merchant Bank Ltd.
A.P. Bank Ltd.
Arbuthnot Latham Bank Ltd.
Australia and New Zealand Banking group Ltd.
B.A.I.I. plc
Banca Nazionale del Lavoro
Banco de Vizcaya S.A.
Banco Espirito Santo e Comercial de Lisboa
Bank für Gemeinwirtschaft A.G.
Bank Hapoalim B.M.
Bank Julius Baer & Company Limited
Bank of America National Trust and Saving Association
Bank of England, The
Bank of Ireland, The
Bank of Leumi (U.K.) plc
Bank of Montreal
Bank of New Zealand
Bank of New York, The
Bank of Nova Scotia, The
Bank of Scotland
Bank of Tokyo Ltd., The
Bankers Trust Company
Banque Belge Ltd.
Banque Bruxelles Lambert S. A.
Banque Indosuez
Banque Nationale de Paris plc

Banque Nationale de Paris S.A. London Branch
Banque Paribas
Barclays Bank plc
Barclays de Zoete Wedd Ltd.
Baring Brothers & Company Ltd.
Bayerische Landesbank Girozentrale
Bayerische Vereinsbank A.G.
British Bank of the Middle East, The
British Linen Bank Ltd., The
Brown, Shipley & Company Ltd.
Canadian Imperial Bank of Commerce
Cassa di Risparmio delle Provincie Lombarde
Cater Allen plc
Chartered Trust plc
Charterhouse Bank Ltd.
Chase Manhattan Bank N.A., The
Chemical Bank
Christiana Bank (UK) Ltd.
Chuo Trust and Banking Company Ltd., The
C.I.C.-Union Europeenne, International et Cie
Citibank N.A.
Citicorp Investment Bank Ltd.
City Merchants Bank Ltd.
Clive Discount Company Ltd.
Clydesdale Bank plc
Clydesdale Bank Finance Corporation Ltd.
Commerzbank A.G.
Commercial Bank of Wales plc
Continental Illinois National Bank and Trust Company of Chicago
Co-operative Bank plc

Coutts & Company
Coutts Finance Company
Crédit Commercial de France
Crédit du Nord
Crédit Lyonnais
Crédit Suisse
Crédit Suisse First Boston Ltd.
Creditanstalt-Bankverein
Credito Italiano
Dai-Ichi Kangyo Bank Ltd.,
  The
Deutsche Bank A.G.
Deutsche
  Genossenschaftsbank
Dresdner Bank A.G.
Euro-Latinamerican Bank plc
European Arab Bank Ltd.
First Interstate Bank of
  California
First National Bank of Boston,
  The
First National Bank of
  Chicago, The
Forward Trust Ltd.
Fuji Bank Ltd., The
Gerrard & National plc
Girobank plc
Girozentrale und Bank der
  österreichischen Sparkassen
  A.G.
Grindlays Bank plc
Guinness Mahon & Company
  Ltd.
Gulf International Bank
  B.S.C.
Hambros Bank Ltd.
Hessische Landesbank-
  Girozentrale-
Hill Samuel & Company Ltd.
Hoare & Company, C
Hongkong and Shangai
  Banking Corporation, The
HongkongBank Ltd.
Industrial Bank of Japan Ltd.,
  The
International Commercial
  Bank plc
International Mexican Bank
  Ltd.
International Westminster
  Bank plc
Irving Trust Company
Italian International Bank plc
King and Shaxson Ltd.
Kleinwort Benson Ltd.

Lazard Brothers & Company
  Ltd.
Leopold Joseph & Sons Ltd.
Libra Bank plc
Lloyds Bank plc
Lloyds Bank International
  Ltd.
Lloyds Merchant Bank Ltd.
Lombard North Central plc
London Interstate Bank Ltd.
Long-Term Credit Bank of
  Japan, Ltd, The
Malayan Banking Berhad
Manufacturers Hanover Trust
  Company
Marine Midland Bank N.A.
Mellon Bank N.A.
Mercantile Credit Company
  Ltd.
Midland Bank plc
Midland Bank Finance
  Corporation Ltd.
Mitsubishi Bank, The
Mitsui Bank Ltd., The
Mitsui Trust and Banking
  Company Ltd., The
Morgan Guaranty Trust
  Company of New York
Morgan Grenfell & Company
  Ltd.
Moscow Narodny Bank Ltd.
National Bank of Abu Dhabi
National Australia Bank Ltd.
National Bank of Canada
National Bank of Detroit
National Bank of New Zealand
  Ltd., The
National Savings Bank
National Westminister Bank
  plc
Natwest Investment Bank Ltd.
Nedbank Ltd.
Nederlandsche
  Middenstandsabnk N.V.
Nippon Credit Bank Ltd., The
Noble Grossart Ltd.,
Northern Bank Development
  Corporation Ltd.
Northern Bank Ltd.
Northern Trust Company
  London Branch, The
Postipankki (U.K.) Ltd.
Privatbanken Ltd.
Rea Brothers plc
RepublicBank Dallas N.A.

Republic National Bank of New York

Robert Fleming and Company Ltd.

Rothschild & Sons Ltd., N.M.

Royal Bank of Canada, The

Royal Bank of Scotland plc, The

Royal Trust Company of Canada, The

Saitama Bank Ltd., The

Samuel Montagu & Company Ltd.

Sanwa Bank Ltd., The

Saudi International Bank (Al-Bank Al-Saudi Al-Alami Ltd.)

Scandinavian Bank plc

Schroder Wagg & Company Ltd., J Henry

Seccombe Marshall & Campion plc

Singer & Friedlander Ltd.

Smith St Aubyn & Company Ltd.

Société Générale

Société Générale Merchant Bank plc

Standard Chartered Bank

Standard Chartered Merchant Bank Ltd.

Sumitomo Trust and Banking Company Ltd., The

Sumitomo Bank Ltd., The

Swiss Bank Corporation

Taiyo Kobe Bank Ltd., The

Texas Commerce Bank N.A.

Thai Farmers Bank Ltd., The

Tokai Bank Ltd., The

Toronto-Dominion Bank, The

Toyo Trust and Banking Company Ltd., The

Trustee Savings Bank (any)

TSB England and Wales plc

UBAF Bank Ltd.

Ulster Bank Ltd.

Ulster Investment Bank Ltd.

Union Discount Company of London plc, The

Union Bank of Switzerland

United Dominions Trust Ltd.

Warburg & Company Ltd. S.G.

Westdeutsche Landesbank Girozentrale

Westpac Banking Corporation

Wintrust Securities Ltd.

Yorkshire Bank plc

Appendix C

GUARANTEE   D № 255660

To: (Name and Address of Vendor's Representative) _____

_____

In this document the following words have the following meanings:

The Vendor: (Name and Address) _____

_____

The Purchaser: (Name and Address) _____

_____

The Deposit: The sum of £ _____

The Property: (Address of the property being purchased) _____

_____

The Gross Premium: £ _____ (not exceeding 10% of the purchase price of the Property)

The Insurer: Lombard Continental Insurance plc, whose registered office is at 31-35 Fenchurch Street, London EC3M 3DX and Eagle Star Insurance Company Limited, whose registered office is at 1 Threadneedle Street, London EC2R 8BE.

In consideration of the Vendor foregoing the receipt of the Deposit under a contract (hereinafter called "the said Contract") intended to be made between the Vendor and the Purchaser for the sale and purchase of the Property the Insurer hereby guarantees to the Vendor that if the Purchaser refuses or fails to complete the said Contract in conformity with the conditions thereof and the whole or any part of the Deposit that would have been paid by the Purchaser under the terms of the said Contract but for the acceptance of this Guarantee by the Vendor in lieu thereof is forfeited under the terms of the said Contract to the Vendor the Insurer will thereupon pay to the Vendor the amount of the Deposit or the part thereof to which the Vendor shall be entitled under the terms of the said Contract PROVIDED THAT:

i)   the liability of the Insurer hereunder shall be limited to the amount of the Deposit stated above and no more;

ii)   if the Purchaser shall complete the said Contract in accordance with the terms provisions and conditions thereof and in accordance with any statute or court order applicable thereto this Guarantee shall be at an end;

iii) no allowance of time by the Vendor nor any forbearance or forgiveness in or in respect of any matter concerning the said Contract on the part of the Vendor shall in any way release the Insurer from liability under this Guarantee.

Dated this   day of   198

Signed _____ (A Practising Solicitor)

(Solicitor to sign all three copies)

Authorised agent for and on behalf of the Insurer

CLAIMS PROCEDURE

In the event of a claim arising under this Guarantee, please forward a copy of this Guarantee and a copy of the Sale Contract, together with details of the circumstances giving rise to the claim to Legal & Professional Indemnity Ltd., 3 Clanricarde Gardens, Tunbridge Wells, Kent TN1 1PE. Tel: (0892) 862345. DX 3923.

Name of organisation from whom purchaser has received a mortgage offer (if any): _____

INDEMNITY BY PURCHASER

I/We the Purchaser hereby offer the Insurer the Gross Premium and request that in consideration thereof the Insurer give a guarantee on my/our behalf in the form above. I/We will indemnify the Insurer from and against all actions damages claims costs charges and expenses sustained by the Insurer under the provisions of this Guarantee and if the Insurer is called upon to make any payment under or in respect of this Guarantee I/We will forthwith on demand pay the Insurer the amount of any such payment.

Signed by the Purchaser(s) _____

Date

WARNING TO PURCHASER

Please note that the Insurer has a right to recover from you a claim paid by the Insurer under the terms of the Guarantee. Please ask your solicitor to advise you.

Conditions

DEPOSIT GUARANTEE SCHEME

(1) Only a Solicitor holding a current Practising Certificate issued by the Law Society is permitted to bind the Companies to the form of guarantee

(2) The form of guarantee is to be that provided by the Companies from time to time and may not be varied without the consent in writing of the Companies

(3) The person or persons on whose behalf this guarantee is given (the purchaser) must, at the same time as contracting to purchase a property, contract to sell a property

(4) The properties being purchased and sold by the purchaser must both be situated in England and/or Wales and in both cases must be freehold, or leasehold with not less than 50 years unexpired

(5) The completion date in the contract for the property being purchased by the purchaser must be not more than ten weeks from the date of exchange

(6) The amount of the guarantee must not be more than £30,000

(7) The amount of the guarantee must not exceed 10% of the purchase price of the property

(8) The payment of premium must be in accordance with Scale 1 of the table of premiums published from time to time by the Companies or their authorised agents

(9) The purchaser under the contract for the purchase of the property and on whose behalf the guarantee is being given must be a person or persons and not a limited company or corporation

(10) The premium must be forwarded to Legal and Professional Indemnity Limited on the same day that the guarantee is forwarded to the vendor's solicitor

(11) All guarantee books belong to the Companies and must be surrendered to the Companies if the Solicitor's authority is terminated

(12) The guarantee must be in the names of the person or persons having a legal or equitable interest as purchaser(s) in the property to which the guarantee relates and the indemnity given to the Companies must be signed by all such persons. A copy of the guarantee signed by the purchaser(s) must be forwarded to Legal and Professional Indemnity Limited with the net premium

DEPOSIT GUARANTEE SCHEME – FIRST-TIME PURCHASER EXTENSION

In cases where the purchaser(s) cannot satisfy Condition (3) set out above (ie. the purchaser(s) is/are not selling another property) authority is hereby given for guarantees to be given on behalf of the Companies subject to the following terms, conditions, limits and premiums:–

(13) The person or persons on whose behalf the guarantee is given (the purchaser) must, prior to contracting to purchase the property, be in receipt of a mortgage offer in a sum not exceeding 100% of the purchase price or lender's valuation of the property whichever is the less. The mortgage offer must have been made by a building society, a registered friendly society, a bank registered under the Banking Act 1979 or a registered insurance company and must not be subject to any condition relating to work to be carried out to the property before the mortgage advance can be made

(14) The payment of premium must be in accordance with Scale 2 of the table of premiums published from time to time by the Companies or their authorised agents.

(15) The amount of the guarantee must be not more than £5,000

(16) The terms, conditions, limits and premiums set out in paragraphs numbered (1)-(12) above shall apply except as varied in paragraphs (13)-(15) above

Any variation of the said terms, conditions, limits and premiums will be such as may be notified in writing by the Companies. The authorised agents of the Companies for the purposes stated above are:–

Leggett, Porter and Howard Limited, 88/89 Gracechurch Street, London EC3V 0DN and Legal and Professional Indemnity Limited of 3 Clanricarde Gardens, Tunbridge Wells, Kent TN1 1PE.

"the Companies" mean Lombard Continental Insurance plc and Eagle Star Insurance Company Limited.

Appendix D

International Drilling Ltd. v. Louisville Investments (C.A.) Balcombe L.J.

From the authorities I deduce the following propositions of law.

(1)   The purpose of a covenant against assignment without the consent of the landlord, such consent not to be unreasonably withheld, is to protect the lessor from having his premises used or occupied in an undesirable way, or by an undesirable tenant or assignee: *per* A. L. Smith L.J. in *Bates v. Donaldson* [1896] 2 Q.B. 241, 247, approved by all the members of the Court of Appeal in *Houlder Brothers & Co. Ltd. v. Gibbs* [1925] Ch. 575.

(2)   As a corollary to the first proposition, a landlord is not entitled to refuse his consent to an assignment on grounds which have nothing whatever to do with the relationship of landlord and tenant in regard to the subject matter of the lease: see *Houlder Brothers & Co. Ltd. v. Gibbs*, a decision which (despite some criticism) is binding on this court: *Bickel v. Duke of Westminster* [1977] Q.B. 517. A recent example of a case where the landlord's consent was unreasonably withheld because the refusal was designed to achieve a collateral purpose unconnected with the terms of the lease is *Bromley Park Gardens Ltd. v. Moss* [1982] 1 W.L.R. 1019.

(3)   The onus of proving that consent has been unreasonably withheld is on the tenant: see *Shanly v. Ward* (1913) 29 T.L.R. 714 and *Pimms Ltd. v. Tallow Chandlers Company* [1964] 2 Q.B. 547 at 564.

(4)   It is not necessary for the landlord to prove that the conclusions which led him to refuse consent were justified, if they were conclusions which might be reached by a reasonable man in the circumstances: *Pimms Ltd. v. Tallow Chandlers Company* [1964] 2 Q.B. 547 at 564.

(5)   It may be reasonable for the landlord to refuse his consent to an assignment on the ground of the purpose for which the proposed assignee intends to use the premises, even though that purpose is not forbidden by the lease: see *Bates v. Donaldson* [1896] 2 Q.B. 241, 244.

(6)   There is a divergence of authority on the question, in considering whether the landlord's refusal of consent is reasonable, whether it is permissible to have regard to the consequences to the tenant if consent to the proposed assignment is withheld. In an early case at first instance, *Sheppard v. Hongkong and Shanghae Banking Corporation* (1872) 20 W.R. 459 at 460, Malins V.-C. said that by withholding their consent the lessors threw a very heavy burden on the lessees and they therefore ought to show good grounds for refusing it. In *Houlder Brothers & Co. Ltd. v. Gibbs* [1925] Ch. 575 at 584, Warrington L.J. said:

> "An act must be regarded as reasonable or unreasonable in reference to the circumstances under which it is committed, and when the question arises on the construction of a contract the outstanding circumstances to be considered are the nature of the contract to be construed, and the relations between the parties resulting from it."

In a recent decision of this court, *Leeward Securities Ltd. v. Lilyheath Properties Ltd.* (1983) 271 E.G. 279 concerning a sub-letting which would attract the protection of the Rent Act, both Oliver L.J. and O'Connor L.J. made it clear in their judgments that they could envisage circumstances in which it might be unreasonable to refuse consent to an underletting, if the result would be that there was no way in which the tenant (the sub-landlord) could reasonably exploit the premises except by creating a tenancy to which the Rent Act protection would apply, and which inevitably would affect the value of the landlord's reversion. O'Connor L.J. said at 283:

> "It must not be thought that, because the introduction of a Rent Act tenant inevitably had an adverse effect upon the value of the reversion, that that is a sufficient ground for the landlords to say that they can withhold consent and that the court will hold that that is reasonable."

To the opposite effect are the dicta, *obiter* but nevertheless weighty, of Viscount Dunedin and Lord Phillimore in *Viscount Tredegar v. Harwood* [1929] A.C. 72 at 78, 82. There are numerous other dicta to the effect that a landlord need consider only his own interests: see, *e.g. West Layton Ltd. v. Ford* [1979] Q.B. 593 at 605, and *Bromley Park Garden Estates Ltd. v. Moss* [1982] 1 W.L.R. 1019 at 1027. Those dicta must be qualified, since a landlord's interests, collateral to the purposes of the lease, are in any event ineligible for consideration: see proposition (2) above. But in my judgment a proper reconciliation of those two streams of authority can be achieved by saying that while a landlord need usually only consider his own relevant interests, there may be cases where there is such a disproportion between the benefit to the landlord and the detriment to the tenant if the landlord withholds his consent to an assignment that it is unreasonable for the landlord to refuse consent.

(7) Subject to the propositions set out above, it is in each case a question of fact, depending upon all the circumstances, whether the landlord's consent to an assignment is being unreasonably withheld: see *Bickel v. Duke of Westminster* [1977] Q.B. 517 at 524, and *West Layton Ltd. v. Ford* [1979] Q.B. 593 at 604, 606–607.

Appendix E

The Law Society's Code for Completion by Post (1984 Edition)

Preamble The code provides a procedure for postal completion which practising solicitors may adopt by reference.

First, each solicitor must satisfy himself that no circumstances exist that are likely to give rise to a conflict between this code and the interests of his own client (including where applicable a mortgagee client).

The code, where adopted, will apply without variation except so far as recorded in writing beforehand.

The Code 1. Adoption hereof must be specifically agreed by all the solicitors concerned and preferably in writing.

2. On completion the vendor's solicitors will act as agent for the purchaser's solicitor without fee or disbursements.

3. The vendor's solicitor undertakes that on completion, he:

(1) will have the vendor's authority to receive the purchase money; and

(2) will be the duly authorised agent of the proprietor of any charge upon the property to receive the part of the money paid to him which is needed to discharge such charge.

4. The purchaser's solicitor shall send to the vendor's solicitor instructions as to:

(1) documents to be examined and marked;

(2) memoranda to be endorsed;

(3) deeds, documents, undertakings and authorities relating to rents, deposits, keys, *etc*; and

(4) any other relevant matters.

In default of instructions, the vendor's solicitor shall not be under any duty to examine, mark or endorse any documents.

5. The purchaser's solicitor shall remit to the vendor's solicitor the balance due on completion specified in the vendor's solicitor's completion statement or with written notification; in default of either, the balance shown due by the contract. If the funds are remitted by transfer between banks, the vendor's solicitor shall instruct his bank to advise him by telephone immediately the funds are received. The vendor's solicitor shall hold such funds to the purchaser's solicitor's order pending completion.

6. The vendor's solicitor, having received the items specified in paras 4 and 5, shall forthwith, or at such later times as may have been agreed, complete. Thereupon he shall hold all documents and other items to be sent to the purchaser's solicitor as agent for such solicitor.

7. Once completion has taken place, the vendor's solicitor shall as soon as possible thereafter on the same day confirm the fact to the purchaser's solicitor by telephone or telex and shall also as soon as possible send by first class post or document exchange written confirmation to the purchaser's solicitor, together with the enclosures referred to in para 4 hereof. The vendor's solicitor shall ensure that such title deeds and any other items are correctly committed to the post or document exchange. Thereafter, they are at the risk of the purchaser's solicitor.

8.   If either the authorities specified in para 3 or the instructions specified in para 4 or the funds in para 5 have not been received by the vendor's solicitor by the agreed completion date and time, he shall forthwith notify the purchaser's solicitor and request further instructions.

9.   Nothing herein shall override any rights and obligations of parties under the contract or otherwise.

10.   Any dispute or difference which may arise between solicitors that is directly referable to a completion agreed to be carried out in accordance herewith, whether or not amended or supplemented in any way, shall be referred to an arbitrator to be agreed, within one month of any such dispute or difference arising between the solicitors who are party thereto, and, in default of such agreement, on the application of any such solicitor, to an arbitrator to be appointed by the President of The Law Society.

11.   Reference herein to vendor's solicitor and purchaser's solicitor shall, where appropriate, be deemed to include solicitors acting for parties other than vendor and purchaser.

Appendix F

The Law Society's Formulae for Exchanging Contracts by Telephone/Telex (1986)

Law Society Telephone/Telex Exchange—Formula A (1986) (for use where one solicitor holds both signed parts of the contract)

A. A completion date of   19   is agreed. The solicitor holding both parts of the contract confirms that he holds the part signed by his client(s), which is identical to the part he is also holding signed by the other solicitor's client(s) and will forthwith insert the agreed completion date in each part.

Solicitors mutually agree that exchange shall take place from that moment and the solicitor holding both parts confirms that, as of that moment, he holds the part signed by his client(s) to the order of the other. He undertakes that day by first-class post or, where the other solicitor is a member of a document exchange (as to which the inclusion of a reference thereto in the solicitor's letterhead shall be conclusive evidence) by delivery to that or any other affiliated exchange or by hand delivery direct to that solicitor's office, to send his signed part of the contract to the other solicitor, together, where he is the purhaser's solicitor, with a banker's draft or a solicitor's client account cheque for the deposit amounting to £..........

Law Society Telephone/Telex Exchange—Formula B (1986) (for use where each solicitor holds his own clients signed part of the contract)

B.   A completion date of   19   is agreed. Each solicitor confirms to the other that he holds a part contract in the agreed form signed by his client(s) and will forthwith insert the agreed completion date.

Each solicitor undertakes to the other thenceforth to hold the signed part of the contract to the other's order, so that contracts are exchanged at that moment. Each solicitor further undertakes that day by first-class post, or, where the other solicitor is a member of a document exchange (as to which the inclusion of a reference thereto in the solicitor's letterhead shall be conclusive evidence) by delivery to that or any other affiliated exchange or by hand delivery direct to that solicitor's office, to send his signed part of the contract to the other together, in the case of a purchaser's solicitor, with a banker's draft or a solicitor's client account cheque for the deposit amounting to £..........

Notes

1. A memorandum should be prepared, after use of a formula, recording:

(*a*) date and time of exchange;
(*b*) the formula used and exact wording of agreed variations;
(*c*) the completion date;
(*d*) the (balance) deposit to be paid;
(*e*) the identities of those involved in any conversation.

2. In Formula B cases, those who are going to affect the exchange must first confirm the details in order to ensure that both parts are identical. This means, in particular, that if either part of the contract has been amended since it was originally prepared, the solicitor who holds a part contract with amendments must disclose them, so that it can be confirmed that the other part is similarly amended.

Appendix G

THE LAW SOCIETY'S GENERAL CONDITIONS OF SALE (1984 REVISION)

1 DEFINITIONS

In these conditions—
(*a*) "completion notice" means a notice served under condition 23 (2)
(*b*) "the contract rate" means the rate specified in a special condition or, if none is so specified, the rate prescribed from time to time under section 32 of the Land Compensation Act 1961 for interest payable thereunder
(*c*) "contractual completion date" has the meaning given in condition 21
(*d*) "conveyance" includes an assignment and a transfer under the Land Registration Acts
(*e*) "lease" includes underlease
(*f*) "normal deposit" means the sum which, together with any preliminary deposit paid by the purchaser, amounts to ten per centum of the purchase money (excluding any separate price to be paid for any chattels, fixtures or fittings)
(*g*) "working day" means any day from Monday to Friday (inclusive) other than—
(i) Christmas Day, Good Friday and any statutory bank holiday, and
(ii) any other day specified in a special condition as not a working day
(*h*) a reference to a statute includes any amendment or re-enactment thereof.

2 SERVICE AND DELIVERY

(1) Section 196 of the Law of Property Act 1925 applies to any notice served under the contract, save that—
(*a*) a notice shall also be sufficiently served on a party if served on that party's solicitors
(*b*) a reference to a registered letter shall include a prepaid first class ordinary letter
(*c*) if the time at which a letter containing a notice would in the ordinary course be delivered is not on a working day, the notice shall be deemed to be served on the next following working day
(*d*) a notice shall also be sufficiently served if—
(i) sent by telex or by telegraphic facsimile transmission to the party to be served, and that service shall be deemed to be made on the day of transmission if transmitted before 4 p.m. on a working day, but otherwise on the next following working day
(ii) when the addressee is a member of a document exchange (as to which the inclusion of a reference thereto in the solicitors' letterhead shall be conclusive evidence) delivered to that or any other affiliated exchange, and that service shall be deemed to have been made on the first working day after that on which the document would, in the ordinary course, be available for collection by the addressee.
(2) Sub-condition (1) applies to the delivery of documents as it applies to the service of notices.

3 MATTERS AFFECTING THE PROPERTY

(1) In this condition—
(*a*) "competent authority" means a local authority or other body exercising powers under statute or Royal Charter
(*b*) "requirement" includes (whether or not subject to confirmation) any notice, order or proposal
(*c*) "relevant matter" means any matter specified in sub-condition (2) whenever arising.
(2) The property is sold subject to—
(*a*) all matters registrable by any competent authority pursuant to statute
(*b*) all requirements of any competent authority
(*c*) all matters disclosed or reasonably to be expected to be disclosed by searches and as a result of enquiries formal or informal, and whether made in person, by writing or orally by or for the purchaser or which a prudent purchaser ought to make
(*d*) all notices served by or on behalf of a reversioner, a tenant or sub-tenant, or the owner or occupier of any adjoining or neighbouring property.
(3) (*a*) Notwithstanding sub-condition (2), the vendor warrants that he has informed the purchaser of the contents of any written communication received by, or known to, the vendor on or before the working day preceding the date of the contract relating to any relevant matter. Failure to give such information before the contract is made shall be deemed to be an omission in a statement in the course of the negotiations leading to the contract, but shall give rise to no right to compensation to the extent that the purchaser has a claim for damages against a competent authority
(*b*) In the event of any conflict or variation between information in fact received from any competent authority relating to any relevant matter and any statement made by the vendor in respect of the same matter, the purchaser shall rely on the information received from the competent authority to the exclusion of that given by the vendor
(*c*) The vendor shall forthwith inform the purchaser of the contents of any written communication received by him after the working day preceding the date of the contract and before the day of actual completion which if received on or before the former day would have fallen within paragraph (*a*).
(4) The purchaser (subject to any right or remedy arising under sub-condition (3)) will indemnify the vendor in respect of any liability under any requirement of a competent authority (whether made before or after the date of the contract), including the reasonable cost to the vendor of compliance after reasonable notice to the purchaser of the vendor's intention to comply, such sum to be payable on demand. The provisions of this sub-condition shall prevail in the event of conflict with any other condition.

4 OPPORTUNITY TO RESCIND

(1) This condition only applies if a special condition so provides.
(2) Within such period as is specified in a special condition or, if none is so specified, within twenty working days from the date of the contract (as to which, in either case, time shall be of the essence), the purchaser shall be entitled, notwithstanding condition 3 (2), to rescind the contract by service of notice on the vendor specifying a matter to which this condition applies affecting the property.
(3) This condition applies to any of the following matters of which the purchaser had no knowledge on or before the working day preceding the date of the contract—
(*a*) a financial charge which the vendor cannot or has not at the purchaser's written request agreed to discharge on or before actual completion
(*b*) a statutory provision prohibiting, restricting or imposing adverse conditions upon the use or the continued use of the property for such purpose as is specified in a special condition or, if none is so specified, the purpose for which the vendor used it immediately before the date of the contract
(*c*) a matter which is likely materially to reduce the price which a willing purchaser could otherwise reasonably be expected to pay for the relevant interest in the property in the open market at the date of the contract.
(4) For the purposes of this condition, the purchaser's knowledge—
(*a*) includes everything in writing received in the course of the transaction leading to the contract by a person acting on his behalf from the vendor, a person acting on the vendor's behalf, or a competent authority (as defined in condition 3 (1) (*a*))
(*b*) does not include anything solely because a statute deems that registration of a matter constitutes actual notice of it.

5 EASEMENTS, RESERVATIONS, RIGHTS AND LIABILITIES

(1) The vendor warrants that he has disclosed to the purchaser the existence of all easements, rights, privileges and liabilities affecting the property, of which the vendor knows or ought to know, other than the existence of those known to the purchaser at the date of the contract, or which a prudent purchaser would have discovered by that date.
(2) Without prejudice to the generality of sub-condition (1)—
(*a*) the purchaser shall purchase with full notice of the actual state and condition of the property and shall take it as it stands, save where it is to be constructed or converted by the vendor
(*b*) the property is sold, and will if the vendor so requires be conveyed, subject to all rights of way, water, light, drainage and other easements, rights, privileges and liabilities affecting the same.
(3) (*a*) In this sub-condition "the retained land" means land retained by the vendor—
(i) adjoining the property, or
(ii) near to the property and designated as retained land in a special condition.
(*b*) The conveyance of the property shall contain such reservations in favour of the retained land and the grant of such rights over the retained land as would have been implied had the vendor conveyed both the property and the retained land by simultaneous conveyances to different purchasers.

6 TENANCIES

(1) This condition applies if the property is sold subject to any lease or tenancy and shall have effect notwithstanding any partial, incomplete or inaccurate reference to any lease or tenancy in the special conditions or the particulars of the property.
(2) Copies or full particulars of all leases or tenancies not vested in the purchaser having been furnished to him, he shall be deemed to purchase with full knowledge thereof and shall take the property subject to the rights of the tenants thereunder or by reason thereof. The purchaser shall indemnify the vendor against all claims, demands and liability in respect of such rights, notwithstanding that they may be void against a purchaser for want of registration.
(3) The vendor gives no warranty as to the amount of rent lawfully recoverable from any tenant, as to the effect of any legislation in relation to any lease or tenancy or as to the compliance with any legislation affecting the same.
(4) The vendor shall inform the purchaser of any change in the disclosed terms and conditions of any lease or tenancy.
(5) If a lease or tenancy subject to which the property is sold terminates for any reason, the vendor shall inform the purchaser and, on being indemnified by the purchaser against all consequential loss, expenditure or liability, shall act as the purchaser may direct.

7 ERRORS, OMISSIONS AND MISSTATEMENTS

(1) No error, omission or misstatement herein or in any plan furnished or any statement made in the course of the negotiations leading to the contract shall annul the sale or entitle the purchaser to be discharged from the purchase.
(2) Any such error, omission or misstatement shown to be material shall entitle the purchaser or the vendor, as the case may be, to proper compensation, provided that the purchaser shall not in any event be entitled to compensation for matters falling within conditions 5 (2) or 6 (3).
(3) No immaterial error, omission or misstatement (including a mistake in any plan furnished for identification only) shall entitle either party to compensation.
(4) Sub-condition (1) shall not apply where compensation for any error, omission or misstatement shown to be material cannot be assessed nor enable either party to compel the other to accept or convey property differing substantially (in quantity, quality tenure or otherwise) from the property agreed to be sold if the other party would be prejudiced by the difference.
(5) The purchaser acknowledges that in making the contract he has not relied on any statement made to him save one made or confirmed in writing.

8 LEASEHOLDS

(1) This condition applies if the property is leasehold.
(2) In all cases the immediate title to the property shall begin with the lease. Where the lease, unless registered with absolute title, is dated not more than fifteen years before the date of the contract and was granted for a term exceeding twenty-one years, the freehold title and all other titles superior to the lease shall be deduced for a period beginning not less than fifteen years prior to the date of the contract and ending on the date of the lease.
(3) A copy of the lease and a copy of, sufficient extract from, or abstract of, all superior leases, the contents of which are known to the vendor, having been supplied or made available to the purchaser, he shall be deemed to purchase with full notice of the contents thereof, whether or not he has inspected the same.
(4) Where any consent to assign is necessary—
(*a*) the vendor shall forthwith at his own cost apply for and use his best endeavours to obtain such consent
(*b*) the purchaser shall forthwith supply such information and references as may reasonably be required by the reversioner before granting such consent
(*c*) if any such consent is not granted at least five working days before contractual completion date, or is subject to any condition to which the purchaser reasonably objects, either party may rescind the contract by notice to the other.
(5) Any statutory implied covenant on the part of the vendor shall not extend to any breach of the terms of the lease as to the state and condition of the property and the assignment shall so provide. This sub-condition applies notwithstanding that a special condition provides for the vendor to convey as beneficial owner.
(6) Where the property is sold subject to an apportioned rent specified as such in a special condition, the purchaser shall not require the consent of the reversioner to be obtained, or the rent to be otherwise legally apportioned.
(7) The purchaser shall assume that any receipt for the last payment due for rent under the lease before actual completion was given by the person then entitled to such rent or his duly authorised agent.

9 DEPOSIT

(1) The purchaser shall on or before the date of the contract pay by way of deposit to the vendor's solicitors as stakeholders the normal deposit, or such lesser sum as the vendor shall have agreed in writing. On a sale by private treaty, payment shall be made by banker's draft or by cheque drawn on a solicitors' bank account.
(2) Upon service by the vendor of a completion notice, the purchaser shall pay to the vendor any difference between the normal deposit and any amount actually paid (if less).
(3) If any draft, cheque or other instrument tendered in or towards payment of any sum payable under this condition is dishonoured when first presented the vendor shall have the right by notice to the purchaser within seven working days thereafter to treat the contract as repudiated.

10 OPTIONAL METHODS OF EXCHANGE

(1) Exchange of contracts may be effected by a method authorised by condition 2 for the service of notices. If so effected, the contract shall be made when the last part is, as the case may be, posted or delivered to a document exchange.
(2) Where contracts have not been exchanged, the parties' solicitors may agree by telephone or telex that the contract be immediately effective and thereupon the solicitors holding a part of the contract signed by their client shall hold it irrevocably to the order of the other party.

11 INSURANCE

(1) If the property is destroyed or damaged prior to actual completion and the proceeds of any insurance policy effected by or for the purchaser are reduced by reason of the existence of any policy effected by or for the vendor, the purchase price shall be abated by the amount of such reduction.
(2) Sub-condition (1) shall not apply where the proceeds of the vendor's policy are applied towards the reinstatement of the property pursuant to any statutory or contractual obligation.
(3) This condition takes effect in substitution for section 47 of the Law of Property Act 1925.
(4) The vendor shall be under no duty to the purchaser to maintain any insurance on the property, save where the property is leasehold and the vendor has an obligation to insure.

12 ABSTRACT OF TITLE

(1) Forthwith upon exchange of contracts the vendor shall deliver to the purchaser—
(*a*) where the title is not registered, an abstract of the title to the property or an epitome of the title together with photocopies of the relevant documents
(*b*) where the title is registered—
(i) the documents, particulars and information specified in sub-sections (1) and (2) of section 110 of the Land Registration Act 1925, save that copies of the entries on the register, the filed plan and any documents noted on the register and filed in the registry shall be office copies, and
(ii) such additional authorities to inspect the register as the purchaser shall reasonably require for any sub-purchaser or prospective mortgagee or lessee.
(2) Where the title is not registered, the vendor shall at his own expense produce the relevant documents of title or an abstract, epitome of title or copy thereof (bearing in each case original markings of examination of all relevant documents of title or of examined abstracts thereof).
(3) Where before the date of the contract any abstract, epitome or document has been delivered to the purchaser, he shall not, save as provided by conditions 6 (2) or 8 (3), be deemed to have had notice before the date of the contract of any matter of title thereby disclosed.

13 IDENTITY AND BOUNDARIES

(1) The vendor shall produce such evidence as may be reasonably necessary to establish the identity and extent of the property, but shall not be required to define exact boundaries, or the ownership of fences, ditches, hedges or walls, nor, beyond the evidence afforded by the information in his possession, separately to identify parts of the property held under different titles.

(2) If reasonably required by the purchaser because of the insufficiency of the evidence produced under sub-condition (1), the vendor shall at his own expense provide and hand over on completion a statutory declaration as to the relevant facts, in a form agreed by the purchaser, such agreement not to be unreasonably withheld.

14 MORTGAGES IN FAVOUR OF FRIENDLY AND OTHER SOCIETIES

Where the title includes a mortgage or legal charge in favour of trustees on behalf of a friendly society, a building society or a society registered under the Industrial and Provident Societies Acts, the purchaser shall assume that any receipt given on the discharge of any such mortgage or legal charge and apparently duly executed was in fact duly executed by all proper persons and is valid.

15 REQUISITIONS

(1) In this condition "abstract" means all the documents, particulars and information required to be delivered by the vendor under condition 12.

(2) Subject to sub-condition (4), the purchaser shall deliver any requisitions or objections relating to the title, evidence of title or the abstract, in writing within six working days of receipt of the abstract (or, in the case of an abstract delivered before the date of the contract, within six working days of the date of contract). Within four working days of such delivery the vendor shall deliver his replies in writing.

(3) The purchaser shall deliver any observations on any of the vendor's replies in writing within four working days of their receipt.

(4) Where some but not all parts of the abstract have been delivered, and defects in title are not disclosed by such parts of the abstract as have been delivered, then in respect only of the undelivered parts or undisclosed defects (as the case may be) the abstract shall be deemed to be received for the purpose of sub-condition (2) at the time or respective times when any previously undelivered part is delivered.

(5) Time shall be of the essence for the purposes of this condition.

16 RESCISSION

(1) If the vendor is unable, or on some reasonable ground unwilling, to satisfy any requisition or objection made by the purchaser, the vendor may give the purchaser notice (specifying the reason for his inability or the ground of his unwillingness) to withdraw the same. If the purchaser does not withdraw the same within seven working days of service, either party may thereafter, notwithstanding any intermediate negotiation or litigation, rescind the contract by notice to the other.

(2) Upon rescission under any power given by these conditions or any special condition—

(*a*) the vendor shall repay to the purchaser any sums paid by way of deposit or otherwise under the contract, with interest on such sums at the contract rate from four working days after rescission until payment

(*b*) the purchaser shall forthwith return all documents delivered to him by the vendor and at his own expense procure the cancellation of any entry relating to the contract in any register.

17 PREPARATION OF CONVEYANCE

(1) The purchaser shall deliver the draft conveyance at least twelve working days before contractual completion date, and within four working days of such delivery the vendor shall deliver it back approved or revised.

(2) The purchaser shall deliver the engrossment of the conveyance (first executed by him, where requisite) at least five working days before contractual completion date.

(3) The purchaser shall not, by delivering the draft conveyance or the engrossment, be deemed to accept the vendor's title or to waive any right to raise or maintain requisitions.

(4) Save to the extent that a covenant for indemnity will be implied by statute, the purchaser shall in the conveyance covenant to indemnify the vendor and his estate (and any estate of which the vendor is personal representative or trustee) against all actions, claims and liability for any breach of any covenant, stipulation, provision or other matter subject to which the property is sold and in respect of which the vendor or any such estate will remain liable after completion.

(5) The vendor shall give an acknowledgment for production and, unless in a fiduciary capacity, an undertaking for safe custody of documents of title retained by him. Where any such document is retained by a mortgagee, trustee or personal representative, the vendor shall procure that such person shall give an acknowledgment for production, and the vendor, unless in a fiduciary capacity, shall covenant that if and when he receives any such document he will, at the cost of the person requiring it, give an undertaking for safe custody.

(6) The vendor shall be entitled on reasonable grounds to decline to convey the property to any person other than the purchaser, by more than one conveyance, at more than the contract price or at a price divided between different parts of the property.

18 OCCUPATION BEFORE COMPLETION

(1) This condition applies if the vendor authorises the purchaser to occupy the property before actual completion, except—

(*a*) where the purchaser already lawfully occupies any part of the property, or

(*b*) where the property is a dwellinghouse and the authority for the occupation is only for the purpose of effecting works of decoration, repair or improvement agreed by the vendor.

(2) The purchaser occupies the property as licensee and not as tenant. The purchaser may not transfer his licence or authorise any other person save members of his immediate family to occupy any part of the property.

(3) The purchaser shall not, by taking such occupation, be deemed to accept the vendor's title or to waive any right to raise or maintain requisitions.

(4) While the purchaser is in occupation of the whole or any part of the property under this condition, he shall—

(*a*) pay and indemnify the vendor against all outgoings and any other expenses in respect of the property and pay to the vendor in respect of such occupation a sum calculated at the contract rate on the amount of the purchase money (less any deposit paid)

(*b*) be entitled to receive any rents and profits from any part of the property not occupied by him

(*c*) insure the property in a sum not less than the purchase price against all risks in respect of which premises of the like nature are normally insured.

(5) The purchaser's licence to occupy the property shall end—

(*a*) on contractual completion date, or

(*b*) upon termination of the contract, or

(*c*) upon the expiry of five working days' notice given by either party to the other,

and thereupon the purchaser shall give up occupation of the property and leave the same in as good repair as it was in when he went into occupation.

(6) If the purchaser, after his licence has ended under sub-condition 5(*a*), remains in occupation with the express or implied consent of the vendor, he shall thereafter occupy on the other terms of this condition and on the further term that the vendor's rights under condition 22 shall not thereby be affected.

19 APPORTIONMENTS

(1) In this condition—

(*a*) "the apportionment day" means—

  (i) if the property is sold with vacant possession of the whole, the date of actual completion

  (ii) in any other case, contractual completion date

(*b*) "payment period" means one of the periods for which a sum payable periodically is payable, whether or not such periods are of equal length.

(2) This condition shall not apply to any sum if—

(*a*) the purchaser cannot, by virtue only of becoming the owner of the property, either enforce payment of it or be obliged to pay it, or

(*b*) it is an outgoing paid in advance, unless the vendor cannot obtain repayment and the purchaser benefits therefrom or is given credit therefor against a sum that would otherwise be his liability.

(3) On completion the income and outgoings of the property shall, subject to sub-condition (2) and conditions 3 and 22(4) and to any adjustment required by condition 18(4), be apportioned as at the apportionment day.

(4) For the purposes of apportionment only, it shall be assumed—

(*a*) that the vendor remains owner of the property until the end of the apportionment day, and

(*b*) that the sum to be apportioned—

  (i) accrues from day to day

  (ii) is payable throughout the relevant period at the same rate as on the apportionment day.

(5) Sums payable periodically shall be apportioned by charging or allowing—

(*a*) for any payment period entirely attributable to one party, the whole of the instalment payable therefor

(*b*) for any part of a payment period, a proportion on an annual basis.

(6) (*a*) This sub-condition applies to any sum payable in respect of any period falling wholly or partly prior to the apportionment day, the amount of which is not notified to either party before actual completion

(*b*) A provisional apportionment shall be made on the best estimate available. Upon the amount being notified, a final apportionment shall be made and one party shall thereupon make to the other the appropriate balancing payment.

20 ENDORSEMENT OF MEMORANDUM

Where the vendor does not hand over all the documents of his title, he shall at completion endorse a memorandum of the sale to the purchaser on the last such document in each relevant title and thereupon produce the endorsed documents for inspection.

21 COMPLETION

(1) Contractual completion date shall be as stated in the special conditions but if not so stated shall be the twenty-fifth working day after the date of the contract. Completion shall take place in England or Wales either at the office of the vendor's solicitors or, if required by the vendor at least five working days prior to actual completion, at the office of the vendor's mortgagee or his solicitors.

(2) The vendor shall not be obliged to accept payment of the money due on completion otherwise than by one or more of the following methods—

(*a*) legal tender

(*b*) a banker's draft drawn by and upon a settlement bank for the purposes of the Clearing House Automated Payments System or any other bank specified in a special condition

(*c*) an unconditional authority to release any deposit held by a stakeholder

(*d*) otherwise as the vendor shall have agreed before actual completion.

(3) If completion is effected otherwise than by personal attendance the time for completion is when on a working day

(*a*) the money due on completion is paid to the vendor or his solicitors, and

(*b*) the vendor's solicitors hold to the order of the purchaser all the documents to which he is entitled on completion.

(4) For the purposes of this condition money is paid when the vendor receives payment by a method specified in sub-condition (2). Where the parties have agreed upon a direct credit to a bank account at a named branch, payment is made when that branch receives the credit.

(5) (*a*) This sub-condition applies if the money due on completion is not paid by 2.30 p.m. on the day of actual completion or by such other time on that day as is specified in a special condition

(*b*) For the purposes of condition 22 only, completion shall be deemed to be postponed by reason of the purchaser's delay from the day of actual completion until the next working day

(*c*) The purchaser shall not as a result of the deemed postponement of completion be liable to make any payment to the vendor unless the vendor claims such payment by giving notice at completion or within five working days thereafter (as to which period time shall be of the essence). Payment shall be due five working days after receipt of such notice.

22 COMPENSATION FOR LATE COMPLETION

(1) For the purposes of this condition—

(*a*) "delay" means failure to perform or lateness in performing any obligation of the contract which causes or contributes to lateness in completion

(*b*) a party is "in default" if and to the extent that the period, or the aggregate of the periods, of his delay exceeds the period, or the aggregate of the periods, of delay of the other party

(*c*) "the period of default" means the length of the excess defined in paragraph (*b*) or, if shorter, the period from contractual completion date to the date of actual completion.

(2) If the sale shall be completed after contractual completion date, the party in default (if any) shall be liable to compensate the other for loss occasioned to him by reason of that default.

(3) Before actual completion, or within five working days thereafter (as to which period time shall be of the essence), the party entitled to compensation may, by notice to the other party, opt to be paid or allowed a sum calculated at the contract rate on the amount of the purchase money (less any deposit paid) for the period of default as liquidated damages in settlement of his claim for compensation.

(4) If the vendor is entitled to compensation, he may, before actual completion, by notice to the purchaser, opt to take the net income of the property for the period of default in lieu of such compensation.

(5) The right to recover any compensation under this condition shall not be prejudiced by completion of the sale, whether before or after the commencement of proceedings.

23 COMPLETION NOTICE

(1) This condition applies unless a special condition provides that time is of the essence in respect of contractual completion date.

(2) If the sale shall not be completed on contractual completion date, either party, being then himself ready able and willing to complete, may after that date serve on the other party notice to complete the transaction in accordance with this condition. A party shall be deemed to be ready, able and willing to complete—

(*a*) if he could be so but for some default or omission of the other party

(*b*) notwithstanding that any mortgage on the property is unredeemed when the completion notice is served if the aggregate of all sums necessary to redeem all such mortgages (to the extent that they relate to the property) does not exceed the sum payable on completion.

(3) Upon service of a completion notice it shall become a term of the contract that the transaction shall be completed within fifteen working days of service and in respect of such period time shall be of the essence.

(4) If the purchaser does not comply with a completion notice—

(*a*) the purchaser shall forthwith return all documents delivered to him by the vendor and at his own expense procure the cancellation of any entry relating to the contract in any register

(*b*) without prejudice to any other rights or remedies available to him, the vendor may—

  (i) forfeit and retain any deposit paid and/or

  (ii) re-sell the property by auction, tender or private treaty.

(5) If on any such re-sale contracted within one year after contractual completion date the vendor incurs a loss and so elects by notice to the purchaser within one month after the contract for such re-sale, the purchaser shall pay to the vendor liquidated damages. The amount payable shall be the aggregate of such loss, all costs and expenses reasonably incurred in any such re-sale and any attempted re-sale and interest at the contract rate on such part of the purchase money as is from time to time outstanding (giving credit for all sums received under any re-sale contract on account of the re-sale price) after contractual completion date.

(6) If the vendor does not comply with a completion notice, the purchaser, without prejudice to any other rights or remedies available to him, may give notice to the vendor forthwith to pay to the purchaser any sums paid by way of deposit or otherwise under the contract and interest on such sums at the contract rate from four working days after service of the notice until payment. On compliance with such notice the purchaser shall not be entitled to specific performance of the contract, but shall forthwith return all documents delivered to him by the vendor and at the expense of the vendor procure the cancellation of any entry relating to the contract in any register.

(7) Where after service of a completion notice the time for completion shall have been extended by agreement or implication, either party may again invoke the provisions of this condition which shall then take effect with the substitution of "seven working days" for "fifteen working days" in sub-condition (3).

24 CHATTELS

The property in any chattels agreed to be sold shall pass to the purchaser on actual completion.

25 AUCTIONS

(1) This condition applies if the property is sold by auction.

(2) The sale is subject to a reserve price for the property and, when the property is sold in lots, for each lot.

(3) The vendor reserves the right—

(*a*) to divide the property into lots and to sub-divide, re-arrange or consolidate any lots

(*b*) to bid personally or by his agent up to any reserve price

(*c*) without disclosing any reserve price, to withdraw from the sale any property or lot at any time before it has been sold, whether or not the sale has begun.

(4) The auctioneer may—

(*a*) refuse to accept a bid

(*b*) in the case of a dispute as to any bid, forthwith determine the dispute or again put up the property or lot at the last undisputed bid.

(5) The purchaser shall forthwith complete and sign the contract and pay, but not necessarily by the means specified in condition 9(1), the normal deposit.

Appendix H

The National Conditions of Sale

20th Edition
first published
December 1981

THESE CONDITIONS ARE COPYRIGHT AND MAY NOT BE REPRODUCED

Construction of the conditions

In these conditions, where the context admits—
(1) The "vendor" and the "purchaser" include the persons deriving title under them respectively
(2) "Purchase money" includes any sum to be paid for chattels, fittings or other separate items
(3) References to the "Special Conditions" include references to the particulars of sale and to the provisions of the contract which is made by reference to the conditions
(4) The "prescribed rate" means the agreed rate of interest or, if none, then the rate of interest prescribed from time to time under Land Compensation Act 1961, s. 32
(5) "Solicitor" includes a barrister who is employed by a corporate body to carry out conveyancing on its behalf and is acting in the course of his employment
(6) "Working day" means a day on which clearing banks in the City of London are (or would be but for a strike, lock-out, or other stoppage, affecting particular banks or banks generally) open during banking hours Except in condition 19(4), in which "working day" means a day when the Land Registry is open to the public
(7) "Designated bank" means a bank designated by the Chief Registrar under Building Societies Act 1962, s. 59
(8) The "Planning Acts" means the enactments from time to time in force relating to town and country planning
(9) On a sale by private treaty references to the "auctioneer" shall be read as references to the vendor's agent
(10) On a sale in lots, the conditions apply to each lot
(11) "Abstract of title" means in relation to registered land such documents as the vendor is required by Land Registration Act 1925, s. 110, to furnish

The conditions

1. The Sale: by Auction: by Private Treaty
(1) Paragraphs (2) to (5) of this condition apply on a sale by auction and paragraphs (6) and (7) on a sale by private treaty
(2) Unless otherwise provided in the Special Conditions, the sale of the property and of each lot is subject to a reserve price and to a right for the vendor or any one person on behalf of the vendor to bid up to that price
(3) The auctioneer may refuse any bid and no person shall at any bid advance less than the amount fixed for that purpose by the auctioneer
(4) If any dispute arises respecting a bid, the auctioneer may determine the dispute or the property may, at the vendor's option, either be put up again at the last undisputed bid, or be withdrawn
(5) Subject to the foregoing provisions of this condition, the highest bidder shall be the purchaser and shall forthwith complete and sign the contract, the date of which shall be the date of the auction
(6) Where there is a draft contract, or an arrangement subject to contract, or a negotiation in which there are one or more outstanding items or suspensory matters (which prevent there being yet a concluded agreement of a contractual nature), a solicitor, who holds a document signed by his client in the form of a contract of sale in writing and embodying this condition, shall (unless the other party or his solicitor is informed to the contrary) have the authority of his client to conclude, by formal exchange of contracts, or by post, or by telex or other telegraphic means, or by telephone, and in any case with or without involving solicitors' undertakings, a binding contract in the terms of the document which his client has signed
(7) The date of the contract shall be—
(i) the date, if any, which is agreed and put on the contract, but if none, then
(ii) on an exchange of contracts by post (unless the parties' solicitors otherwise agree), the date on which the last part of the contract is posted, or
(iii) in any other case, the date on which, consistently with this condition, a binding contract is concluded

2. Deposit
(1) Unless the Special Conditions otherwise provide, the purchaser shall on the date of the contract pay a deposit of 10 per cent. of the purchase price, on a sale by auction, to the auctioneer, or on a sale by private treaty, to the vendor's solicitor and, in either case, as stakeholder
(2) In case a cheque taken for the deposit (having been presented, and whether or not it has been re-presented) has not been honoured, then and on that account the vendor may elect—
either (i) to treat the contract as discharged by breach thereof on the purchaser's part
or (ii) to enforce payment of the deposit as a deposit, by suing on the cheque or otherwise

3. Purchaser's short right to rescind
(1) This condition shall have effect if the Special Conditions so provide, but not otherwise
(2) If the property is affected by any matter to which this condition applies, then the purchaser may by notice in writing (hereinafter referred to as a "Condition 3 Notice") given to the vendor or his solicitor and expressly referring to this condition and the matter in question, and notwithstanding any intermediate negotiation, rescind the contract on the same terms as if the purchaser had persisted in an objection to the title which the vendor was unable to remove
(3) A Condition 3 Notice shall not be given after the expiration of 16 working days from the date of the contract, time being of the essence of this condition
(4) This condition applies to any matter materially affecting the value of the property, other than—
(i) a matter which was not yet in existence or subsisting at the date of the contract
(ii) a specific matter to which the sale was expressly made subject, or
(iii) a matter of which the purchaser had at the date of the contract express notice or actual knowledge, not being notice or knowledge imputed to the purchaser by statute solely by reason of a registration of such matter, or notice or knowledge which the purchaser is only deemed to have had by the conditions
(5) This condition and condition 15 are additional to each other

4. Chattels, etc., and separate items
If the sale includes chattels, fittings or other separate items, the vendor warrants that he is entitled to sell the same free from any charge, lien, burden, or adverse claim

5. Date and manner of completion
(1) The completion date shall be the date specified for the purpose in the contract or, if none, the 26th working day after the date of the contract or the date of delivery of the abstract of title, whichever be the later
(2) Unless the Special Conditions otherwise provide, in respect of the completion date time shall not be of the essence of the contract, but this provision shall operate subject and without prejudice to—
(i) the provisions of condition 22 and
(ii) the rights of either party to recover from the other damages for delay in fulfilling his obligations under the contract
(3) The purchaser's obligations to pay money due on completion shall be discharged by one or more of the following methods—
(i) authorisation in writing to release a deposit held for the purposes of the contract by a stakeholder
(ii) banker's draft issued by a designated bank
(iii) cheque drawn on and guaranteed by a designated bank
(iv) telegraphic or other direct transfer (as requested or agreed to by the vendor's solicitor) to a particular bank or branch for the credit of a specified account
(v) legal tender
(vi) any other method requested or agreed to by the vendor's solicitor
(4) Completion shall be carried out, either formally at such office or place as the vendor's solicitor shall reasonably require, or (if the parties' solicitors so arrange) by post, or by means of solicitors' undertakings concerning the holding of documents or otherwise Provided that on a sale with vacant possession of the whole or part of the property, if the conveyance or transfer will not, by overreaching or otherwise, discharge the property from interests (if any) of persons in, or who may be in, actual occupation of the property or such part of it, then (subject always to the rights of the purchaser under Law of Property Act 1925, s. 42 (1)), the purchaser may, by giving reasonable notice, require that on, or immediately before the time of, completion possession of the property or part be handed over to the purchaser or his representative at the property
(5) The date of actual completion shall be the day on which, the contract being completed in other respects, the purchaser has discharged consistently with the provisions of this condition the obligations of the purchaser to pay the money due on completion Provided that—
(i) for the purposes only of conditions 6, 7 and 8, if but for this proviso the date of actual completion would be the last working day of a week (starting on Sunday) and the purchaser is unable or unwilling to complete before 2.15 p.m. on that day, then the date of actual completion shall be taken to be the first working day thereafter
(ii) a remittance sent by post or delivered by hand shall be treated as being made on the day on which it reaches the vendor's solicitor's office, unless that day is not a working day in which case the remittance shall be treated as being made on the first working day thereafter

6. Rents, outgoings and apportionments
The purchase being completed (whether on the completion date or subsequently), the income and outgoings shall be apportioned as follows (the day itself in each case being apportioned to the vendor):—
(1) In a case to which proviso (i) to condition 7 (1) applies apportionment shall be made as at the date of actual completion
(2) In a case in which the purchaser is in possession of the whole of the property as lessee or tenant at a rent apportionment shall be made as at the date of actual completion unless proviso (ii) to condition 7 (1) applies, when apportionment shall be made as at the date of the purchaser's notice under that proviso
(3) In any other case apportionment shall be made as from the completion date Provided nevertheless that, if delay is attributable to the vendor's failure to obtain the reversioner's licence, where necessary, or if the vendor remains in beneficial occupation of the property after the completion date, the purchaser may by notice in writing before actual completion elect that apportionment shall be made as at the date of actual completion
(4) Rates shall be apportioned according to the period for which they are intended to provide and rents (whether payable in advance or in arrear) according to the period in respect of which they have been paid or are payable; and apportionment of yearly items (whether or not the same are payable by equal quarterly, monthly or other instalments) shall be according to the relevant number of days relatively to the number of days in the full year
(5) Service charges under leases, in the absence of known or readily ascertainable amounts, shall be apportioned according to the best estimate available at the time of completion and, unless otherwise agreed, the vendor and the purchaser shall be and remain mutually bound after completion to account for and pay or allow to each other, within 15 working days after being informed of the actual amounts as ascertained, any balances or excesses due

7. Interest
(1) If the purchase shall not be completed on the completion date then (subject to the provisions of paragraph (2) of this condition) the purchaser shall pay interest on the remainder of his purchase money at the prescribed rate from that date until the purchase shall actually be completed Provided nevertheless—
(i) That (without prejudice to the operation of proviso (ii) to this paragraph) the vendor may by notice in writing before actual completion elect to take the income of the property (less outgoings) up to the date of actual completion instead of interest as aforesaid
(ii) That, if the delay arises from any cause other than the neglect or default of the purchaser, and if the purchaser (not being in occupation of the property in circumstances to which condition 8 applies) places the remainder of his purchase money (at his own risk) at interest on a deposit account in England or Wales with any designated bank, and gives written notice thereof to the vendor or his solicitor, then in lieu of the interest or income payable to or receivable by the vendor as aforesaid, the vendor shall from the time of such notice be entitled to such interest only as is produced by such deposit
(iii) That the vendor shall in no case be or become entitled in respect of the same period of time both to be paid interest and to enjoy income of the property, or to be paid interest more than once on the same sum of money
(2) The purchaser shall not be liable to pay interest under paragraph (1) of this condition—
(i) so long as, or to the extent that, delay in completion is attributable to any act or default of the vendor or his mortgagee or Settled Land Act trustees
(ii) in case the property is to be constructed or converted by the vendor, so long as the construction or conversion is unfinished

8. Occupation pending completion
(1) If the purchaser (not being already in occupation as lessee or tenant at a rent) is let into occupation of the property before the actual completion of the purchase, then, as from the date of his going into occupation and until actual completion, or until upon discharge or rescission of the contract he ceases to occupy the property, the purchaser shall—
(i) be the licensee and not the tenant of the vendor
(ii) pay interest on the remainder of the purchase money at the prescribed rate
(iii) keep the property in as good repair and condition as it was in when he went into occupation
(iv) pay, or otherwise indemnify the vendor against, all outgoings and expenses (including the cost of insurance) in respect of the property, the purchaser at the same time taking or being credited with the income of the property (if any)
(v) not carry out any development within the meaning of the Planning Acts
(2) Upon discharge or rescission of the contract, or upon the expiration of 7 working days' or longer notice given by the vendor or his solicitor to the purchaser or his solicitor in that behalf, the purchaser shall forthwith give up the property in such repair and condition as aforesaid
(3) A purchaser going into occupation before completion shall not be deemed thereby to have accepted the vendor's title
(4) Where the purchaser is allowed access to the property for the purpose only of carrying out works or installations, the purchaser shall not be treated as being let into occupation within the meaning of this condition

9. Abstract, requisitions and observations
(1) The vendor shall deliver the abstract of title not later than 11 working days after the date of the contract but, subject and without prejudice as mentioned in condition 5 (2), that time limit shall not be of the essence of the contract
(2) Subject always to the rights of the purchaser under Law of Property Act 1925, s. 42(1), the vendor may be required by the purchaser to deal with requisitions and observations concerning persons who are or may be in occupation or actual occupation of the property, so as to satisfy the purchaser that the title is not, and that the purchaser will not be, prejudicially affected by any interests or claims of such persons

(3) The purchaser shall deliver in writing his requisitions within 11 working days after delivery of the abstract, and his observations on the replies to the requisitions within 6 working days after delivery of the replies
(4) In respect of the delivery of requisitions and observations, time shall be of the essence of the contract, notwithstanding that the abstract may not have been delivered within due time
(5) The purchaser shall deliver his requisitions and observations on the abstract as delivered, whether it is a perfect or an imperfect abstract, but for the purposes of any requisitions or observations which could not be raised or made on the information contained in an imperfect abstract, time under paragraph (3) of this condition shall not start to run against the purchaser, until the vendor has delivered the further abstract or information on which the requisitions or observations arise
(6) Subject to his requisitions and observations, the purchaser shall be deemed to have accepted the title.

10. Vendor's right to rescind
(1) If the purchaser shall persist in any objection to the title which the vendor shall be unable or unwilling, on reasonable grounds, to remove, and shall not withdraw the same within 10 working days of being required so to do, the vendor may, subject to the purchaser's rights under Law of Property Act 1925, ss. 42 and 125, by notice in writing to the purchaser or his solicitor, and notwithstanding any intermediate negotiation or litigation, rescind the contract
(2) Upon such rescission the vendor shall return the deposit, but without interest, costs of investigating title or other compensation or payment, and the purchaser shall return the abstract and other papers furnished to him.

11. Existing leaseholds
(1) Where the interest sold is leasehold for the residue of an existing term the following provisions of this condition shall apply
(2) The lease or underlease or a copy thereof having been made available, the purchaser (whether he has inspected the same or not) shall be deemed to have bought with full notice of the contents thereof
(3) On production of a receipt for the last payment due for rent under the lease or underlease, the purchaser shall assume without proof that the person giving the receipt, though not the original lessor, is the reversioner expectant on the said lease or underlease or his duly authorised agent
(4) No objection shall be taken on account of the covenants in an underlease not corresponding with the covenants in any superior lease
(5) The sale is subject to the reversioner's licence being obtained, where necessary. The purchaser supplying such information and references, if any, as may reasonably be required of him, the vendor will use his best endeavours to obtain such licence and will pay the fee for the same. But if the licence cannot be obtained, the vendor may rescind the contract on the same terms as if the purchaser had persisted in an objection to the title which the vendor was unable to remove
(6) Where the property comprises part only of the property comprised in a lease or underlease, the rent, covenants and conditions shall, if the purchaser so requires, be legally apportioned at his expense, but completion shall not be delayed on that account and in the meantime the apportionment by the auctioneer shall be accepted, or the property may at the option of the vendor be sub-demised for the residue of the term, less one day, at a rent apportioned by the auctioneer and subject to the purchaser executing a counterpart containing covenants and provisions corresponding to those contained in the lease or underlease aforesaid
(7) Any statutory covenant to be implied in the conveyance on the part of a vendor shall be so limited as not to affect him with liability for a subsisting breach of any convenant or condition concerning the state or condition of the property, of which state and condition the purchaser is by paragraph (3) of condition 13 deemed to have full notice, and where Land Registration Act 1925, s. 24, applies the purchaser, if required, will join in requesting that an appropriate entry be made in the register.

12. Vendor's duty to produce documents
(1) If an abstracted document refers to any plan material to the description of the property, or to any covenants contained in a document earlier in date than the document with which the title commences, and such plan or earlier document is in the possession or power of the vendor or his trustees or mortgagee, the vendor shall supply a copy thereof with the abstract
(2) If the property is sold subject to restrictive covenants, the deed imposing those covenants or a copy thereof having been made available, the purchaser (whether he has inspected the same or not) shall be deemed to have purchased with full knowledge thereof
(3) The vendor shall not be required to procure the production of any document not in his possession or not in the possession of his mortgagee or trustees, and of which the vendor cannot obtain production, or to trace or state who has the possession of the same.

13. Identity: boundaries: condition of property
(1) The purchaser shall admit the identity of the property with that comprised in the muniments offered by the vendor as the title thereto upon the evidence afforded by the descriptions contained in such muniments, and of a statutory declaration, to be made (if required) at the purchaser's expense, that the property has been enjoyed according to the title for at least twelve years
(2) The vendor shall not be bound to show any title to boundaries, fences, ditches, hedges or walls, or to distinguish parts of the property held under different titles further than he may be able to do from information in his possession
(3) The purchaser shall be deemed to buy with full notice in all respects of the actual state and condition of the property and, save where it is to be constructed or converted by the vendor, shall take the property as it is.

14. Property sold subject to easements, etc.
Without prejudice to the duty of the vendor to disclose all latent easements and latent liabilities known to the vendor to affect the property, the property is sold subject to any rights of way and water, rights of common, and other rights, easements, quasi-easements, liabilities and public rights affecting the same.

15. Town and Country Planning
(1) In this condition, where the context admits, references to "authorised use" are references to "established use", or to use for which permission has been granted under the Planning Acts, or to use for which permission is not required under those Acts, as the case may be
(2) The purchaser shall be entitled to deliver, with his requisitions in respect of the title, requisitions concerning the authorised use of the property for the purposes of the Planning Acts. The vendor in reply shall give all such relevant information as may be in his possession or power
(3) Where the property is in the Special Conditions expressed to be sold on the footing of an authorised use which is specified, then if it appears before actual completion of the purchase that the specified use is not an authorised use of the property for the purposes of the Planning Acts, the purchaser may by notice in writing rescind the contract, and thereupon paragraph (2) of condition 10 shall apply. But, subject to the foregoing provisions of this condition, the purchaser shall be deemed to have accepted that the specified use is an authorised use of the property for the purposes of the Planning Acts
(4) Save as mentioned in the Special Conditions, the property is not to the knowledge of the vendor subject to any charge, notice, order, restriction, agreement or other matter arising under the Planning Acts, but (without prejudice to any right of the purchaser to rescind the contract under paragraph (3) of this condition) the property is sold subject to any such charges, notices, orders, restrictions, agreements and matters affecting the interest sold
(5) Subject as hereinbefore provided, and without prejudice to the obligations of the vendor to supply information as aforesaid, the purchaser shall be deemed to buy with knowledge in all respects of the authorised use of the property for the purposes of the Planning Acts.

16. Requirements by local authority
(1) If after the date of the contract any requirement in respect of the property be made against the vendor by any local authority, the purchaser shall comply with the same at his own expense, and indemnify the vendor in respect thereof: in so far as the purchaser shall fail to comply with such requirement, the vendor may comply with the same wholly or in part and any money so expended by the vendor shall be repaid by the purchaser on completion
(2) The vendor shall upon receiving notice of any such requirement forthwith inform the purchaser thereof.

17. Errors, mis-statements or omissions
(1) Without prejudice to any express right of either party, or to any right of the purchaser in reliance on Law of Property Act 1969, s. 24, to rescind the contract before completion and subject to the provisions of paragraph (2) of this condition, no error, mis-statement or omission in any preliminary answer concerning the property, or in the sale plan or the Special Conditions, shall annul the sale, nor (save where the error, mis-statement or omission relates to a matter materially affecting the description or value of the property) shall any damages be payable, or compensation allowed by either party, in respect thereof
(2) Paragraph (1) of this condition shall not apply to any error, mis-statement or, omission which is recklessly or fraudulently made, or to any matter or thing by which the purchaser is prevented from getting substantially what he contracted to buy
(3) In this condition a "preliminary answer" means and includes any statement made by or on behalf of the vendor to the purchaser or his agents or advisers, whether in answer to formal preliminary enquiries or otherwise, before the purchaser entered into the contract.

18. Leases and tenancies
(1) Abstracts or copies of the leases or agreements (if in writing) under which the tenants hold having been made available, the purchaser (whether he has inspected the same or not) shall be deemed to have notice of and shall take subject to the terms of all the existing tenancies and the rights of the tenants, whether arising during the continuance or after the expiration thereof, and such notice shall not be affected by any partial or incomplete statement in the Special Conditions with reference to the tenancies, and no objection shall be taken on account of there not being an agreement in writing with any tenant
(2) Where a lease or tenancy affects the property sold and other property, the property sold will be conveyed with the benefit of the apportioned rent (if any) mentioned in the Special Conditions or (if not so mentioned) fixed by the auctioneer, and no objection shall be taken on the ground that the consent of the tenant has not been obtained to the apportionment and the purchaser shall not require the rent to be legally apportioned
(3) The purchaser shall keep the vendor indemnified against all claims by the tenant for compensation or otherwise, except in respect of a tenancy which expires or is determined on or before the completion date or in respect of an obligation which ought to have been discharged before the date of the contract
(4) Land in the occupation of the vendor is sold subject to the right (hereby reserved to him) to be paid a fair price for tillages, off-going and other allowances as if he were an outgoing tenant who had entered into occupation of the land after 1st March 1948, and as if the purchaser were the landlord, and in case of dispute such price shall be fixed by the valuation of a valuer, to be nominated in case the parties differ by the President of the Royal Institution of Chartered Surveyors.

19. Preparation of conveyance: priority notices: indemnities
(1) Where the interest sold is leasehold for a term of years to be granted by the vendor, the lease or underlease and counterpart shall be prepared by the vendor's solicitor in accordance (as nearly as the circumstances admit) with a form or draft annexed to the contract or otherwise sufficiently identified by the signatures of the parties or their solicitors
(2) In any other case the conveyance shall be prepared by the purchaser or his solicitor and the following provisions of this condition shall apply
(3) The draft conveyance shall be delivered at the office of the vendor's solicitor at least 6 working days before the completion date and the engrossment for execution by the vendor and other necessary parties (if any) shall be left at the said office within 3 working days after the draft has been returned to the purchaser approved on behalf of the vendor and other necessary parties (if any)
(4) Where the property is unregistered land not in an area of compulsory registration and the conveyance is to contain restrictive covenants, and the purchaser intends contemporaneously with the conveyance to execute a mortgage or conveyance to a third party, he shall inform the vendor of his intention and, if necessary, allow the vendor to give a priority notice for the registration of the intended covenants at least 15 working days before the contract is completed
(5) Where the property is sold subject to legal incumbrances, the purchaser shall covenant to indemnify the vendor against actions and claims in respect of them; and the purchaser will not make any claim on account of increased expense caused by the concurrence of any legal incumbrancer
(6) Where the property is sold subject to stipulations, or restrictive or other covenants, and breach thereof would expose the vendor to liability, the purchaser shall covenant to observe and perform the same and to indemnify the vendor against actions and claims in respect thereof
(7) Paragraphs (5) and (6) of this condition shall have effect without prejudice to the provisions of Law of Property Act 1925, s. 77, and Land Registration Act 1925, s. 24, where such provisions respectively are applicable, and in respect of matters covered by a covenant implied under either of those sections no express covenant shall be required.

20. Severance of properties formerly in common ownership
Where the property and any adjacent or neighbouring property have hitherto been in common ownership, the purchaser shall not become entitled to any right to light or air over or in respect of any adjacent or neighbouring property which is retained by the vendor and the conveyance shall, if the vendor so requires, reserve to him such easements and rights as would become appurtenant to such last-mentioned property by implication of law, if the vendor had sold it to another purchaser at the same time as he has sold the property to the purchaser.

21. Insurance
(1) With respect to any policy of insurance maintained by the vendor in respect of damage to or destruction of the property, the vendor shall not (save pursuant to an obligation to a third party) be bound to keep such insurance on foot or to give notice to the purchaser of any premium being or becoming due
(2) The purchaser shall be entitled to inspect the policy at any time
(3) The vendor shall, if required, by and at the expense of the purchaser obtain or consent to an endorsement of notice of the purchaser's interest on the policy, and in such case the vendor (keeping the policy on foot) may require the purchaser to pay on completion a proportionate part of the premium from the date of the contract.

22. Special notice to complete
(1) At any time on or after the completion date, either party, being ready and willing to fulfil his own outstanding obligations under the contract, may (without prejudice to any other right or remedy available to him) give to the other party or his solicitor notice in writing requiring completion of the contract in conformity with this condition
(2) Upon service of such notice as aforesaid it shall become and be a term of the contract, in respect of which time shall be of the essence thereof, that the party to whom the notice is given shall complete the contract within 16 working days after service of the notice (exclusive of the day of service): but this condition shall operate without prejudice to any right of either party to rescind the contract in the meantime
(3) In case the purchaser refuses or fails to complete in conformity with this condition, then (without prejudice to any other right or remedy available to the vendor) the purchaser's deposit may be forfeited (unless the court otherwise directs) and, if the vendor resells the property within twelve months of the expiration of the said period of 16 working days, he shall be entitled (upon crediting the deposit) to recover from the purchaser hereunder the amount of any loss occasioned to the vendor by expenses of or incidental to such resale, or by diminution in the price

INDEX